# CELLULOID ADVENTURES 2
## Artistic Triumphs—Box Office Bombs

# CELLULOID ADVENTURES 2
## Artistic Triumphs— Box Office Bombs

by Nicholas Anez

Midnight Marquee Press, Inc.
Baltimore, Maryland

ISBN 978-1-936168-12-5
Library of Congress Catalog Card Number  2010938650
Manufactured in the United States of America
First Printing by Midnight Marquee Press, Inc., January 2011

For John and Mary,
For Kathy
and
Again, for Margaret,
who has to live with me, while I return to a better time,
cinematic and otherwise

I am the way, the truth and the life;
no one comes to the Father except through me.—John 14:6

*The Egyptian*

# CONTENTS

Spanish poster for *The Chase*

# INTRODUCTION

In the 1960s, soldiers and their families living on United States Army bases often had the opportunity to see major motion pictures prior to their official release dates. This type of audience could be difficult to entertain. Soldiers were unsure of their future and family members did not like being a part of the military community. As a result, many audience members were already in a foul mood before buying their tickets. If they did not like a movie, they would make their opinions known loud and clear.

In January 1966, one month before it was nationally released, *The Chase* was presented at a theater on the Fort Dix Army base in New Jersey. For its two-hour-plus running time, it held the attention of the audience. Soldiers and civilians were totally absorbed by the dramatic events of the story. There was not a single hiss or jeering of any kind, which was unusual. No one left the theater before the movie was over, which was even more unusual.

As a draftee on the Army base, I predicted that when *The Chase* was officially released it would be a huge commercial and critical success. A few weeks later, I was proven classically wrong. It received terrible reviews from most critics and played to half-empty theaters. Why was it a hit on military bases and a flop in civilian theaters? Was it the victim of bad timing? Perhaps the themes were too disturbing for mainstream audiences in 1966. It is possible that only the Vietnam-era military audience could relate to the film's themes of societal turmoil, political hypocrisies and legal injustices, as well as sudden death which could occur without any warning.

*The Chase* is one of the 11 "Celluloid Adventures" discussed in this book. In the previous volume, *Celluloid Adventures*: *Good Movies Bad Timing*, I discussed several movies within various categories of films that had suffered similar commercial fates. Entries in the Tarzan and James Bond series, along with Westerns, Wyatt Earp movies and Hammer horror movies, were resurrected from diverse levels of oblivion in an attempt to provide some recognition. In this volume, individual movies are presented and represent a wide range of genres, including Westerns, science fiction, film noir, spy films, historical epics, suspense films, social message films and spiritual dramas. All of the movies share the stigma of being failures or disappointments at the box office. But these movies deserved a better fate at the time of their release and they deserve one now.

It is disappointing to see a good movie play to meager audiences. It is even more discouraging to read a bad review of a good movie. And it is most disheartening to see a good movie end its run as a commercial bomb. However, as gloomy as this might be for fans of the movies, it must be extremely depressing for the creative talents involved. An exorbitant amount of personal involvement is often invested into the production of a motion picture. At least it was in the 1950s and 1960s, before conglomerates took over the major studios and turned them into subsidiaries whose only objective is to churn out a profitable product for mass consumption.

From a relatively small film like *Try and Get Me!* to a spectacle like *The Egyptian*, the creative filmmakers attempted to make a good movie and one in which they could have justified pride. In the former film, violence was depicted without resorting to graphic displays of gore, while in the latter film, sensuality was conveyed without relying on nudity or soft-core pornography. Of course, censorship decreed such restraint but the filmmakers also had respect for their audiences and did not condescend to them.

*In a Lonely Place* and *Pitfall* were made over half a century ago but yet depict their subjects of sex and violence with far more maturity than films do today. *The Last Hunt* illustrates the injustices involved in the Winning of the West without either patronizing Native Americans or demonizing Whites. *Cape Fear* and *The Last Sunset* feature potentially disturbing themes to audiences in the early 1960s but yet depict them without sensationalizing them. *The Singer Not the Song* explores the covert collusion between good and evil as well as between love and hate. *First Men in the Moon* proves that science fiction is more memorable when the story and characters are front and center instead of computerized special effects. And *The Quiller Memorandum* displays the inhumanity of espionage while illuminating the humanity of its characters.

All of these movies were subjected to unfair attacks from critics who too often brought their agendas to their criticism. Not all critics should be condemned since many were perceptive as well as objective. But too many others lacked such insight and often judged a movie based upon their own personal views or expectations and not on the movie's entertainment or artistic value. And in the 1950s and 1960s, the opinions of critics had more of an impact upon a film's box office performance than they do today. Adults comprised a much larger share of the audience population in the past and paid more attention to reviews than today's younger audiences.

Equally important to a film's commercial success is the timing of its release. A movie that failed during one period may have been a commercial hit if released during another period. Bad timing could be due to any number of factors, from unpopular political themes to disturbing social messages, from overabundance of a particular genre to bad publicity, from a lack of proper promotion to an ill-conceived publicity campaign. Regardless of the factor, the movie suffered at the box office.

Quite often, the circumstances surrounding a movie's production are so acrimonious that it is astonishing that the film emerged as so exemplary. The legendary star of *In a Lonely Place* envisioned only his actress-wife as his co-star and became irate when her studio refused to allow her to play opposite him. Shortly before the start of filming *The Egyptian*, the disappearance of the acclaimed actor who had been signed to play the title role placed an undeserved stigma upon the entire production. Regarding *The Last Sunset*, the subsequent denunciation of the film by its director and its writer would have a distinct effect upon its reception and its reputation. Prior to the filming of *The Singer Not the Song*, its lead actor furiously expressed his intent to sabotage the production because of his resentment of his co-star. During production of *The Chase*, the numerous reports of discord on the set were directly responsible for the negative reviews that greeted the film upon its release. These stories—along with many others—are told within the following pages.

Of course, when discussing films released in the 1950s and 1960s, there is the strong possibility that the subject of the Hollywood blacklist will rear its ugly head. Though it was not illegal to be a Communist in the 1940s and 1950s, the status of Russia as an enemy of the United States resulted in the suspicion that American Communists were in fact subversive agents of a foreign nation. This suspicion gave rise to the blacklist, which many believed was as un-American as foreign agents. This political scourge was a film industry nightmare with its tentacles affecting movies for more than a decade. Within this book, the blacklist will make sporadic appearances, but its impact will be widespread and powerful. Thus, a brief overview of the subject will be provided, from its origin to its impact upon the lives and careers of some of the artists responsible for the films under discussion.

Once again, I have attempted to provide a complete portrait of the individual films by providing a summary of the plots as well as significant factors that led to their production. Where applicable, it can be helpful to appreciating the movies by summarizing the source material upon which they are based. Also included are reviews to give examples of their critical reception. Finally, the domestic theatrical rentals earned by each movie, which are approximately 40% of the total gross, are included to illustrate its fate at the box office, particularly compared to films that were far more successful during the respective year.

The commercial failure of these movies does not reflect their quality. They are noteworthy achievements and represent the best efforts of talented filmmakers on both sides of the camera. They are like lost treasures that are just waiting to be discovered.

# PITFALL

John Forbes is tired of being an average person. He is bored and in a rut. He wishes that he could add some excitement to his routine life. He wishes something different would happen to him. He gets his wish and it destroys his life.

"Film noir" is a phrase coined by French film critics to refer to a certain kind of American film that became popular after World War II. The term means, literally, "black film" and refers to stories that occur within a world of shadows, uncertainty and moral corruption. It is an indigenous American type of film that suggests that a very dangerous world co-exists with the superficial world of security. It implies that decadence exists just beneath the conventional morality that represented American life after the war.

The action in a film noir frequently takes place at night on dark streets with neon lights. The main character is often a victim of circumstances or of a cruel fate over which he has no control. He may be a good man with a flaw that makes him susceptible to temptation. He could be a pawn in the hands of a sexually uninhibited woman. He could be a frightened man struggling to survive in a hostile environment. He may feel alienated within his own society or he may be the victim of some invisible force. More often than not the endings of these films are bleak. If the ending is positive for the main character, it has been achieved at great expense to his body and to his soul.

Film historians may differ on the specific time period that encompasses the era of film noir but they generally agree that the most productive years occurred after World War II. From 1946 to 1950, between 20 and 30 movies were produced each year that fit within this category. Such a significant amount provides an indication of how pervasive the genre was.

The year 1948 witnessed the release of at least a couple of dozen noir films. *The Big Clock* from Paramount, *The Lady from Shanghai* from Columbia, *Cry of the City* from 20th Century Fox, *Force of Evil* from MGM, *A Double Life* from Universal-International and *Raw Deal* from Eagle-Lion are just a few of the many noir films released. And there was an independent film released through United Artists called *Pitfall*, which did not light any fires at the box office. However, it is a terrific movie and an evocative example of film noir.

*Pitfall* is based upon a novel entitled *The Pitfall* by Jay Dratler that was published by The Thomas Y. Crowell Company in 1947. Dratler was a successful novelist and screenwriter who was considered an influential figure in the field of film noir. He wrote his first novel, *Manhattan Side Street*, in 1936. Moving to Hollywood in 1940, he wrote the first Boston Blackie movie along with other programmers and also contributed to musicals and comedies. However, his real skill was in the field of crime thrillers and he did his best

work at 20th Century Fox. He is credited with co-writing such movies as *Laura* (1944), *The Dark Corner* (1946) and *Call Northside 777* (1948).

*The Pitfall* is the story of John Forbes who, like Dratler, is a successful screenwriter for 20th Century Fox. John lives happily with his pregnant wife Sue and their four-year-old daughter, Ann. He has a loyal secretary who takes his dictation, two agents who consider him a friend and a producer, Mr. Brawley, whom he considers a father-figure. John's life changes forever when he takes a phone call from MacDonald, a police officer whom he knows from a previous film assignment. Mac has arrested Bill Smiley for theft and has become interested in Smiley's wife, Mona. Since Mac cannot approach Mona directly because of his position, he asks John to become involved with her. Mac figures that if John first becomes her lover, Mac will then have knowledge to hold over her in case she tries to compromise him because of his position. John initially refuses but, being bored with his life and intrigued because of Mac's description of Mona, he eventually contacts her. This is his first of many mistakes he will make.

Mona and Bill Smiley are both models who came to California from New York to hopefully break into the movies. After Bill was unable to find work, he turned to crime. Now Mona is lonely and vulnerable. John quickly becomes enamored of Mona and the two begin an emotional as well as a physical relationship. She becomes angry when she learns that he is married, but he convinces her that he loves her. John believes that he can maintain a happy home and have a mistress, but he does not count on MacDonald who gives him a savage beating when John backs out of their arrangement.

John feels increasingly guilty for his betrayal of Sue, but he cannot break away from Mona. Meanwhile, Mac is visiting Smiley in jail and needling him with information about Mona's cheating. When Smiley is released from jail, he returns to Mona and angrily demands to know the name of her lover. Simultaneously, Mac is telling John how dangerous Smiley can be and advises him to get a gun to protect himself. Increasingly tortured by fear and guilt, John takes pills to calm his nerves. Feeling that he is on the verge of a breakdown, he confesses to Brawley who advises him not to tell Sue because the knowledge of his affair would devastate her and possibly affect her pregnancy.

Eventually, Mona asks John to come to her home. Worried and depressed, she tells him that she has to end their relationship and try to repair her marriage. She also tells him that Smiley has a gun and is still threatening to go to John's home. John becomes furious and threatens to kill Smiley if he comes near his family. John asks Mac for help and Mac tells him that he will put extra police protection on his house. But Smiley arrives and after an angry confrontation at the front door returns to the back door. Frightened for his family, John fires his gun through the door, instantly killing Smiley.

When the police arrive, John tells them that he thought Smiley was a burglar and the police accept the statement, even though Smiley was not armed. However, when they discover John's fingerprints all over Mona's apartment, they arrest him for murder. John's attorney assures him that they have a good case for self-defense, in view of Smiley's criminal record. When both Sue and Mona testify on his behalf, an acquittal verdict seems a good possibility. But then the prosecution brings out their surprise witness, who happens to be Mac.

Mac tells the court that he overheard Smiley in jail planning crimes and, after his release, planted a dictaphone in his apartment. The recordings are then played in the courtroom. They reveal Mona's conversation with John in which she tells him that she is going to stay with her husband. This is followed by John's angry declaration that he will kill Smiley if he comes near his family. Finally realizing that Mac set him up and that he will be convicted, John breaks down hysterically in the courtroom. He knows that he will lose his case, his family and probably his life. He also knows that the path is now clear for Mac to get Mona.

*The Pitfall* is a cleverly plotted novel and doesn't feature run-of-the-mill characters. John Forbes narrates, probably from death row, though this is not known until the last page, and the book moves at such a quick pace that the lapses in plot are not initially noticed. For instance, the fact that John continues to ask Mac for help even after Mac beats him strains credibility. It also seems strange that he accepts Mac's assurance that he has nothing to do with Smiley's suspicions and that the guards at the jail are the ones who are instigating the prisoner. But these are minor quibbles and are far outweighed by the virtues. The novel is far more than just a crime thriller. It is an engrossing human drama about very real people that remains spellbinding six decades after its publication.

Despite the highly sexual tone of the novel, it was inevitable that Hollywood would beckon in view of the story's cinematic potential. Samuel Bischoff began his career as a Hollywood producer during the silent era with comedy shorts and eventually graduated to features. Throughout his career, he would produce over 100 motion pictures from 1922 to 1964. He worked at various times at Columbia Pictures, Warner Bros. and RKO Radio Pictures, mostly producing programmers. Reportedly, while Bischoff was a producer at Columbia in 1945, he submitted an early manuscript of Dratler's novel for evaluation but was informed that it could not be approved under the provisions of the Production Code.

Bischoff apparently persevered and production was eventually approved. Regal Films was an independent company owned by Bischoff that was incorporated in 1947 with Dick Powell on the company's board of directors. The film version of Dratler's novel was announced as the first production of Regal films and would be released by United Artists. Dick Powell agreed to star and André de Toth was signed to direct.

Karl Kamb is given credit for the script but whether he actually wrote it or not is subject to dispute. Kamb began his career writing shorts for MGM in the late 1930s and graduated to features in the mid-1940s. His movies include undistinguished programmers until *Pitfall*. Subsequent movies are more impressive and include co-writing credits for the fine Alan Ladd Western *Whispering Smith* (also 1948) and *The Captive City* (1952), a good crime exposé film with noir elements.

In his autobiography *Fragments: Portraits from the Inside* (Faber and Faber; 1994), André de Toth claims that he and William Bowers wrote the screenplay for *Pitfall*. But according to de Toth, since Bowers could not be given credit because he was under contract to another studio, de Toth refused to take sole credit. He adds that the credited screenwriter "probably never even read the script." But this could be just one man's biased opinion and it would be beneficial if Kamb could have provided his own account.

On the other hand, the script is closer in tone and style to Jay Dratler's other film noirs. Dratler was known to be a script doctor and reportedly worked uncredited on many films. In 2006, Dratler's daughter reported that she has documents that prove that her father actually wrote the screenplay for *Pitfall* and adds that, although he wrote the novel first, he wrote the screenplay prior to its publication. However, William Bowers subsequently wrote two noirs for Powell, *Cry Danger* (1951) and *Split Second* (1953), which Powell directed. This may indicate that he could have made some contributions to the script. Nevertheless, the story and characters belong to Jay Dratler.

The main plot of the film remains basically the same, though with a different resolution. Other changes include the profession of the main character. John Forbes is no longer a screenwriter but works for an insurance company. His wife is not pregnant or confined to bed and they have a six-year-old son instead of a three-year-old daughter. MacDonald is transformed from a uniformed police officer into former cop who is now a private detective and does occasional work for the insurance company. A summary of the plot will indicate other differences as well as similarities to the novel.

DICK
POWELL
LIZABETH
SCOTT "PITFALL"

JANE WYATT and Raymond Burr · Byron Barr · John Litel
Ann Doran · Jimmy Hunt · Selmer Jackson
Based on the novel "The Pitfall" by Jay Dratler · Screenplay by Karl Kamb
Directed by ANDRE de TOTH · Produced by SAMUEL BISCHOFF · Released thru United Artists

John Forbes is bored with his routine life and his routine job. On the fateful day that his life will change, he is in an irritable mood. He is abrupt with his devoted wife Sue and impatient with his son Tommy. He wonders what happened to the two people who were going to build a boat and sail around the world. When Sue tells him that they got married, it seems to increase his irritability. He is still short-tempered when he arrives at his office. Being a claims adjustor for an insurance company has become dull and unexciting. When he finds private detective MacDonald waiting for him, his distaste for the man is obvious. MacDonald tells him that he solved an embezzlement case involving a man named Bill Smiley who stole money for which the company was bonded and spent it on lavish gifts for his girl friend, Mona Stephens. MacDonald raves about Mona and states that he has fallen for her. But John tells him to stay away from her and that his detective work is completed. It is John's job to try to obtain some of the money back for the company.

John isn't initially attracted to Mona. She is a model who works for a local department store and belittles John. She has no desire to keep the gifts Smiley gave her and will cooperate with John if it may mean an early release for Smiley. When Mona informs him that Smiley also bought her a boat, John's words earlier that morning to Sue come back to him and he impulsively agrees to go for a ride with Mona. He wants to show her that he isn't just a little man with a briefcase, which is what she called him. The ride seems to unleash something in John, and when she asks him if he has anything to do

**Lisabeth Scott and Dick Powell in a studio publicity shot for *Pitfall*.**

that evening, he is eager to show her that he is not bound by any schedule even though he is expecting his boss, Ed Brawley, and his wife over to their home. The dinner John shares with Mona is harmless, but not to Mac, who is watching them.

The next day John finds an angry Mac waiting for him at his office. Mac quickly tells him that he knows about the boat that John hasn't reported. Since he now has to report the boat to his company, John visits Mona again to tell her directly instead of telephoning her with the bad news. The kindness of the act makes Mona impulsively kiss him and the fade-out signifies intimacy. John has proven to himself that he is not just an average person leading an average life, that his life is not dreary. But he has started down a road that will lead to disaster.

Mac, who has continued to spy on Mona, is waiting for John at his home and beats him furiously. After telling Sue that he was attacked by strangers who tried to rob him, John recuperates from the beating at home. Meanwhile, Mona finds John's briefcase at her apartment. Informed by his secretary that he is sick, she drives to his home and learns that he is a husband and father. Once he is well enough to return to work, John meets with Mona. Though she is hurt, she is not a vindictive woman and promises to let John off the hook, telling him angrily to stay home with his family.

John regrets hurting Mona but is relieved that the affair is over. His shame for his single indiscretion was difficult to endure and he intends to make it up to Sue and Tommy. But Mac begins to hound Mona, initially posing as a customer at her department store and then appearing at her home. When she tells him that she is not interested in him, he replies by threatening to tell John's family about her. Mona is forced to ask John for help and John angrily beats Mac in his apartment, warning him not to go near his family. Both John and Mona hope that they can now get on with their lives.

However, Mac retaliates for the beating by telling Smiley about Mona's relationship with John. Mona is forced to call John for help again, worried over what Smiley may do when he is released. John tries to visit Smiley in jail but learns that he has obtained an early release. Plagued by guilt and fear, John confesses to Ed Brawley, who advises him not to tell Sue and hope that Smiley will forget his anger now that he is out of jail. But Smiley is furious when he returns to Mona, who discovers that he has a gun—given to him by Mac. After Smiley leaves, Mona frantically calls John to tell him that Smiley is looking for him. John arms himself while he tries to keep his family away from danger. When Smiley appears at his home, John forces him to leave. But Smiley returns and breaks into the house, forcing John to shoot him.

Knowing that his plan has worked, Mac cheerfully visits Mona to tell her that John has killed Smiley. He didn't really care who killed whom as long as both men were removed from his path to Mona. Now he informs her that there is no one else for her and she belongs to him. She knows now that Mac is responsible for Smiley's death. Mac already has a trip planned for her, but, as he starts to pack, Mona pulls out a gun and fires at him.

Tortured by the fact that he killed a man, John confesses to Sue about his affair. Devastated, Sue warns him not to further harm his family by admitting his guilt to the police. But after wandering in despair all though the night, John reveals the entire story to the District Attorney. The D.A. contemptuously berates him for his act and reluctantly tells him that he is free to go since Smiley was armed and broke into his house. He also informs John that Mona has been arrested, her fate dependent upon whether Mac dies. Crushed even further, John leaves the office and sees Mona being led away.

As he leaves the building, John finds Sue waiting for him. She tells him that she had considered divorcing him but decided against it. She adds that their lives will never be the same, but she is willing to try to save their marriage if he is agreeable. Grateful for the chance to make up for the pain he caused and the harm he did, he quickly agrees. But, as they drive away, their future is uncertain.

*Pitfall,* and the novel that it is based upon, are both excellent works. Dratler's novel is out of print today but deserves to be re-published. It is the kind of book that is hard to put down. It is also a very moral story with a horrifying ending. The movie is equally powerful and equally moral. It is related to the novel in a way that fraternal twins are related. The stories are not identical but they are similar in some ways and different in others. The movie's ending is not as brutal as the novel's, but it is fairly bleak.

The title of *Pitfall* is certainly appropriate for the destiny of John Forbes, despite the fact that he is spared the fate of the novel's counterpart. By straying off the path of convention with a simple boat ride, he believes he is opening a door to excitement and doesn't realize that he is stepping into a pit that has no way out. Once he is intimate with Mona, he has violated not only his marriage oath but also the code of morality which allows him to face himself in the mirror. As he falls into the pit, there is nothing for him to hang onto. It is only because Sue offers her hand to him at the end that he has any hope to climb out of the morass that surrounds him.

At least, though he has hurt them terribly, John still has Sue and Tommy. But Mona is totally alone. The first man who was ever kind to her is dead and the second man who treated her with gentleness can never see her again. As she is led away by a matron, she conveys the impression that her life is over. Whether Mac lives or dies is irrelevant to her because she has nothing to live for. Life has been tough on Mona but now it can only get worse. She will have to go to prison and the only question is for how long. It is obvious that she doesn't care.

The novel's Mona Smiley has a much happier fate. She has lost both men that she loved but she has Mac waiting to take their place. Unaware of the extent of Mac's duplicity as her counterpart is in the film, she is obviously susceptible to his advances at the end of the novel. Indeed, there are indications that she will accept Mac as a replacement for John just as she accepted John as a replacement for Smiley. In contrast, the film's Mona Stephens is a truly tragic character whose vulnerability and string of bad luck condemns her to hopelessness and despair.

In the novel, Mac emerges triumphant. His devious plan worked perfectly and he is the only character to survive unscathed. Evil truly has its rewards for the Mac of the novel, while in the film, he pays for his duplicity with a bullet. Ironically, the Mac of the film is menacing but he is also pathetic. He can be vicious, as his beating of John proves, but his motive for his actions are different. In the novel, he wants only to possess Mona physically. But in the film, he falls in love with Mona. This makes his actions slightly more understandable, though not forgivable. Unlike his counterpart in the novel, Mac of the film doesn't get what he wants and his future is as uncertain as Mona's.

It is also of interest that, in the novel, Mac is primarily responsible for John's fate by sensing his weakness and tempting him with his description of Mona. Mac's awareness of John's vulnerability is clear when, after initially refusing Mac's offer, John tracks Mac down to ask for Mona's telephone number. It is revealing that Mac is not surprised to see John and has the number ready for him. Thus, Mac is more of a Machiavellian character in the novel, making his surname far more appropriate.

John in the novel is perhaps more responsible for his fate than John of the film, particularly since he doesn't just have a one-night stand but a long-term affair which he would like to maintain. They both suffer the same torturous

John Forbes (Dick Powell) is unhappy but his wife Sue (Jane Wyatt) does not know why.

guilt, but the novel's John is more naïve and culpable than the film's John. As a result, Sue and Anne in the novel suffer a terrible and permanent fate while Sue and Tommy in the film will have emotional scars but may survive. It is also interesting that Sue in the novel cries when John tells her of his affair and blames herself because of her invalidity. Sue in the film doesn't cry but gets justifiably angry and places the blame on John, which is where it belongs.

There is one small gap in the movie that perhaps may indicate some cutting prior to release. When John impulsively decides to have dinner with Mona to show her that he has some independence, he has apparently forgotten that the Brawleys are having dinner with Sue and him that evening. The fact that he misses the dinner is never raised as expected. Such a scene would perhaps have illustrated the friendship between John and Brawley, which would explain why Brawley is the person to whom John confesses his indiscretion. It would also demonstrate the first sign of Sue's suspicion of John's behavior, which she later expresses when she asks him what is bothering him. But this is a slight flaw that doesn't impact the course of the story.

The incisive screenplay is brought to life by a director whose skills were often taken for granted. André de Toth directed some films in his native Hungary before World War II and then fled to England at the outbreak of the war, eventually immigrating to the United States in 1942. The following year, he directed his first U.S. film, *Passport to Suez*, and worked quite steadily thereafter. His films over the next 25 years included crime thrillers, mysteries and

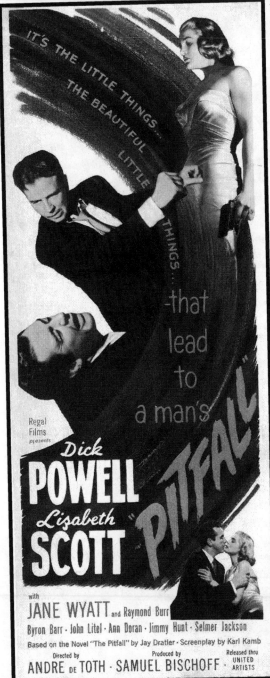

IT'S THE LITTLE THINGS... THE BEAUTIFUL LITTLE THINGS... that lead to a man's

Regal Films presents

*Dick* POWELL
*Lisabeth* SCOTT *in* "PITFALL"

with

JANE WYATT and Raymond Burr

Byron Barr · John Litel · Ann Doran · Jimmy Hunt · Selmer Jackson

Based on the Novel "The Pitfall" by Jay Dratler · Screenplay by Karl Kamb

Directed by
ANDRE DE TOTH

Produced by
SAMUEL BISCHOFF

Released thru
UNITED ARTISTS

Westerns, most of which were located somewhere between A movies and B movies. He first attracted attention with the potent drama *None Shall Escape* in 1944. The Western *Ramrod* in 1947 also received acclaim due to the realism of the violence, which would become one of his trademarks. His most famous movie is *House of Wax* in 1953, which was the first major studio production in 3-D.

Samuel Bischoff designed *Pitfall* as a top-of-the-bill film and serves as a fine showcase for de Toth's skill in handling adult material. His direction keeps the plot moving progressively without any superfluous distractions. More than any of de Toth's other films, this one most clearly illustrates his theme of the complexity of human relationships. It also serves as an attack upon the malaise of the middle class that seemed to simmer beneath the fulfillment of the American dream. John Forbes has everything but it isn't enough for him. He only learns the value of what he has after he loses it. De Toth records his fall from grace dispassionately, reserving his sympathy for his wife and son who are grateful for what they have and for Mona who longs for what he has.

Even Mac is accorded some degree of understanding. Compared to John, he has very little. He lives in a seedy room, has an equally sleazy office with an obnoxious secretary (unlike John's loyal secretary) and wants to give Mona everything she desires. But Mona falls for John who already has everything Mac lacks. His subsequent fury is understandable.

De Toth underscores Mac's complexity by focusing on his expression when he tells John that he has fallen in love. John's slightly veiled contempt for Mac, which his secretary more overtly expresses, makes Mac almost sympathetic at this stage of the story. This is not to excuse Mac for the violence he displays or for his actions that lead directly to the tragic outcome. Though de Toth records his savage beating of John with restraint, the sounds and the expression on Mac's face are all that is needed to reflect the viciousness of his actions. The director keeps his camera upon Mac and doesn't show either John's reaction or any of the blows being struck. However, though Mac is clearly the villain of the piece, he is still accorded some pathos.

De Toth uses both day and night scenes to amplify the film noir aspects of the story. The exteriors at the beginning of the movie, in John's home and office, as well as during the drive to work, are all naturalistic in their lighting but they become purposefully noir for they reveal John's frustration with his dreary environment. Only during the boat ride with Mona does the daylight seem to promise excitement, though the peril of the excitement will soon become apparent. In contrast, as John's fate becomes increasingly fraught with danger and uncertainty, more scenes take place at night and the noir elements become more apparent. There is an almost claustrophobic atmosphere within John's home as he anxiously waits for Smiley. His feeling of desolation reaches its climax as he walks the dark streets alone with the realization that he has destroyed his family and killed a man.

The players are without exception at the top of their form. Dick Powell is very compelling as John Forbes. Powell has to be one of the most versatile personalities in Hollywood history. He started as a song and dance man, starred in many musicals in the 1930s and was a natural for lightweight comedy roles. Then in the early 1940s, he completely changed his image by playing hardboiled private detective Philip Marlowe in *Murder My Sweet*. This led to a string of equally tough characters in which he was extremely effective. But acting was only one part of his career. In the 1950s, he started directing and producing movies and was one of the first major stars to enter television, producing several series. He was exceptionally talented in a variety of areas and deserves more credit than he is usually given.

In *Pitfall*, Powell provides a full-rounded characterization for John Forbes. Initially, he is not very likeable as he sarcastically responds to his wife's pleasantries. His ingratitude for his relatively luxurious life verges on inviting contempt and it is to the actor's credit that he still manages to provide some degree of warmth to his character. It is interesting that, upon driving John to work, Sue tells him that she hopes his mood will be better when she picks him up. This indicates that his irritable mood is unusual, which makes his later meeting with Mona fateful. Perhaps if he had met her any other day nothing would ever have happened between them. When Mona mentions her boat, John's eyes light up and perhaps he wouldn't have been excited if he hadn't been reminiscing about a boat earlier that morning. Fate seems to be closing in on John and Powell registers the boyish enthusiasm in the boat that makes his subsequent lapse in morality inevitable.

Powell's skill is displayed quite superbly after his fall from grace. The scene in which Mona tells him that she knows he is married could have been a cliché but stands out due to the mixture of both embarrassment and relief that are evident in his expression. He is equally convincing at displaying rage when he returns the beating he received from Mac. The misery on his face after he has killed Smiley, however, erases the negative feelings his character may have evoked prior to this time. More impressively, the guilt and shame in his expression and voice when he confesses to Sue are almost agonizing to view. When he sees Mona for the last time, after being subjected to the scorn of the district attorney, his helplessness and self-contempt are almost palpable. And in the last scene, he projects an image of total devastation that is alleviated by only a small glimmer of hope as he appreciatively accepts Sue's offer to try to save their marriage.

Lizabeth Scott projects both sensuality and sensitivity as Mona. The role is quite different than the wicked seductress associated with her image. Her character's basic loneliness and fragility are established when she tells John that Smiley is the first man who ever gave her an engagement ring, adding ironically that she later learned that it was bought with stolen money. When she confronts John with knowledge of his marriage, her tone and manner reflect a mixture of emotions convincingly, including anger as well as pain. And she is particularly credible during her final confrontation with Mac when her expression and tone signify her complete despair and foreshadows her firing the gun.

Jane Wyatt as Sue displays the expected warmth of a loving wife but there is a suggestion of strength beneath the tenderness. This strength, mixed with pain and disbelief, will be displayed when John confesses. In the final scene, even her voice sounds devastated as she stares ahead, not wanting to even look at John because he has destroyed everything she valued. In fact, it is her character's strength that has to make the final decision and carry her errant husband at the end, signifying a permanent change in the relationship that his behavior has caused. Wyatt is quite affecting in an unappreciated performance of subtlety and intelligence.

Raymond Burr is chilling, crafty and remorselessly vindictive as Mac. As he spies on John and Mona, he registers smoldering anger that erupts first in brutal violence toward John and then in cunning manipulation of the hapless Smiley. But yet he also conveys the loneliness behind the cruelty. Just before he is shot, there is an pitiable enthusiasm in his voice as he starts to pack Mona's bags while telling her that he really loves her. This recalls his initial appearance in the film when he tells John, "I bet you never thought of me as a man who could fall in love." John responded to his romantic words with indifference and Mona responded with a bullet. Though his character may be slimy and sinister, the pathetic side as envisioned by the script is also revealed.

**Lizabeth Scott, Dick Powell and Raymond Burr in** *Pitfall*

The supporting cast is more than adequate. Jimmy Hunt gives a natural performance as Tommy and is quite believable in the scene in which he has a nightmare. This scene is particularly important because of John's attempts to blame the bad dreams on comic books, while denying the possibility that his own behavior might be a factor, however symbolically. John Litel is effectively contemptuous of John in his brief scene as the District Attorney, while Byron Barr makes an impression as Bill Smiley, though his scenes are relatively few.

Production qualities are top notch. There is a realism to the settings that belies the usual noir environment. A southern Californian suburban neighborhood takes the place of rain-swept dark streets and squalid hotel residences. The sets, from the Forbes residence to the insurance company, from Mona's department store to the jail visiting room, all look natural and realistic. The editing is quite brisk and the film moves along at a steady pace, spending just enough time on each scene to achieve its purpose.

*Pitfall* received mixed reviews. "Brog" in *Variety* didn't like the movie which, he writes, "never lives up to its promise of a tight, suspenseful melodrama; the promise of exciting stuff is always present but never delivered." Brog's criticism of the "weak-kneed scripting and tritely projected ending" is difficult to comprehend since there is nothing even remotely weak-kneed or trite about the film. The reviewer for *Newsweek* gave a sarcastically

**John learns that Bill Smiley has been released from jail.**

negative review, writing that it was "snoopopathic" and adding that "Powell's comeuppance may stick in the craw of anyone not well within the inner circle of the Production Code." Thomas Pryor in *The New York Times* proved to be far more perceptive. "This is a neatly-constructed film that builds suspense as it goes along," Pryor wrote, "(and) is as palatable and effective a sample of cinematic sermonizing on marital mores as the screen has presented in some time." All of the above reviews, incidentally, singled out Raymond Burr's performance as being particularly impressive.

*Pitfall* didn't do well at the box office. *Variety*'s annual list of Top-Grossing Films for 1948 includes 93 films that earned domestic theatrical rentals exceeding the minimum figure of $1 million. As an accompanying article explains, "the minimum figure is considered to be the point at which a film begins to make a substantial impact upon the box office." *Pitfall* failed to make the list. Possibly the hypocrisy and malaise of the middle-class it depicted were too discomforting for many potential audiences. As an indication of what kinds of films were most popular that year, the top film was the comedy *The Road to Rio* with $4.5 million. The musical *Easter Parade* and the Western *Red River* followed with over $4 million each.

The surplus of noir films may have had an impact upon its reception and major studio films may have had an advantage over an independent production. The most commercially successful noir movies on the list included *Key Largo* from Warner Bros. at Number 18 with $3.25 million, *Sorry Wrong Number* from Paramount at Number 25 with $2.85 million, *Road House* from Fox at Number 46 with $2.3 million, *The Street With No Name* from Fox at Number 47 with $2.35 million and *Kiss the Blood Off My Hands* from Universal-International at Number 83 with $1.6 million. Incidentally, two other movies—non-noirs—that starred Dick Powell also made the list: the Western *Station West* was Number 80 with $1.7 million and the thriller *To the Ends of the Earth* was Number 82, also with $1.7 million.

Nevertheless, *Pitfall* is a memorable motion picture, not only because of its many qualities, but because it remains in the mind long after viewing it, particularly regarding the fate of its main characters. Did John and Sue overcome this problem as they had overcome less serious problems? Did Tommy continue to have even worse nightmares? Were they able to start a new life in another city? Could John ever forgive himself for killing Smiley? It's possible, but even if luck is on their side, Sue was correct when she said that their lives would never be the same.

When Sue told John why she decided against divorcing him, she explained that, "If a man has always been a good husband, except for 24 hours, how long should he pay for it?" She didn't know the answer and John didn't know either. They will definitely find out. Sue has the last words when she tells him, "That's what we'll do. We'll try." But we will never know if they succeed or not, just that they may have a chance.

As for Mona, she has no chance at all.

CREDITS: Producer: Samuel Bischoff; Director: André de Toth; Screenplay: Karl Kamb, Based Upon the Novel by Jay Dratler; Cinematographer: Harry Wild; Editor: Walter Thompson; Music: Louis Forbes

CAST: Dick Powell (John Forbes); Lizabeth Scott (Mona Stevens); Jane Wyatt (Sue Forbes); Raymond Burr (MacDonald); Byron Barr (Bill Smiley); John Litel (District Attorney); Jimmy Hunt (Tommy Forbes); Ann Doran (Maggie); Selmer Jackson (Ed Brawley); Margaret Wells (Terry); Dick Wassel (Desk Sergeant)

# IN A LONELY PLACE

I was born when she kissed me
I died when she left me
I lived a few weeks while she loved me.

These hauntingly romantic poetic lines are from the 1950 film, *In a Lonely Place*, one of the most incisive portraits of an artistic personality ever brought to the screen. It is also a murder mystery, a psychological thriller and a film noir. But above all, it is a romance and its story can be encapsulated in these three poetic lines that foreshadow the fate of its protagonist and his love interest.

Nicholas Ray directed *In a Lonely Place* and the movie stars Humphrey Bogart and Gloria Grahame. Andrew Solt wrote the screenplay from an adaptation by Edmund H. North, based upon a novel by Dorothy B. Hughes. However, except for the names of the main characters and the murder that generates the storyline, the novel and film are almost entirely different in plot, characterizations and resolution.

Duell, Sloane & Pearce published the novel in 1947. In the preface, Hughes quotes a line from a play by J. M. Synge entitled *In the Shadow of the Glen* about a young woman whose elderly husband pretends to be dead in order to obtain proof of her infidelity. Trapped in a loveless marriage of inconvenience, the woman recites the line, "It's in a lonesome place that you do have to be talking to someone, and looking for someone, in the evening of the day." These sad words reflect her need to be close to someone, to anyone, as an escape from her isolated and unhappy life.

The novel concerns a young man named Dickson Steele who, upon his discharge from the service after the war, has come to Los Angeles ostensibly to write a novel, thanks to the generosity of a rich uncle who has agreed to support his literary efforts for one year. Steele is an unpleasant man who seems to despise everyone, particularly the wealthy. Temporarily living in the vacated apartment of Mel Terriss, an acquaintance from college, he has few, if any, literary capabilities and abhors honest work. And he is also leading a double life, for he is a serial strangler who has been terrorizing the city. At the beginning of the novel, he murders his sixth victim, Mildred Atkinson, a stenographer he chances to sight when prowling the streets in search of victims.

Steele meets neighbor Laurel Grey, a would-be actress to whom he is attracted but yet realizes is a greedy and callous woman. While engaging in an affair with Laurel, he follows the murder investigation by renewing his friendship with police officer Brub Nicolai, a friend from the service. Brub initially seems unaware of the contradictions in Steele's personality, though his wife Sylvia notices them. While the police develop their psychological profile of the killer, Laurel begins to lose interest in Steele. Knowing that he

THE BOGART SUSPENSE PICTURE WITH THE SURPRISE FINISH—

COLUMBIA PICTURES presents

HUMPHREY BOGART

IN A LONELY PLACE

with GLORIA GRAHAME

Frank LOVEJOY · Carl Benton REID · Art SMITH · Jeff DONNELL · Martha STEWART

Screen Play by ANDREW SOLT · A SANTANA PRODUCTION

Produced by ROBERT LORD · Directed by NICHOLAS RAY

must have money to keep Laurel, Steele unsuccessfully tries to trick his uncle into increasing his allowance. Laurel is also becoming suspicious of Steele due to the disappearance of her former lover, Mel Terriss. Angered by both

Laurel and his uncle, Steele strangles another woman because she reminded him of Brucie, a woman he loved in England during the war. With the help of both Laurel and Sylvia, Brub sets a trap for Steele which leads to his arrest and the disclosure that he is not only the Los Angeles strangler, but that he also killed Mel and six more women in England, including Brucie.

The author of the novel provides logical explanations for the actions of Steele, who is clearly a sociopath with a hatred for women and who is incapable of genuine emotion. Born into poverty, he developed a loathing for "the stinking rich." At Princeton, which he attended only to ingratiate himself with his rich uncle, he sponged off wealthy students and befriended the alcoholic Mel Terriss, for whom he procured women in exchange for money and acceptance. With the outbreak of World War II, he enlisted in the air corps and found that his uniform obliterated class differences and enabled him to meet his one true love, Brucie. But his childhood experiences combined with the effects of the war, and the resulting psychological disturbances, created a serial killer.

Dorothy B. Hughes was a distinguished writer of mystery fiction as well as an acclaimed biographer, poet and book reviewer. In 1950, she received the Edgar Allan Poe award from the Mystery Writers of America and, in 1978, she was named a Grand Master by the same organization. Her 14 novels include *The Fallen Sparrow* in 1942 and *Ride the Pink Horse* in 1946, both of which were made into successful films. *In a Lonely Place* was her 11th novel and received excellent reviews, the most typical of which was the one in the *Saturday Review of Literature* that called it, "an excellently written and chilling study of periodic blood lust." The title of the novel refers not only to the Synge play but to the mind of a killer, a lonely place in which he is trapped forever. The novel was written shortly after the war and reflects the national concern of the period with the emotional effects of war upon servicemen, as well as the growing interest of the public in the field of psychiatry.

Though the novel is suspenseful, it contains coincidences and contrivances that strain credibility. At the beginning, Steele just happens to find himself in the neighborhood of his old friend Brub, who just happens to be the police officer in charge of the case. Prior to that time, he just happened to run into Mel, another old acquaintance. Though he has traveled all across the country, he has managed to meet two old friends under improbable circumstances. Also, Brub just happens to learn of Brucie's death and Steele just happens to keep seeing the woman who resembles her. Equally detrimental to the novel is the fact that both Steele and Laurel are self-centered and unlikable. Steele lacks the fascination of, for instance, Patricia Highsmith's psychopathic Ripley who retains interest through several novels despite his homicidal amorality.

It would be three years before *In a Lonely Place* reached the screen and the film version would be barely recognizable to readers of the novel. *In a Lonely Place* was the third film produced by Humphrey Bogart's Santana productions for release by Columbia Pictures. Bogart had reached the height of his popularity through a series of movies made at Warner Bros. in the 1940s. In movies such as *The Maltese Falcon*, *Casablanca* and *To Have and Have Not* he developed a screen persona that made him extremely popular. But he wanted more challenging roles, as well as more control over future movies, and formed Santana in 1947 with writer and producer Mark Hellinger, who died shortly afterward.

Robert Lord produced *In a Lonely Place* and had previously been a writer and producer at Warner Bros. Lord functioned in the same role for the four Santana films made from 1948 to 1951. As executive producer, however, Bogart probably had the right to approve the ultimate decision to use the Hughes novel as merely an inspiration for a totally different story. Perhaps he realized that if the novel had been faithfully adapted to the screen, the main character would have been similar to roles he had played in some of his more forgettable Warner movies, such as *Conflict* and *The Two Mr. Carrolls*.

The screenplay was subjected to several modifications before production began and, pertaining to the climax, significantly altered during filming. The original treatment by Edmund H. North was reportedly a fairly straightforward adaptation of the novel while Solt's later screenplay is closer to the finished film, though it climaxes with Steele killing Laurel out of jealousy. According to reports, Ray and Bogart agreed to eliminate the final killing during production and changed the resolution at the last moment to the more powerful and poignant one that exists in the completed film. The decision to change the character of Steele from the novel's untalented writer who has nothing to do with the film industry into a Hollywood screenwriter adds another dimension to the story, for Hollywood is almost a character in itself. The superficiality and commercialism of the film colony is blatantly represented, as is the slightly veiled antagonism and nastiness of its denizens.

In the film, the character of Dixon Steele is more psychologically complex and enigmatic than the Dickson Steele of the novel, despite the thorough psychosocial portrait provided by the author in the novel. Unlike the novel, the screenplay provides no explanations or solutions for its protagonist's problems. He is not a murderer, at least not an actual one despite his potential, but he is an extremely volatile person who explodes violently at the slightest affront. His mood swings and periodic uncontrollable rage are due not to his childhood, to greed or to the war but to his artistic personality, which is frustrated by the business in which he is employed and the inartistic people with whom he must work.

The title of the movie remains appropriate, for it is about a man who is hopelessly trapped within the isolated place that is his mind. It refers as well, per Synge, to the desperate need of both Dix and Laurel to be close to someone. Bernard Eisenschitz, in his book *Nicholas Ray: An American Journey* (Faber and Faber; 1993), feels that it also refers to the film's depiction of Hollywood as a place of isolation, particularly for its protagonist. And Dix makes the most literal reference in the film, describing the lonely place in which the murder victim's body is found.

Dixon Steele is a middle-aged screenwriter whose quick temper and his disdain for the commercial demands of the film industry have made him virtually unemployable. Working in a profession in which he is judged by the financial success of his last film, he appears to be past the peak of his career and has become morose and cynical. However, there is another side of Dix, a side that is warm and charming, one that inspires loyalty, affection and love. He can be compassionate and kind to the defenseless, especially those that have been cast off by the Hollywood elite. But he is very guarded with these emotions and only allows those closest to him to be aware of them. In return, he expects that small circle of friends to live up to his high standards of integrity. The failure of others to live according to his standards will often be the impetus for his violence.

The opening sequence establishes the characterization of Dixon Steele. He is introduced under the main titles, the camera fixed on the back of his head as he drives through the night. His eyes are visible in the rear-view mirror, surrounded by darkness, alone. At the slightest provocation from another motorist, instantly he is ready to fight. A few moments later, he self-effacingly tolerates youngsters waiting for autographs in front of Paul's Restaurant, his favorite hangout, frequented by members of the film colony. Once inside

**Humphrey Bogart, Art Smith, Robert Warwick and Gloria Grahame all provide fine performances**

Paul's, the two sides of his personality are shown once again as he displays his quick temper to Junior, an arrogant son of a studio executive, and his kindness to Charlie Waterman, an elderly actor now ostracized by the film capital. To Lloyd Barnes, a director, he is brutally direct about the reasons for the director's success, none of which have to do with artistry.

Dix's devoted friend and agent, Mel Lippman, has good news for him. He has secured a contract for Dix to write the screenplay for a current bestseller, an assignment that will enable him to reclaim his former glory. Though he needs the work, Dix lacks the motivation to read the novel, knowing that it is trash and reluctant to compromise his integrity. A chance conversation with a hatcheck girl, Mildred Atkinson, provides a way out of his dilemma since she has read the novel and accepts his offer to give him a summary. Taking her to his apartment, he is momentarily distracted by the sight of a new neighbor, Laurel Grey, who passes by them. Inside his apartment, he is amused by Mildred's dramatic recreations of scenes from the novel but disgusted by its obvious lack of quality. Looking out of his window, he again sights Laurel on her balcony. Instantly attracted to her, he politely dismisses Mildred and gives her taxi money to get home.

The scenes with Mildred are amusing and once again Dix shows how charming he can be. The anger seething beneath the charm is obvious from the manner in which he throws his shoes to the floor. The anger is not directed

**Things turn grim when Dix and Laurel share an evening with Brub and Sylvia at the beach.**

toward Mildred but is just beneath the surface, waiting for someone like the belligerent motorist or Junior to bring it to the surface. Since Mildred is innocent and naïve, her off-screen murder will be shocking when it is revealed in the next sequence.

The film initially implies that Dix cannot be Mildred's killer because he sent her home, but some critics have suggested that, by not showing the crime, it leaves open the possibility that he may be guilty, a possibility that will become stronger as the film progresses. But such an evaluation, though valid to some degree, leaves out two important points. The audience has seen both the softer side of Dix and the fact that someone always provokes his explosive temper, particularly the person against whom he vents his rage. Mildred has done nothing to anger Dix and he even seems to like her. In view of this, it seems almost certain that Dix is not the killer. But this clarity is only for the audience, not for Laurel or the police. And as Dix's violence is increasingly displayed, even audiences begin to wonder along with Laurel if he may be the killer. The filmmakers awaken audience suspicion of Dix despite knowledge that he cannot be guilty.

When Dix's friend from the service, Detective Brub Nicolai, asks him to come to the station the next morning, Dix assumes that Junior may have pressed charges against him. After being told of Mildred's murder by Brub's superior, Captain Lochner, Dix keeps his true feelings to himself and replies to official questions with amusement and sarcasm. Initially unable to provide an alibi, Dix remembers his new neighbor who is brought down to the station and corroborates Dix's story that he sent Mildred away alone. But the film has not shown what Dix did after he sent Mildred away and the possibility is left open that Laurel may be providing a false alibi since she seems to be responding to Dix personally. However, despite her apparent interest, she lets him know that she is not easy and declines his invitation to share a cab home. Significantly, once he is alone, Dix anonymously sends flowers to Mildred's funeral, a gesture that he doesn't allow anyone to see.

The film's Laurel Grey, unlike the character in the novel, is sensitive and vulnerable. She has never been married but is just ending a relationship with a wealthy man. She is also a hopeful actress with small parts to her credit. Like Dix, she seems jaded to some degree and lonely as well. When she visits him to ask him if he can keep her name out of the newspapers, she doesn't initially respond to his romantic overtures but tells him that she will consider the offer. One of the film's most poignant scenes occurs when they next meet. Anxious for her answer, Dix doesn't try to contain his happiness when Laurel tells him that she is as interested in him as he is in her. While the Dix of the novel could only tell Laurel that "I knew you before I even saw you," the film's Dix is far more romantic and sincere in his emotions. "I've been looking for you all my life," he tells her. "I didn't know her name, where she lived, what she looked like. And then a girl was killed. And now I know your name, where you live, what you look like." When he kisses her, it is obvious that Dix has found not only the woman of his dreams but his salvation. Sadly and prophetically, Dix's words have also revealed his unconscious association of love with violence.

Once the romance begins, Dix and Laurel seem to be truly in love, each bringing the other happiness and fulfillment. Dix no longer seems to be on the verge of exploding at the slightest offense and starts adapting the novel into a superior screenplay. But his history of violence, combined with the fact that he was the last person seen with Mildred, makes him a prime suspect in her murder. Brub doesn't believe that Dix is guilty but cannot dissuade Lochner from ordering a closer investigation of his friend. Initially only mildly annoyed, Dix becomes increasingly agitated as suspicion of him begins to affect his relationship with Laurel. The rage within his character, now submerged by Laurel's love, will soon boil over due to the pressure of the surveillance and investigation.

Brub's wife Sylvia is a former psychology student and more educated than her husband. However, she tends to over-analyze and interpret even innocent behavior as symptoms of a disorder. After Dix re-enacts the murder as he believes it may have occurred, she tells Brub that Dix is a "sick man." His apparent excitement during the re-enactment causes Sylvia to wonder if the

**Dix and Laurel's happiness becomes increasingly threatened.**

specific details are due only to supposition. Sylvia's instant diagnosis can also be seen as an example of society's misunderstanding and distrust of artists whose behavior does not conform. Sylvia's behavior is particularly annoying because Dix is visiting one of his few friends and is exposing his true feelings because of his affection for both Brub and Sylvia, who grievously abuses the friendship. She will do this again later when she advises Laurel to end the relationship.

In defense of Dix, Brub explains that his friend is "an exciting guy" who was respected by the men under his command during the war and that his somewhat unusual behavior does not mean that he is a killer. But Brub feels obliged to convey Sylvia's opinions to Lochner, whose suspicions increase. Brub's reference to the war is not meant to explain Dix's behavior but to show how such behavior can be a positive trait. Similarly, later in the film, Mel tells Laurel that he hasn't seen Dix work so hard since before the war. While some may construe these words to imply that the war turned Dix into a killer, they could also mean that the war stifled his creativity, which has been reawakened by love. The words can be interpreted in either a positive or negative way by not only the characters in the film but by audiences who are once again being manipulated into assuming the best or worst about Dix.

During the course of the film, it becomes apparent that Dix presents a facade to the world that is the opposite of his true self. This façade keeps the world from intruding into his privacy and knowing how vulnerable he is. Dix knows that he is different, that he is an outsider. He sees things differently than most people because the same qualities that have made him an artist have given him this vision. He uses only the highest standards when writing, but the film industry doesn't want such high standards anymore because they won't sell tickets or popcorn. He refuses to compromise his art and he cannot tolerate people who sell out, as Lloyd Barnes has obviously done. He creates honesty and truthfulness in his scripts and he expects these qualities from people with whom he associates. But he works in an environment in which people who lack such principles have been rewarded with success, though they lack the artistry Dix possesses.

Dix wants to be close to someone but most people fear his dark side and he, in turn, rejects them for their hypocrisy. Dix allows only a few people to see beyond his facade because they accept him as he is. Mel Lippman and Charlie Waterman respond to the warmth they see within Dix and even Brub Nicolai, though he is not as close to him since he is not in the film industry, knows from past experiences that the real Dix is hidden from public view. And now, most meaningfully, Dix has allowed Laurel to see beyond the facade. But by exposing his real emotions, he is also exposing his wounds and scars. By fully revealing himself so completely to Laurel, he is placing all of his trust in her because he desperately wants the kind of happiness that only she can bring him.

However, there is a sense of fatalism throughout the film. Dix's happiness becomes increasingly threatened as society, represented not only by the police but by Laurel's masseuse Martha, who seems intent on punishing him whether he is guilty or not. It is significant that, while Dix's reactions to the provocations are extreme, it is also true that the provocations are unjustified. Martha's resentment of Dix is due not to the rumors she has heard but by his intrusion into her relationship with Laurel. Lochner's anger toward Dix may be due to the suspect's apparently callous attitude as much as his history.

Dix's explosive reactions increase primarily because he can sense the gradual changes in Laurel's behavior, and these changes are due directly to the seeds of distrust that are being planted within her. Ironically, now that he has found happiness with Laurel, fear of losing her and being forced back into that lonely place will increase his propensity for violence and give truth to the lies and suspicions that are being spread about him.

The scene at the beach, during which Dix and Laurel share an initially pleasurable evening with Brub and Sylvia, is momentous. Dix is almost euphoric in Laurel's company as he looks forward to the same happiness and stability that is represented by the Nicolais. In the midst of this idyllic scene, a remark by Sylvia reveals to Dix that Lochner has again interviewed Laurel about him. In Dix's mind, the three people with whom he is sharing his innermost feelings have been keeping secrets from him while he has been entirely open with them. But, more significantly, he now understands that the subtle changes in Laurel's behavior are due to the fact that he is still the prime suspect. This unleashes the anger that has been suppressed since he fell in love with Laurel.

Infuriated, Dix drives away with Laurel and sideswipes a car driven by a college student. In the altercation that follows, he loses control and beats the young man into unconsciousness. For a fraction of a second, it appears that he could actually kill the student, if not for Laurel's intervention. Dix's savagery frightens Laurel and forces her latent insecurity and doubts about Dix's innocence to the surface. Dix's outburst, precipitated by the web of suspicion that has infected everyone around him, seems almost irrelevant because of its ferocity.

Driving away, Dix is aware that Laurel has seen his dark side in all its ugliness. Regretting his outburst and sensing her fear, he recites the lines from his screenplay that expresses his love for her: "I was born when she kissed me; I died when she left me; I lived a few weeks while she loved me." He tells her that he wants to put the lines in his screenplay, but he is actually saying that if she leaves him, his life will be over. He asks her to repeat the lines, as though wanting her to re-affirm her love for him and hopefully forget what she has just witnessed. After she recites the lines, the car ominously disappears into the darkness. This is the turning point in the film and in Dix's relationship with Laurel. For Laurel, it is over, though she is too afraid to admit it to Dix or to herself. For Dix, he can only try to hold on to her, unwilling to admit that it is too late.

After that evening, Laurel seriously believes that Dix could have killed Mildred Atkinson. Lochner's warnings to her, Martha's spiteful rumors and Dix's fury have made the possibility all too real for her. She doesn't know, or perhaps wouldn't care, that Dix has tried to apologize to the student by sending him money. She doesn't realize that his intensity of love for her and the fear of losing her combined with the pressure of the investigation are driving Dix to extremes. Unable to sleep at night, she reverts to her habit of taking sleeping pills, thus indicating that society is forcing not only Dix back to his formerly unstable state but Laurel as well.

Frightened that he is losing her and aware that forces beyond his control are taking her away from him, Dix pressures Laurel into accepting his proposal of marriage. Laurel's acceptance is a deceitful one, for she has already decided to leave him. Unable to withstand the pressure and the fears driven into her, she secretly makes plans that will take her away. She confides in Mel who pleads with her to give Dix another chance, but her nerves are shattered. Her

COLUMBIA PICTURES present
HUMPHREY **BOGART**
In A
Lonely Place

**Dix is unable to control his dark side as the evidence against him grows.**

insecurity has made her all too susceptible to the malignant forces that have destroyed their relationship.

The penultimate scene at Paul's is painful for everyone in attendance. Sensing that he has already lost Laurel but being unable to accept it, Dix is suspicious of every word and gesture and is on the verge of exploding in fury. Laurel, fearful that he will learn of her plans to leave, is tense and quiet. Mel, aware of Laurel's intentions, dreads the effect the knowledge will have on Dix. Charlie Waterman is oblivious to the causes of the tension at the table but the concern on his face indicates his awareness of Dix's mood.

The appearance of Dix's former lover adds to the tension. Then Lloyd Barnes arrives and informs Dix that he loves his script. But Dix's anger increases with the knowledge that Laurel and Mel have given his screenplay to the director without his permission, instinctively suspecting their motives. Professional success means nothing to him and, once again, in his view, those closest to him have deceived him. Impulsively, he strikes out at Mel, shattering what is left of Laurel's attempt to conceal her feelings. Immediately regretful of hitting his closest friend, Dix follows Mel to the lounge and apologizes. The scene indicates Dix's true remorse for his actions, but the worst is yet to come. When he returns to his table and finds that Laurel has left, Dix furiously races after

**Laurel (Gloria Grahame) lovingly persuades Dix (Humphrey Bogart) to get some sleep.**

her, missing by moments that telephone call that could have salvaged their relationship.

Dix catches up with Laurel at her apartment as she is hastily packing. The scene is extremely suspenseful since Dix, already pushed to his breaking point, may learn at any moment of Laurel's plans. Laurel, fearful perhaps for her life, desperately tries to conceal her intentions but she seems increasingly unable to maintain her self-control. The scene is also emotionally wrenching because these two people, who seem to belong together, have been pushed to such a dangerous point. It is an indication of the skill of the actors and director that there still exists hope that the love Dix and Laurel shared will return and triumph, that the happiness they shared together should not be destroyed. Though the suspicion still exists that Dix could be the killer, particularly in view of his unbridled fury, there is the hope that he isn't. If Mel can forgive and retain his trust in Dix, then perhaps Laurel can. But her fear and his anger steadily increase with each passing moment. And then all hope is lost.

The telephone rings but it is not the call that could save them. It is the airline agent confirming Laurel's reservation and Dix now knows with certainty that he has lost her. The rage that has been building up within him explodes and he throws her savagely to the bed and nearly kills the only woman he will ever love. Whether it is the ringing of the telephone or his realization that he cannot commit murder that stops him—is insignificant. The call from the police that informs Dix of the actual murderer's confession has no effect on him for he knows that it is too late. He gives the telephone to a bruised Laurel who tearfully tells an apologetic Lochner, "Yesterday this would've meant everything; now it means nothing at all."

Drained of emotion, Dix looks back one last time at Laurel and then walks out of the apartment and down the stairway. In pain and in tears, Laurel looks down at him and recites the line that represented their love: "I lived a few weeks while you loved me." Then she adds, "Good-bye, Dix." Under the end title, separated from Laurel, Dix stands alone in the darkness as if frozen in time and space, looking ahead to a life of emptiness and desolation.

*In a Lonely Place* is an uncompromising vision of alienation and loss. The complex and mature screenplay by Andrew Solt is brilliantly brought to the screen by Nicholas Ray, whose unique talent was never more evident in this film, his fourth as director. His proficiency is particularly notable for the manner in which he balances the romantic scenes with the suspense of the murder investigation, the tension of which gradually intrudes upon the tenderness of the romance and eventually destroys it. Despite the undercurrent of violence that pervades the entire film, his depiction of the doomed romance is extremely gentle and memorable because it is so understated. An example of this is the scene in which Dix busily works on his screenplay while Laurel is careful not to disturb him and Mel happily spies upon them. Like the other scenes of intimacy, it is meaningful due to its simplicity and the implication that the relationship shouldn't end because these two people genuinely love one another.

However, Dix and Laurel do not exist in a vacuum. Ray skillfully creates the distinct impression of an unwholesome atmosphere permeating the world in which they must exist. Beneath the superficial glamour of Hollywood, pettiness and slightly veiled hostility always seems to be evident. And the zeal with which the representatives of law and order, represented more by Lochner than Brub, hound an innocent man implies a perversion of official authority. The world that Dix and Laurel inhabit is diseased and will eventually infect them and their love for one another. In Ray's cinematic world, the violence that Dix displays may be symptomatic of his pathology, but that same pathology is nourished by the hypocrisy around him, as well as the clouds of suspicion and hatred that can only flourish in an unhealthy environment.

Ray's visual style frequently uses light and shadows to convey Dix's inner turmoil. This style is particularly striking during the mock strangulation scene as well as the actual near-strangulation at the finale. Other scenes, including those at the restaurant, are emphasized by a visual directness that connotes the superficiality of the supposedly sophisticated setting. Ray's pacing is excellent and seamlessly combines pathos and suspense, tenderness and brutality from the beginning to the somber conclusion. The director's distinctive style is assisted tremendously by Burnett Guffey's cinematography and Viola Lawrence's editing.

Also notable is George Antheil's restrained and brooding score. Antheil was a composer of symphonies and operas, who was notorious for his iconoclastic compositions and daring instrumentation. Today, classical fans of the composer snobbishly feel that his work in Hollywood tarnished his reputation, an unjust assessment that is unfortunately bolstered by the fact that Columbia frequently used his scores as stock music for cheap programmers. He composed the scores for all four Santana productions and his music for *In a Lonely Place* is the most notable. The score includes a main theme that conveys the despondency and fatalism of the character of Dixon Steele but yet it is also marked by a suggestion of hope, particularly when Laurel enters his life. At the finale, however, the emotionalism of the images on screen is complemented perfectly by a reprise of the main theme, which builds to a climactic note of futility and despair.

Throughout his subsequent career, Nicholas Ray would often probe psychologically disturbed characters whose violent actions were caused by a hostile society. His body of work is commendable and contains many noteworthy films including *On Dangerous Ground* (1952), *Johnny Guitar* (1954) and *Party Girl* (1958). However, *In a Lonely Place* may be his most personal movie. Perhaps because his marriage to Gloria Grahame was falling apart during production, he was able to invest compassion and fragility into the romance. Of equal significance, Ray may have identified with Dixon Steele. Over the next decade, he found it increasingly difficult working within the commercial demands of the film capital and eventually left Hollywood for Europe. Except for small, independent films and a documentary, his last commercial movie was made in 1963, which is unfortunate, since he had many more productive years ahead of him. He was one of cinema's most gifted talents who was rarely afforded the freedom given today to directors of far less skill.

*In a Lonely Place* is perfectly cast. All of the supporting actors are fine with especially touching performances by Art Smith as Mel Lippman and Robert Warwick as Charley Waterman. Frank Lovejoy and Jeff Donnell are effectively sincere as Brub and Sylvia while Martha Stewart makes the most out of her brief role as the unfortunate Mildred Atkinson. Also notable are Paul Geray as Paul and Alice Talton as Dix's former lover. The expressions of concern displayed by Geray and Warwick upon seeing Dix slowly self-destruct, and the smug expression on Talton's face as she witnesses Dix direct his anger toward Laurel are just a few examples of the many little touches that contribute to the film's overall impact. The fact that Warwick and Mike Romanoff, who plays himself in the restaurant scenes, were close friends of Bogart adds to the believability of the relationships.

As Laurel Gray, Gloria Grahame provides just the right amount of both sensuality and vulnerability to make her character touchingly credible. Through her expressions and intonations, she manages to suggest sophistication that gradually crumbles into helplessness. The accomplished manner in which she conveys Laurel's steadily increasing doubts and fears make her betrayal of Dix lamentable but understandable. Prior to production, it was reported that executive producer Bogart initially wanted Lauren Bacall for the role but that Warner Bros. wouldn't release her. This is fortunate because Bacall's screen presence lacks the delicacy that Grahame exudes and which is so necessary for the character. Grahame's performance is an exceptional and memorable one.

At the center of the film is Humphrey Bogart's electrifying portrayal of Dixon Steele. Bogart completely captures the character's enigmatic and

**Dix and Laurel share a happy evening — but not for long.**

often contradictory emotions, from callous brutality to tender consideration, from arrogant self-confidence to anxious insecurity. His performance never falters and perfectly projects the ambiguity of a tortured artist at war with not only society but himself. It is a multi-faceted characterization that few actors could portray in such a laudable manner. While the menace he displays in some scenes is frighteningly real, the underlying warmth and sensitivity of the character are remarkably conveyed and make Steele, though unpredictably dangerous, ultimately highly sympathetic.

Several scenes illustrate the strength of conviction that Bogart brings to the role. When he makes breakfast for Laurel and tells her what she means to him by describing an ideal love scene in a movie, his expression and tone reflect not only love but anxiety, hope, regret and fear. The actor is also especially moving in the climactic restaurant scene, making Dix quite pitiful as each word and incident from everyone else at the table gradually augment his suspicions and fears. The expression of shame and contrition on his face as he apologizes to Mel for hitting him is painful to watch. And in the final scene, in which he almost becomes a murderer, he is terrifying, while the heartbreaking emptiness of the soul displayed afterward is truly affecting.

At the end of the film, it is clear from Bogart's expression that for Dixon Steele life no longer has any meaning. Whether he continues to write or

Humphrey Bogart

# Manden uden hemninger

···han går gennem livet som en ladt pistol

Produceret af **ROBERT LORD**    iscenesat af **NICHOLAS RAY**

**SKANDINAVISK FILM**

completely withdraws from human society is irrelevant. The actor creates the unmistakable impression that Dix's few weeks of happiness are over and will never return. With this role, Humphrey Bogart proves that he is a consummate artist.

In a Lonely Place was greeted by mixed reviews. In The New York Times, Thomas Pryor called it "a dandy film" and "a superior cut of melodrama."

Philip Hartung in *Commonweal* praised the cast, direction and script and called the movie "exciting cinema." Other reviews are somewhat puzzling. The reviewer for *Time* wrote that the movie "seems to take forever getting to the point," adding that the film concerns "the over-familiar love story of a hero-heel and a good-bad girl." This is such an absurd description of the film that it boggles the mind. The equally erroneous reviewer for *Newsweek* demonstrated his lack of understanding of the story's complexities by writing that "Dix is a war veteran and script-writer suffering from a touch of battle-rattle." The reviewer for *The New Yorker* called it "a pretty sharp commentary on Hollywood practices" but added that "as a murder mystery [it] suffers from being a trifle incredible." Which it isn't at all. Unfortunately, such misguided reviews probably had an effect upon the film's fate at the box office.

The film was not a financial success. On *Variety*'s annual list of Top-Grossing Films for the year 1950, 95 movies earned domestic theatrical rentals of more than $1 million. *In a Lonely Place* ranked 85th with only $1.4 million. This poor reception by the public may have been due to a number of factors other than some poor reviews. Columbia did not seem to know how to sell the film. On advertisements for the film, the tagline read, "Suspense in the night, intrigue at dawn, suspicion around the clock." This gave the impression that the movie was a typical mystery tale. Audiences expecting a crime thriller had to be disappointed to be viewing a tragic romance in which the crime is secondary to the main theme. In fact, neither the murder nor the killer's apprehension are even shown. The posters for the movie also featured the line, "The Bogart picture with the surprise ending." This is equally misleading since the revelation of the actual killer is secondary to the story's real focus, which is the relationship between Dix and Laurel.

Religious spectacles were immensely popular during this period. The top grossing film on the *Variety* list was *Samson and Delilah* (which had been released in December 1949 in New York City but in January 1950 in the rest of the country) with $11 million. Also at the top of the 1950 list, earning between $4.5 and $3.5 million, was a World War II movie (*Battleground*), an adventure film (*King Solomon's Mines*), a musical (*Annie Get Your Gun*) and two comedies (*Cheaper By the Dozen* and *Father of the Bride*). Furthermore, movies about Hollywood didn't seem to appeal to audiences in 1950. Released the same year, Billy Wilder's acclaimed *Sunset Boulevard* received much more careful promotion but earned only a respectable 2.3 million to rank 29th on the list.

Another factor may have been the reluctance of audiences to accept Humphrey Bogart in such a different role. Prior to 1950, his most commercially successful films were those in which he perfected the familiar Bogart persona of a tough, independent hero, whether as a private detective, an owner of a nightclub or the skipper of a boat. *The Treasure of the Sierra Madre* also provided him with a markedly different characterization but was advertised as an adventure film; yet, despite critical plaudits for his performance as a crazed killer, it was still disappointing at the box office compared to his other movies of the period such as *The Big Sleep*, *To Have and Have Not* and *Key Largo*. In 1951, audiences would love him as the boozy hero of *The African Queen* but that film is a comedy-adventure with a joyous ending. By 1954, audiences would appreciate the versatility he displayed in *The Caine Mutiny* and make it a major commercial success, but that movie was based upon a best-selling novel and was a pre-sold commodity.

And still another factor may have been the downbeat ending of the film. It is quite possible that audiences of the early 1950s wanted to believe in the redemptive power of love and that love could triumph over all adversity. The message of this film is quite the opposite. The year 1950 may have been too early for such a searing melodrama with a heartrending finale.

Regardless of its commercial fate, *In a Lonely Place* is a superb depiction of loneliness and alienation temporarily relieved by love. It is about a painfully flawed human being who reaches out one last time for salvation and is destroyed by his environment and by his own tortured soul.

*In a Lonely Place* is a masterpiece.

CREDITS: Producer: Robert Lord; Director: Nicholas Ray; Screenplay: Andrew Solt, Adaptation by Edmund H. North, Based on the Novel by Dorothy B. Hughes; Cinematographer: Burnett Guffey; Editor: Viola Lawrence; Music: George Antheil

CAST: Humphrey Bogart (Dixon Steele); Gloria Grahame (Laurel Grey); Frank Lovejoy (Brub Nicolai); Art Smith (Mel Lippman); Carl Benton Reid (Captain Lochner); Jeff Donnell (Sylvia Nicolai); Martha Stewart (Mildred Atkinson); Robert Warwick (Charley Waterman); Morris Ankrum (Lloyd Barnes); Stephen Geray (Paul); Alice Talton (Frances Randolph); Jack Reynolds (Henry Kesler); Hadda Brooks (Singer); Ruth Gillette (Martha); Ruth Warren (Effie); Lewis Howard (Junior); William Ching (Ted Barton); Guy Beach (Swan); Don Hamin (John Mason); Robert Davis (Street Waterer)

# TRY AND GET ME!

## AKA: THE SOUND OF FURY

In November 1933, in the small town of San Jose, California, three brutal murders occurred. Jack Holmes and Harold Thurman committed the first murder when they kidnapped and brutally bludgeoned to death 21-year-old department store heir Brooke Hart and then attempted to extort money from his parents. The second and third murders were committed by several hundred citizens of San Jose who stormed the jail, yanked the prisoners out of their cells, dragged them kicking and screaming to a nearby park and hanged them.

It would be convenient to consider the Depression and its accompanying hard times as factors in the murders. However, the two kidnappers were both employed and from families that were financially comfortable. The lynch mob was comprised of people from all strata of society, including prosperous businessmen, working class people and students from nearby Santa Clara University, including a famous former Hollywood child star. And there were thrill-seekers and people looking for an excuse to kill with impunity.

According to his family, Harold Thurman was mentally impaired, the result of an accident in his childhood. He was supposedly easily led and subservient to the more aggressive Holmes, who wanted more money than his salary as an oil company salesman provided. But Thurman knew right from wrong and Holmes planned the horrific deed because of desire for a woman. Both men knew that if they concealed their faces they wouldn't have had to kill Hart, but they decided that killing him would be less troublesome than keeping him prisoner.

And both men understood the cruelty of promising parents the safe return of their son after bludgeoning him to death and throwing his body in a lake. They were undoubtedly sadistic murderers.

In view of their confessions, the two killers would have been convicted in a court of law and legally executed. But the mob would not have had the satisfaction of drawing blood. Though they assumed self-righteousness, the vigilantes destroyed such claims by the savagery they displayed. The mob pummeled the men into bloody messes, burned them, tore their clothes off and then hung them, cheering ecstatically as the faces of the hanged men turned black and their naked bodies swung back and forth. Women held their children up to give them a better view of the lifeless bodies, while men proudly had their pictures taken.

The lynching was the result of many factors. Following the arrests of the two men, a local newspaper and a radio station had inflamed the mood of the townspeople and encouraged the lawlessness that eventually erupted. Prior to the lynching, the political bosses of San Jose had signified their approval of the atrocity through a variety of subtle messages. The governor of California had promised a pardon for anyone charged with lynching, if the act should occur. As the mob gathered around the jail, the governor also refused to send in the National Guard to protect the prisoners, thereby ensuring their fate. Furthermore, the local sheriff had promised that gunfire would not be used against the rioters, further encouraging them.

In 1933, lynching was not an uncommon occurrence. There were 28 lynchings nationwide in that year alone and all but four of the victims were black. Regardless of the race of the victims, the lynchers all shared the same traits of cowardice, lawlessness and savagery. Alone, each person would not have had the courage to act, but as part of a mob, they became emboldened and shed all traces of civilization in order to experience the thrill of killing someone.

A disturbing motivation for members of the mob was advanced by John Steinbeck in his 1936 story "The Lonesome Vigilante," which was inspired by the San Jose lynching. In the story, a man who has taken part in the lynching stops in a bar on his way home, delights in recounting his part in the killing and sells a piece of the victim's clothing to the bartender. (In reality, lynchers tore pieces of clothing from the bodies, cut the ropes into pieces and slashed bark off the trees to keep as souvenirs.) After returning home, the man is greeted by his angry wife who accuses him of being with another woman because of his demeanor. The man suddenly realizes that his sensation has been one of sexual excitement.

The most authoritative account of the atrocity can be found in the book, *Swift Justice* by Harry Farrell (St. Martins Press; 1992). Besides providing the definitive version of the kidnapping and lynching, Farrell raises many questions about the crimes that will never be answered because of the collapse of justice in the town. The author also reveals that Jackie Coogan, beloved child star of the 1920s, was in the forefront of the lynch mob. The dust jacket of *Swift Justice* notes that the lynching "was the basis for the landmark Fritz Lang film, *Fury*," but does not mention a 1950 movie originally called *The Sound of Fury*, and later re-titled *Try and Get Me!*, that was far closer to the actual facts of the case and remains far more impressive, though it is generally unknown.

Lang's *Fury* was released in 1936 and is the story of an honest auto mechanic, Joe Wheeler, who is falsely accused of kidnapping and jailed. As word of the arrest spreads through town, the citizens quickly turn into a mob and set the jail afire. Joe escapes but keeps his survival a secret as he plots revenge against the vigilantes. After various members of the mob are brought to trial, Joe eventually repents due to the pleading of his fiancée. Though still embittered, Joe at least can look forward to starting a new life.

Loosely inspired by the San Jose lynching, *Fury* is an effective indictment of mob psychology and the baseness of human nature, which seems to only need a convenient excuse to be unleashed. Fritz Lang's direction is indicative of his usual expressionism, particularly in the development of the mob and the savagery of their actions. However, the script tends to be contrived with overly melodramatic scenes. *Fury* is a good movie but it is tarnished by the implausible plot twists and the happy ending that doesn't fit in with the tone of the film.

In addition to boasting an esteemed director, *Fury* starred A-list actors Spencer Tracy and Sylvia Sidney, and was released by a major studio, MGM. In contrast, *The Sound of Fury* was helmed by an unknown director, featured lesser-known actors associated with B movies and was an independent production.

The genesis for *The Sound of Fury* was the publication of a novel called *The Condemned* by Jo Pagano (Prentice Hall; 1947). In the early 1930s, Pagano began writing stories that were published in magazines such as *Atlantic Monthly*, *Scribner's* and *Argosy*. His first book was a collection of stories entitled *The Paesanos*, published in 1940, followed by a novel, *Golden Wedding* in 1943; both books were about the Italian-American experience in America and received critical acclaim. Pagano's first credited screenplay is a B movie released in 1938 entitled *Tarnished Angel*. He subsequently either wrote or co-wrote numerous programmers, including everything from a Hopalong Cassidy movie to a couple of Ace the Wonder Dog movies. He came close to an A movie when he did the adaptation for *The Man I Love* in 1947 but was soon back in the B world.

None of Pagano's screenplays or previous books contains the intensity and passion that are displayed in *The Condemned*. Using the San Jose lynching as the basis for his story, Pagano crafted a gripping novel with skillful characterizations and genuine emotion that never crosses over into sensationalism. The setting is Santa Sierra, a small town in California. Unemployed Howard Tyler, hoping to improve his family's life, joins petty crook Jerry Slocum in committing a series of hold-ups. They graduate to a kidnapping and Slocum's brutal murder of the victim, which leads to their lynching by a mob of the town's enraged citizens, who have been aroused by the inflammatory articles of reporter Gil Stanton.

Pagano's novel ambitiously attempts to explore the reasons for the violent behavior of human beings, which he suggests is the direct result of the society that they have created. Through one of his characters, he asserts that humans have lost the moral center of their universe by replacing God with self-centered materialism. The lack of a moral base and the desire for possessions, combined with other environmental factors, give free rein to the suppressed and sordid facets of human nature, illustrated either by the brutal act of the two misfits or the collective act of an angry mob.

Howard Tyler, the product of an impoverished childhood, is a victim of his society. His deprived background and limited capabilities have placed him at a disadvantage since childhood and are responsible for his fate as well as the fate of his wife who, as a result of his lynching, suffers a miscarriage and collapses into madness. Even the repugnant Jerry Slocum is afforded some understanding, if not sympathy, when it is revealed by his autopsy that he had a tumor on his brain. The motivations of the vigilantes are proposed through three of the leaders, whose characterizations provide an insight into the mechanism by which a crowd becomes a lynch mob.

However, the novel is marred by the author's interruptions of the story with philosophical reflections by the unnamed narrator. This exploration of the ethics of crime and punishment occurs so often that it almost relegates the main characters to secondary status. Though Pagano deserves credit for attempting to provide an explanation for violent behavior, it would have been preferable to convey the same messages through the storyline. Nevertheless, the novel remains powerful, especially in its depiction of the horrifying climax toward which the entire narrative has been leading from the first page.

Robert Stillman Productions acquired the motion picture rights to *The Condemned*, for release through United Artists. In the 1940s, Stillman functioned as assistant director on several films, and in 1949, was associate producer to Stanley Kramer on two movies, the boxing drama *Champion* and the searing depiction of racism during World War II, *Home of the Brave*. The social consciousness of those two films had perhaps inspired Stillman to explore further some of the societal ills that were hidden beneath the superficial prosperity and security of post-War American society. In 1950, he formed his own production company and signed Pagano to adapt his novel to the screen. He also signed Cyril Endfield to direct the film version of *The Condemned*, which during production had its title changed to *The Sound of Fury*.

Newspaper headlines deliberately inflame the public.

Cy Endfield was born in 1914 in Pennsylvania and attended Yale University, becoming briefly involved with the Young Communist League as well as becoming an accomplished magician. In the 1930s, he worked with progressive theater groups in New York as drama coach and director. He also directed for extended periods in Montreal and in the Catskills. In the early1940s, he moved to Hollywood where his skills as a magician, particularly with card tricks, brought him to the attention of Orson Welles, who hired him as an apprentice in his Mercury Productions. His first directing effort was a short subject for MGM entitled *Inflation* in 1942, which was perceived by the Chamber of Commerce as anti-capitalist and, after a few showings, was shelved (it would not be shown again until the 1990s.) After several more shorts at MGM, he moved up to low-budget productions at smaller studios. He directed his first feature in 1946, *Gentleman Joe Palooka*, which was followed by additional inauspicious programmers. However, his fifth film was *The Underworld Story* in 1950, an effective B movie about corruption in the press and in politics. Ingrained within the movie was criticism of unscrupulous methods within the House Un-American Activities Committee (HUAC), which had Hollywood in a grip of fear due to its hunt for Communists within the film industry.

Stillman reunited Frank Lovejoy and Lloyd Bridges, who had co-starred in *Home of the Brave*, for *The Sound of Fury*. In its denunciation of mob violence and its indictment of class divisions, the movie is more pessimistic than Kramer's exposés of the brutality of the boxing industry and bigotry in the military. Unlike the two Kramer films, in which the innate goodness of humanity prevailed, this movie contains a sense of futility and despair, due to oppressive environmental factors as well as the potential for evil lurking beneath the surface of civilized human beings once they become part of a mob. The correlation with HUAC "witch-hunters" is obvious.

Pagano's screenplay, with uncredited contributions from director Endfield, improves upon the novel. The narrative is more straightforward and doesn't allow any respite from the tension, which begins immediately and steadily escalates. The film's Howard Tyler is more intelligent and mature than his counterpart in the novel, thus making his dilemma more unjust. In view of his capabilities and his desire to do any kind of work, he should be able to find a job but none is available. Though his impoverished background is eliminated from the film, he remains a sympathetic victim, especially in view of his unwilling participation in the horrific crime. Jerry Slocum's brain tumor is also eliminated, not allowing even a trace of sympathy for a truly despicable character.

The movie opens with a brief but potent pre-credits sequence in which a blind preacher tries in vain to warn a crowd of unconcerned people to be aware of their shared guilt and to repent for their sins. But the people are not listening and this sets the tone for the entire film. The main story then begins with Howard Tyler hitching a ride home after unsuccessfully traveling out of town in hope of finding a job. Already there is a sense of despondency emanating from within Howard as he explains his plight to a truck driver. Having taken his wife and son from Massachusetts to California to find a better life in which to raise his family, he has found only unemployment and poverty.

Back at home in the small town of Santa Sierra, Howard's natural decency is evident as he gives 50 cents to his son, Tommy, knowing that he cannot spare even such a small amount. His rent is overdue and his wife Judy cannot afford to pay a doctor to monitor her pregnancy or even buy groceries. His impulsive gift to his son leads to an argument that reveals the extent of his misery as well as Judy's. Howard's inability to provide even basic needs for his family will drive him out of the home in anger and will lead him to a meeting that will begin his destruction.

Frustrated and depressed, Howard goes to a local bowling alley for a beer. Gil Stanton, reporter for the Santa Sierra Journal, is at the alley but the two men do not notice one another, destined to meet only when Howard is about to face a horrible death due in part to Gil's irresponsibility. Ominously, Howard strikes up a conversation with Jerry Slocum, who projects an appearance of prosperousness. A chance remark by Howard reveals his need for a job to Jerry whose subtle reaction suggests that Howard's desperation just might fit into his plans. Using a possible job as a lure, Jerry entices Howard to his room and eventually tells him that he needs an accomplice for a hold-up. When Howard refuses, Jerry contemptuously humiliates him for his integrity and his fear. The tactic has its desired effect and Howard is ensnared.

**Howard Tyler (Frank Lovejoy) despondently walks into the bowling center — and destroys his life.**

The first hold-up is nerve-wracking for Howard, but he is able to bring food home. After another hold-up, Gil Stanton and his editor Hal Clendenning build up circulation for their newspaper by inventing a crime wave, creating a foundation of fear and anger among the citizens. But Howard only knows that his wife can now get proper care for their unborn child and he doesn't have to hide from the landlord. Telling Judy that he is working nights, Howard takes part in additional hold-ups, but he remains fearful that the chances of getting caught steadily increase with each crime. Thus, when Jerry suggests one big crime that will set them up for life, Howard cannot resist the temptation.

However, Jerry's big crime involves kidnapping Donald Miller, the son of a local wealthy family. Jerry makes it seem so simple since all they will have to do is hold Miller prisoner in an abandoned shack, collect the ransom and then free him. Thinking of his family's security, Howard reluctantly decides to go along, vowing that it will be his last crime. But everything goes wrong and Howard is unable to stop Jerry from brutally murdering Miller. Displaying no remorse, Jerry forces Howard to proceed with the plan. He arranges for two women, Velma and Hazel, to accompany them to a neighboring town, figuring that two couples will not create suspicion, and mails the ransom notes.

Howard initially seems to function like a zombie, as though he cannot believe what has happened. Unable to face Judy, he gets drunk and flees to the lonely Hazel where his tearful agitation betrays his responsibility in the murder. Frantically running away, Howard hides in a shed until he is arrested. It is obvious from his overwhelming anguish that he cannot live with his guilt

**The townspeople turn into an angry lynch mob in the horrifying finale of *The Sound of Fury*.**

and knows that he and Jerry must be punished for what they have done. But he has no idea of what type of inhumane punishment awaits him.

With Howard and Jerry in jail, Gil's articles have exploited the murder and instigated the citizens into a hunger for vengeance. Frantic to save her husband's life, Judy (who is spared the fate of her novel's counterpart) pleads with Gil for help and shows him Howard's letter to her from the jail, in which he begs her to believe that he didn't know of Jerry's intention to murder Miller. Now aware of his recklessness, Gil is helpless to stop the chain of events which are quickly unfolding near the jail. Gradually, the crowd of angry townspeople turns into a lynch mob, each formerly decent citizen feeling strengthened by the increasing size of the mob. Storming the jail, the mob drags Howard and Jerry from their cells and hangs them as a horrified Gil stands powerlessly by, unable to stop the fury that he has helped to unleash. Gil, totally grief-stricken, promises that he will never forgive himself or let the townspeople forget what they have done.

The screenplay for *The Sound of Fury* makes no compromises. Howard Tyler's destruction is as much the result of his environment as of the individual savagery of Jerry Slocum and the collective savagery of the lynch mob. Unable to provide for his family, Howard can only feel increasingly alienated in a hostile and uncaring society. He feels responsible for Judy's increasing despair as her hopes for a better life are repeatedly crushed. He has played by the rules all of his life. He served honorably in the war, risking his life for his country, and then was fully prepared to work hard to fulfill the American dream. But society didn't play by the rules and a chance encounter persuaded him that his only recourse was to break those rules for the survival of his family.

Jerry Slocum, on the other hand, has made his own rules and seems to be enjoying a prosperous life, his pockets so full of money that he can scornfully throw a $10 bill to a desperate Howard. The tragedy of Howard's fate is that he met Jerry when he was most susceptible to the lure of a quick solution to the unbearable weight of the pressures that were crushing his family. Seeing Judy smile again was enough to alleviate his guilt at breaking the law for the first time in his life. He didn't want to see her worry again, not while she was pregnant, and he couldn't see the trap that Jerry had set for him until it was too late.

If there is a fault in the screenplay, it is the same one that is carried over from the novel, though it is not as extensive. The character of Dr. Vido Simone assumes a tutorial tone and lectures Gil on social responsibility. He repeatedly warns Gil of the folly of his actions and periodically expresses the necessity of morality based upon philosophical reasoning. Though not overly intrusive to the storyline, the character and the dialogue are superfluous. The message is clear enough without him, but it is a tolerable flaw. The script's power remains intact.

Cy Endfield's approach to his subject is stark and unrelenting, especially in depicting an increasingly alienated world that corrupts Howard Tyler. The director's visual treatment of despair and helplessness that destroys Howard and his family is effectively realized with great impact. The opening scene takes place at night and the blackness surrounding Howard seems almost suffocating as he expresses his plight to the truck driver. The film noir aspects of this scene, enhanced by the stark black-and-white cinematography, suggest the inevitability of Howard's fate as though he is already trapped by circumstances over which he has no control. Endfield visually underscores the concept of Howard's moral descent through closeups during the first holdup and particularly during the murder. The increasingly frenzied Howard is repeatedly contrasted with the psychopathic Jerry Slocum, as well as the self-righteous Gil Stanton, and Howard emerges with the most sympathy.

However, it is Endfield's staging of the riot and lynching that leaves an indelible memory. Cutting from the bloodthirsty rioters throwing rocks, breaking doors and trampling ineffective lawmen, to the prisoners trapped within their cells as the uncontrolled savagery gets increasingly closer, the director conveys the total collapse not only of justice but of civilization. As the screaming prisoners are dragged from their cells by supposedly law-abiding citizens, the unmistakable impression is made that there is no difference between the mob and Jerry Slocum. The horror of the sequence is so effective that the actual lynching of the two men does not have to be shown. The roar of the crowd as each body is hung is all that is needed to fully convey the unmitigated savagery of the act. This movie should have established Endfield as a major film director and probably would have if not for the political climate enveloping Hollywood.

In the role of Howard Tyler, Frank Lovejoy gives a superlative performance. Lovejoy had acted on the stage and extensively on radio. In 1948, he didn't make an impression as a supporting actor in his first film, a B western entitled *Black Bart*, but he was more noticeable as a decent soldier in *Home of the Brave* the following year. Basically, he seemed to lack the magnetism necessary to be a star and appeared to be a good candidate for supporting roles. However, when he was given star billing for the first time in *The Sound of Fury*, his seventh movie, he proved to be an exceptionally fine actor with a memorable portrayal of the doomed protagonist.

Lovejoy has often been described as a reliable actor who could always be cast in Everyman roles, the kind of guy who doesn't stand out in a crowd. Howard Tyler is deliberately written to be that sort of person, thus making him uncomfortably identifiable to members of the audience who knew in 1950 how easy it would be to become unemployed and desperate. Lovejoy's sincere portrayal of this Average Joe suggests both vulnerability and integrity that makes him immediately deserving of compassion.

Lovejoy initially creates a portrait of a good man whose shame at being unable to find a job makes him prone to behaviors that he would never have otherwise considered. Several sequences in particular showcase a truly fine actor. There is the scene in which Howard, unable to sleep, stares out the window from his darkened room; he doesn't say a word but yet he succinctly conveys fear, anger and quiet desperation. His agonizing expression of panic and disbelief as he is unable to stop Jerry from murdering Miller is horrifyingly convincing. Equally memorable is the confession scene with Hazel that is particularly difficult because it is evident that Howard is filled with remorse and self-hatred. He wants to conceal his crime for his family's sake but simultaneously has a desperate need to confess to be relieved of the unbearable guilt that is consuming him. Lovejoy expertly projects these contradictory emotions. And the terror on his face in the climactic scene as he is dragged from his cell is shocking in its impact. This is a splendid performance from an underrated actor that should have received recognition during the award season but was unjustly ignored.

As Jerry Slocum, Lloyd Bridges is mesmerizing as a psychopath without a trace of conscience. Bridges had started acting in the mid-1930s and appeared in uncredited and small parts for over a decade. In the 1940s, he started getting larger roles, received his first starring billing in a programmer called *Hideout* and then had his first important role in *Home of the Brave*, as a superficially liberal soldier whose latent racism is exposed.

In *The Sound of Fury*, Bridges creates a loathsome character whose exterior bluster masks an amoral and sadistic brute. From his first appearance, Jerry Slocum projects narcissism as he displays his expertise in a bowling alley. Later, in his room, he struts around shirtless as though he is looking for praise for his physique. The manner in which his shallow friendliness quickly turns to contempt for Howard's honesty reveals the true nature that will become increasingly evident until his merciless killing of the hapless Miller betrays the monster within. In the climactic riot scene, he projects the appearance of a terrified animal expertly as he frenetically paces in his cell, his hysteria steadily increasing as the sounds of the lynch mob get louder and closer. This is another performance that should have received an Oscar nomination from Academy members who were probably too frightened to reward a movie with an obvious social message.

Other performers are uniformly fine. Richard Carlson is convincing as Gil Stanton, whose awareness of his own culpability appears too late. Kathleen Ryan is touchingly effective as Judy, particularly in the scene in which she helplessly watches Howard emerge from the shed in which he has been cowering, her expression reflecting confusion and devastation. Katherine Locke makes a strong impression as Hazel, suggesting pathos and loneliness in her few but significant scenes. All of the players bring an emotional commitment to their roles, no matter how small, which adds to the overall impact of the film. Location filming took place in Phoenix, Arizona and many extras during the riot scenes were students from Arizona State College, which is ironic in view of the role played by students from Santa Clara University in the actual San Jose lynching.

Reviews in the trade papers were very encouraging. *Variety* called the movie "shocking but gripping (and) thoroughly effective." *Film Daily* called it "a brilliant achievement." *Box Office* called it "gutsy, uncompromising (and) distinguished." *Motion Picture Daily* called it "excellent entertainment (that) builds to one of the most powerful sequences to be seen on the screen." All of the trade publications predicted a healthy box office. Such predictions would prove to be erroneous.

In view of the movie's bitterness and downbeat ending, United Artists may have been unsure of how to publicize it. Earlier in the year, Paramount had released *The Lawless*, a film about mob violence and discrimination against Mexican fruit pickers in California that, despite good reviews, failed at the box office. Proceeding slowly and hoping that positive word of mouth would publicize the film, United Artists tested *The Sound of Fury* in six cities in November, 1950 prior to its official release in January, 1951. The original ad campaign for the movie was low-key but reflective of its quality. The poster featured a minimum of copy and artwork and had no montages, just a small picture of Lovejoy and Ryan holding one another, surrounded by darkness, expressions of fear on their faces as they seem to be looking toward some unseen terror. There is no such scene in the movie, but it is still an excellent, though symbolic, representation of the film's implication of the uncontrollable forces that destroy the Tylers.

Upon release, *The Sound of Fury* received some positive reviews. *Newsweek* called it "a grim and highly effective melodrama," praised Lovejoy and Bridges for being "completely persuasive in their contrasting roles" and Endfield for his direction of the lynching which "compounds hysteria and sadism into a nerve-shattering climax." *Redbook*'s reviewer also liked it, calling it "engrossing, intensely realistic (and) a film not easily forgotten." But it also received many negative reviews. Bosley Crowther in *The New York Times* called it "a brooding film" and complained that its arguments "are so doleful and negative that they offer no demonstration of correction or hope." The reviewer for *Time* compared the movie unfavorably to both *Fury* and *The Lawless* and criticized its "amateurish script construction, academic soap box speeches and lack of insight into the mechanism of mob violence." *Commonweal*'s reviewer complained "we end up feeling lectured at" while *Library Journal*'s review carped that the film "is based on disputable premises."

The negative reviews may have affected the film's box office performance since initial business was disappointing. In an article in *Variety* in March, 1951, it was reported that "*The Sound of Fury* played several engagements and, on the basis of spotty returns, a change of title was in order." It is also possible that the similarity of the title to *Fury* was a factor. Producer Stillman decided upon *Try and Get Me!* and this is the title under which it was released throughout most of the country, two exceptions being the Los Angeles and San Francisco areas due to earlier ad campaigns for the film in those two cities under the original title.

Accompanying the new action-promising title were new advertisements for the movie that tried to sell it as a lurid thriller and were totally deceptive. In the center of the primary poster was a photograph of B movie femme fatale Adele Jergens (who played the small role of the greedy Velma) in a suggestive dress, accompanied by the taglines: "A blonde with ice-cold nerves and deep warm curves! The hottest dame you ever met!" Underneath a photograph of Lloyd Bridges holding a gun were the words: "A gunman who robbed and killed for this beautiful doll who played him for a sucker!" Another line was equally misleading: "6000 hunt the killer all because of a blonde bombshell!"

The title change didn't help the movie and the new ad campaign probably hurt it. In *Variety*'s chart of Top Grossing Films of 1951, there are 131 movies that earned the minimum of $1 million in domestic theatrical rentals. Topping the list was the religious spectacle *Quo Vadis* with $11.9 million, followed by the musical *Show Boat* with $5.2 million and *David and Bathsheba* with $4.7 million. *Try and Get Me!* did not earn the minimum figure and is not on the list. Another movie about a lynching did better business. *Storm Warning* was a Warner Bros. release about a woman who witnesses a Ku Klux Klan lynching. It received more publicity than *Try and Get Me!* since it was a major studio release with big stars (Ginger Rogers, Ronald Reagan, Doris Day). While earnest, it lacks the power of the United Artists release due to routine direction and a predictable script. But it is 105th on the list with $1.25 million. Also on the list is a movie called *I Was a Communist for the F.B.I* that was 97th with $1.3 million.

*Try and Get Me!* failed to win recognition from the Academy of Motion Picture Arts and Sciences. It received no Academy Award nominations and no acknowledgment from any other organization, at least not in the United States. Upon its subsequent release in England under the title of *The Sound of Fury*, Gavin Lambert wrote in *Sight and Sound* that: "The characterizations and the handling of the drama are remarkable, at times reaching a complexity rare in films of this type." In *Punch*, Richard Mallett apparently was disturbed by the movie, calling it "A strange, uncomfortable sometimes brutal and depressing picture." Though not a major box office success, it received a nomination for a BAFTA (British Academy of Film and Television Arts) Award for Best Film from Any Source. It was also nominated for BAFTA's United Nations Award.

Unfortunately, compared to subsequent events, the commercial failure of *Try and Get Me!* would prove to be a relatively minor problem for Endfield and other personnel associated with the film. In 1947, HUAC had begun its hearings into Communist influence within Hollywood. The hearings resulted in the imprisonment of several artists—the Hollywood Ten—who had refused to testify and were charged with contempt of Congress. Some of the more defiant members of the Ten had practically invited such punishment by their extremely belligerent attitude. In 1951, HUAC launched a second investigation and, as a result, scores of people within the entertainment industry were barred from working. Several of the participants of *Try and Get Me!* came under suspicion by HUAC. In addition to their alleged political sentiments, the film's implied criticism of American society may have been a factor in creating that suspicion.

There was, incidentally, a justified reason for HUAC. During World War II, when the Soviet Union was an ally of the United States, movies such as *Song of Russia*, *The North Star* and *Mission to Moscow* portrayed Joseph Stalin favorably, praised Russia and depicted its collective farmers as cheerful workers devoted to their leaders. After the War, when Russia became an enemy, members of the American Communist Party (CPUSA) within the film industry remained loyal to the Party. Their true status as tools of a foreign power has recently been documented in *The Soviet World of American Communism*, edited by Haynes, Klehr and Anderson (Yale University Press; 1998). This book, based upon newly declassified documents from Soviet Archives, proves that the CPUSA was controlled by Soviets who dictated that party members should use their positions to extol the virtues of Communism, to infiltrate the studios' labor unions, to show the evils of capitalism and to prevent anti-Communist themes from being filmed.

Following the end of the blacklist, revisionists have since described those who cooperated with HUAC as informers while romanticizing the Hollywood Ten as noble defenders of free speech. Actually, the friendly witnesses—including one of the original Ten who decided to cooperate—were truthfully relating how they were deceived by some of the ideological principles used by the Party to entice altruistic personnel into their ranks; it is ironic that these people, because they identified known Communists, have since been defamed by Hollywood radicals in the same way that the blacklist victims were once defamed. The radical members of the Hollywood Ten were not "victimized heroes" but were long-term members of the CPUSA who were devoted to the Party and to their Soviet controllers. These fanatics, along with many other loyal comrades, discounted Stalin's forced starvation in the Ukraine, his Great Purge, his Gulag labor camps and his murder of millions.

The real tragedy of the HUAC hearings is that the committee members persecuted scores of innocent people. These victims were idealistic liberals who, like the friendly witnesses, had been attracted to various positions promoted by the CPUSA but became gradually dismayed by the Party's adherence to the Soviet Union. They were also upset because of the brutal tactics within the Party that would not tolerate deviance from its rigid tenets and demanded strict obedience to its precepts. But the final straw was the shocking revelations about the Soviet system and Stalin's policies, which gradually became known to the rest of the world. Stunned by such horrors, they left the Party. Regrettably, because of their past associations, many of them were unjustly blacklisted by HUAC. Careers and lives were destroyed. And this brings us back to *Try and Get Me!*

Though he had never joined the Communist Party, Cy Endfield was named as a Communist at a HUAC hearing and was blacklisted. Also blacklisted, incidentally, were Endfield's screenwriter and supporting star from *The Underworld Story*, respectively Henry Blankfort and Howard Da Silva. Joseph Losey, director of *The Lawless*, suffered the same fate. Endfield moved to England where he wrote and directed under pseudonyms for several years (as did Losey). Under the name of Charles DeLatour, he reunited with Lloyd Bridges for a British programmer, *The Limping Man*, in 1953. Directing as C. Raker Endfield, he received a BAFTA nomination for co-writing the screenplay for *Hell Drivers*, a hard-hitting and edgy 1957 action film about racketeering in the trucking industry and which featured a pre-James Bond Sean Connery in one of his earliest roles. (Although this film received little attention in the United States, it has recently received overdue acclaim and was presented at

YOU MUST SEE IT...
HEAR IT...
FEEL IT...

THE SOUND OF FURY

ROBERT STILLMAN PRODUCTIONS presents "THE SOUND OF FURY" starring FRANK LOVEJOY  KATHLEEN RYAN  RICHARD CARLSON  LLOYD BRIDGES

the Museum of Modern Art in 2008.) His uncredited work also included the final script for Jacques Tourneur's renowned 1958 horror film, *Night of the Demon* (U.S. title: *Curse of the Demon.*)

Endfield eventually resumed directing and writing under his own name and among his subsequent films were a suspenseful thriller, *Jet Storm*, in 1958, and the first-rate fantasy adventure, *Mysterious Island*, in 1961, which featured the special effects of Ray Harryhausen. He formed a production partnership with actor Stanley Baker, star of *Hell Drivers*, and received acclaim in 1964 for the adventure film, *Zulu*, which was a success in most of the world, except the United States. The following year, Endfield's winning streak continued with the underrated and exciting  *Sands of the Kalahari* with Baker (who, ironically, was also one of Joseph Losey's favorite actors.) His last film as director was *Universal Soldier* in 1971, an anti-war film which starred one-time James Bond George Lazenby and which was not widely released but has since become a cult favorite. His last credit was for co-writing the screenplay for *Zulu Dawn* in 1979, a prequel to *Zulu*.

Though his film career was over, Cy Endfield kept busy with other interests. He became recognized as an authority on the Zulu wars, designed chess sets and invented a pocket-sized computer typewriter called a Microwriter, as well as a computerized pocket organizer. He died in 1995 in England, never having lived again in the country of his birth. He had never revoked his U.S. citizenship and had attempted unsuccessfully to reverse his blacklisting. Because Endfield had been lynched symbolically by sanctimonious politicians and frightened studio heads, the cinematic heights his career might have achieved will never be known.

Lloyd Bridges, briefly blacklisted by HUAC for his political activism, was later cleared after testifying as a cooperative witness. He continued to appear in movies, mostly programmers. He worked more frequently in television and received an Emmy nomination in 1955 as Best Single Performance by an Actor for his role in "Tragedy in a Temporary Town," an episode of *The Alcoa Hour*. Bridges enjoyed tremendous success with a television series, *Sea Hunt*, from 1957 to 1961 and continued working in films and television until his death in 2002. Out of his lengthy career, which included many other fine performances, his brilliant portrayal of Jerry Slocum stands out as one of the screen's most despicable villains.

Art Smith, who played newspaper editor Clendenning, was a veteran Broadway actor and appeared in many plays throughout the 1930s. He made his first film in 1942, working regularly in films throughout the decade. His film career, in which he always provided earnest portrayals, ended when he became another victim of the blacklist. After 1952, he did not appear in a movie until 1961 when he played an uncredited role in *The Hustler* for director Robert Rossen, who had also been blacklisted for over two years until he agreed to testify as a cooperative witness. Smith returned to Broadway and acted fairly regularly in the 1950s and early 1960s. (HUAC had no interest in the Broadway Theater because theater actors were unknown to most of the public; consequently, hearings would not create the publicity that some HUAC members desired.) His role in *Try and Get Me!* is not as significant as his role in *In a Lonely Place*, which had been released earlier in the year, but he provides the required sincerity. He died in 1973.

Frank Lovejoy (in a role totally different from *In a Lonely Place*'s Brub Nicolai) was not involved with HUAC, possibly because he had one significant title in his résumé which may have put him in a favorable light. The same week that *Try and Get Me!* opened in New York City, another Lovejoy film also opened. It was the aforementioned *I Was a Communist for the F.B.I.* and starred Lovejoy in the allegedly true-life story of Matt Cvetic, who does exactly what the title promises. (In real life, Cvetic reportedly was not quite the heroic person depicted in the movie and was eventually fired by the Bureau due to his unreliable behavior; he was discredited as a witness in the mid-1950s.) Since the movie extols HUAC, the committee may have given Lovejoy a pass.

**Lloyd Bridges' portrayal of Jerry Slocum stands out as one of the screen's most despicable villains.**

Lovejoy gave another noteworthy performance in the 1953 movie *The Hitchhiker*. In 1955, the same year Bridges was nominated, he received overdue recognition for his talent with an Emmy nomination for Best Actor in a Single Performance for his starring role in a television version of "Double Indemnity," which was broadcast on *Lux Video Theater*. In 1956, he provided an incisive and memorable portrayal of the title role in "The Country Husband," an adaptation of the John Cheever story that was broadcast on *Playhouse 90*. He also received plaudits for his role in *The Best Man* on Broadway in 1960. Lovejoy continued to provide solid performances in films, on television and on stage, until his death in 1962. Always a dependable actor, he never had another film role that displayed his exemplary skills as much as his role as Howard Tyler.

Richard Carlson also continued his career in films and on television, not only as an actor but as a director and writer. He reunited with Lovejoy in 1952 for *Retreat Hell*, a Korean War movie in which they both fought Communists. Like Lovejoy, Carlson also played a true-life HUAC hero who infiltrated the Communist Party. He starred as Herbert Philbrick in the successful television series *I Led Three Lives*, which was telecast from 1953 to 1956. (Unlike the self-promoting Cvetic, Philbrick was reportedly a humble man whose story was quite authentic, though naturally embellished for a weekly series.) However, despite his multi-talented career which spanned four decades, Carlson will always be known primarily for the memorable science fiction and monster movies he made in the 1950s, especially *Creature from the Black Lagoon*. He died in 1977.

Other artists associated with the movie managed to escape the wrath of the HUAC and continued with their careers. Irish actress Kathleen Ryan, who had made a terrific impression in her debut film, *Odd Man Out* in 1947, distinguished herself in several more movies before retiring from the screen in 1957. Katherine Locke also only made a handful of films, always in supporting roles, having had a more illustrious career on Broadway. Adele Jergens continued playing "tough dames" in B movies, being typecast for the most of her career.

Jo Pagano continued to write forgettable B movies like *Yaqui Drums* and *Jungle Moon Men*. In 1954, he wrote the screenplay for a B movie entitled *Security Risk*, in which FBI agents bring Communist agents to justice. He worked extensively in television, writing teleplays for numerous series. He died in 1982 and is generally unknown today. (*Variety*'s obituary confused him with his brother, screenwriter and producer Ernest Pagano, crediting him with one of his brother's works.) Though *The Condemned* was reissued as a mass market paperback under the title *Die Screaming* in 1958, it has since been out of print. This is unjust because it remains, though flawed, a provocative novel. Pagano deserves praise for both his novel and his screenplay.

Robert Stillman only produced two more movies, including *The Americano* that co-starred Frank Lovejoy. He then worked exclusively in television in various production capacities. He was a production executive on the Western series *Bonanza* for three years, during which time Jo Pagano wrote a couple of episodes. It is perhaps informative that neither of his subsequent films nor his numerous television shows contained the type of controversial social and political themes that distinguished either his films with Stanley Kramer or his first production, *Try and Get Me!* It is unfortunate that he didn't—or perhaps was unable to—make more films like his first one. HUAC cast a long shadow.

The blacklist began to crumble in 1957 and ended in 1960. If *Try and Get Me!* had been released before or after the HUAC reign of terror, it perhaps would have received more commercial and critical success. However, the timing was wrong and the movie suffered an unmerited fate. Since it was an independent production, as well as a commercial failure, it was rarely shown theatrically or on television even after the blacklist ended. But, fortunately, the movie survived. In 1995, Republic Home Video issued a VHS of the film and, hopefully, there will be a DVD release in the future. It is unjust that the contributions of all of its participants remain unrewarded and unacknowledged.

Similarly, there is all too frequently a lack of justice in the real world. Although it is implied in *Try and Get Me!* that many members of the lynch mob will pay for their crime, in actuality none of the San Jose lynchers were ever brought to justice. There were a few token arrests but no actual legal action followed and records were erased. One 18-year-old glory-seeker who had bragged in newspapers about his active participation in the lynching was arraigned, but charges were later dismissed and he eventually became a wealthy real estate developer. Basically, the subject was officially allowed to officially disappear while, unofficially, lynchers and officials who sanctioned the killings congratulated one another and repeatedly celebrated the atrocity.

Of course, there are other kinds of justice. As the vigilantes grew older, did they continue to think of themselves as honorable executioners or did they begin to suspect that they were spineless killers hiding behind mob anonymity? Did grown children, with nightmarish memories about being held high by their mothers to watch their fathers thrashing naked bodies, reproach their parents for subjecting them to such a horror? Did other children ever ask their parents why they kept a patch of bloody clothing framed under glass and react in disgust when they found out what it signified? Did the rioters sneak into a San Jose theater to see *Fury* or *Try and Get Me!* to view how they were portrayed and then pretend that they were not the raging animals depicted? When *Swift Justice* was published, did they lie to their grandchildren and tell them that they were not part of the bloodthirsty rabble? As they approached their final days, did they begin to quake with fear that there might be some kind of justice after death for their acts?

Perhaps there is a small trace of ironic justice. The year *Try and Get Me!* was released, Jackie Coogan's career was at such a low point that he was reduced to supporting two former boxing champions, Max "Slapsie Maxie" Rosenbloom and Max Baer, in something called *Skipalong Rosenbloom*.

*Try and Get Me!* deserves to be re-evaluated. It is time to give belated recognition to this powerful study of mass hysteria and social injustice, as well as to the creative personnel on both sides of the camera who were responsible for its undeniable power.

CREDITS: Producer: Robert Stillman; Director: Cyril Endfield; Screenplay: Jo Pagano, From his Novel, *The Condemned*; Associate producer: Seton I. Miller; Cinematographer: Guy Roe; Editor: George Amy; Music: Hugo Friedhofer

CAST: Frank Lovejoy (Howard Tyler); Kathleen Ryan (Judy Tyler); Richard Carlson (Gil Stanton); Lloyd Bridges (Jerry Slocum); Katherine Locke (Hazel); Adele Jergens (Velma); Art Smith (Hal Clendenning); Renzo Cesana (Dr. Vido Simone); Irene Vernon (Helen Stanton); Lynn Gray (Vi Clendenning); Cliff Clark (Sheriff Demig); Harry Shannon (Mr. Yaeger); Donald Smelick (Tommy Tyler)

# THE EGYPTIAN

In 1954, 20th Century Fox released a lavish historical spectacle in the revolutionary widescreen process called Cinemascope, with the added enticements of De Luxe Color and Stereophonic Sound. Produced by studio chief Darryl F. Zanuck, it was entitled *The Egyptian* and it was based upon a worldwide best-selling novel by Finnish author Mika Waltari. The all-star cast featured Victor Mature, Jean Simmons, Gene Tierney, Michael Wilding, Bella Darvi and Peter Ustinov. In the title role was a relatively unknown actor by the name of Edmund Purdom. Director of the film was Michael Curtiz.

Prior to release, *The Egyptian* received an enthusiastic review by "Hift" in *Variety*. "The decision to bring the masterly, scholarly-detailed novel to the screen," Hift wrote, "must have taken a lot of courage for this is a long way off the standard spectacle beat. It is big, splashy and sometimes breathtaking (but) yet there are many moments of genuine emotion. It all adds up to a solid, alluring can't-fail merchandising package which opens up exciting new vistas for the audience." Hift praised Zanuck as well as the direction and all of the performers, except for Bella Darvi whose "thesping is something less than believable or skilled."

However, upon release, critics almost universally panned *The Egyptian*. Bosley Crowther in *The New York Times* wrote that the film "moves at the pace of a death march across the broad Cinemascope screen (and) the weak screenplay slips off in several directions with no strong dramatic line." Crowther concluded that there was a "thin little story of a mixed-up doctor trying to sneak in but scenic splendor and moral claptrap entomb the young man." *Newsweek*'s reviewer wrote that the movie "remains one Hollywood mummy that might better have been left in its wrappings," adding with equal wittiness of the film's "low jinks on the upper Nile." Other reviewers similarly attempted to display their drollness by scorning the movie.

Today, it is regularly degraded in film reference books. For example, Leonard Maltin in his annual *Movie and Video Guide* calls it a "ponderous, often unintentionally funny biblical-era soaper." Leslie Halliwell in several editions of his *Film Guide* calls it "pretentious (and) more risible than reasonable." Other books are equally dismissive. Douglas Brode in *Lost Films of the Fifties* (Citadel; 1990) calls it, "thuddingly dull (and) a story barely worth telling, much less at such an inordinate length." In his autobiography *Dear Me* (Little Brown; 1977), Peter Ustinov writes that he never saw *The Egyptian* "since I found it so profoundly silly while I was making it." Actually, what is silly is that so many knowledgeable film historians—as well as the multitalented Mr. Ustinov—could be so classically wrong.

The movie's origins date back to a work that had been written three thousand years earlier and is one of the oldest works of literature in human history. "The

Tale of Sinuhe" was first recorded during ancient Egypt's 12th dynasty on papyrus scrolls, stored in clay jars and archived in ancient libraries, to be discovered by archaeologists centuries later. The story recounts the adventures of Sinuhe, who is returning from a military campaign with his commander Senusret. He overhears a plot to assassinate Senusret, who is expected to become the new pharaoh, but instead of warning his friend, flees in shame to Syria. Tormented by his cowardice, he eventually marries the daughter of a chief and rises to power while discovering his courage as a warrior. Forgiven by Senusret, Sinuhe returns to Egypt to again serve his pharaoh.

In 1941, Egyptian writer Naguib Mahfouz wrote a story entitled "The Return of Sinuhe" which was based upon the ancient tale. In this story, Sinuhe returns to Egypt after a 40 year absence. Four decades earlier, when they were young princes, Sinuhe and his brother Senwosret both loved a princess. Their father Pharaoh Amenemhat sent them on a military mission to Libya with Senwosret in command. After defeating the Libyans, the brothers received word of their father's death. Suspecting that Senwosret might kill him, Sinuhe ran away and wandered for years until he reached the land of Amora, where he was befriended by a tribal chieftain. Through his military skills, he defeated the chief's enemies and then married his daughter, eventually succeeding to the role of chieftain. However,

"Every night I see the hunger in men's eyes. With a tavern maid, they don't trouble to hide it."

CINEMASCOPE

20th CENTURY-FOX presents

THE EGYPTIAN

COLOR by DELUXE

Jean SIMMONS · Victor MATURE · Gene TIERNEY
Michael WILDING · Bella DARVI · Peter USTINOV
and Edmund PURDOM as "THE EGYPTIAN"

Darryl F. ZANUCK · Michael CURTIZ · Philip DUNNE and Casey ROBINSON
From the novel by MIKA WALTARI

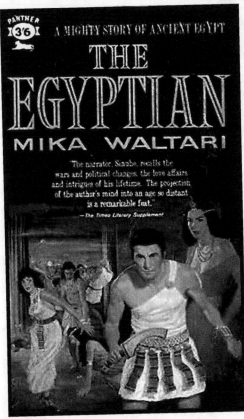

A MIGHTY STORY OF ANCIENT EGYPT

THE EGYPTIAN

MIKA WALTARI

The narrator, Sinuhe, recalls the wars and political changes, the love affairs and intrigues of his lifetime. The projection of the author's mind into an age so distant is a remarkable feat."
— The Times Literary Supplement

he never forgot his homeland or the princess he loved. Aged and frail, Sinuhe returns to Egypt and begs his brother's forgiveness. The Queen then tells him her story. Shortly before the brothers left, she told Senwosret that she loved Sinuhe and Senwosret promised her that he would always be devoted to her and to his brother. After Sinuhe disappeared, the princess mourned for years until she accepted the comfort offered by Senwosret. Stunned and grief-stricken, Sinuhe must now die with the knowledge that he destroyed the love he shared with the princess and with his brother.

In 1945, Mika Waltari used the ancient story as inspiration for his novel *The Egyptian* (G.P. Putnam's; 1949). Waltari was a prolific author who wrote numerous novels, stories, fairy tales, poetry, plays and screenplays. Though he achieved some fame in his native country for his mystery novels, he achieved international eminence for his historical novels, the first of which was *The Egyptian*. The novel was a tremendous success and was translated into more than 40 languages. A recurrent theme of Waltari's novels was the conflict between humanist values and materialism with the latter usually emerging triumphant. This theme is present in *The Egyptian*. Waltari changed the period of the story to the 18th dynasty but kept the name of Sinuhe for his title character. As in the ancient story, Sinuhe leaves his homeland in disgrace and eventually returns after achieving riches and fame in other countries. However, aside from that general theme, the novel is basically original and is far more ambitious in scope.

In 1300 BC, Egypt is in a state of political turmoil amidst threats of famine and war. A newly born baby is set adrift on the Nile and found by the wife of a physician, who tends to the poor. He is adopted and named Sinuhe. Like his foster-father, he studies medicine and becomes a doctor. He also forms a friendship with the modestly born but ambitious soldier, Horemheb. But Sinuhe becomes infatuated with the courtesan Nefer, to whom he gives all of his possessions as well as those of his parents, who subsequently commit suicide. Embittered and shamed, Sinuhe toils in the House of Death in exchange for tombs for his parents. He then departs Egypt in disgrace, accompanied by his loyal servant Kaptah. After several years in Syria and Crete, during which he becomes cynical and self-centered, Sinuhe returns with wealth to Egypt and learns that Horemheb has been appointed commander of the Army. With Horemheb's soldiers as allies, he exacts revenge upon Nefer, though she survives and emerges triumphant again.

Sinuhe becomes royal physician to the Pharaoh Akhnaton and this position brings him in contact with the Queen Mother, who eventually informs him that he is the pharaoh's half-brother and rightful heir to the throne. But Sinuhe has fallen in love with a tavern maid, Merit. He also becomes aware of Horemheb's ambitions to marry the Pharaoh's sister, Bakeneton, and become heir to the throne. Akhnaton is despised by virtually everyone due to his pacifism and his belief in monotheism. Devoted to the principles of love and peace, Akhnaton refuses to wage war with the Hittites and orders all false gods to be destroyed. However, his policies cause the deaths of Merit and Sinuhe's son. Grief-stricken, Sinuhe is persuaded by Horemheb and the priests of the old gods to poison Akhnaton. After another murder, Horemheb succeeds in his plan to marry Bakeneton, who despises him and ultimately shames him. Remorseful for his actions, Sinuhe preaches the wisdom acquired from Akhnaton and is exiled by Horemheb.

A summary of the novel cannot encompass the deep characterizations, the historical detail and the philosophical themes of the novel. Sinuhe is one of historical fiction's truly tragic characters. Deprived of his heritage due to the circumstances of his birth, he subsequently searches for the meaning of life, becoming increasingly pessimistic and cynical as his innate goodness is smothered by the evil and corruption enveloping him and his world. By the end of the novel, he has learned the significance of brotherhood and love, but it is too late to atone for his sins and he dies alone, as he has lived all of his life.

The novel was purchased by 20th Century Fox and was perfect material for the studio's Cinemascope process. In September 1953, Fox's first Cinemascope feature, the religious spectacle *The Robe*, was released and became a tremendous commercial success. The new widescreen process proved to be the single, most innovative discovery to entice audiences away from their new television sets and back into theaters. The previous year, Cinerama had proven to be enormously popular but the process required three cameras during filming and specially designed theaters to showcase the films. Three-dimensional movies had also been introduced but, though the process had potential, it was used mostly as a gimmick to attract younger audiences, while the special glasses required to view the movies were cumbersome. Publicity for Cinemascope implied the benefits of both of those processes, being exhibited on a screen almost as wide as Cinerama's and suggesting some degree of depth due to the curvature of the screen. And it didn't need special theaters or special glasses.

Despite Cinemascope's success with the public, there were still some problems since some portions of the wide screen occasionally displayed a lack of clarity. *The Egyptian* was advertised as the first movie to utilize the improved technology of redesigned Bausch and Lomb anamorphic lenses, which would provide superior density of image and enhanced definition over the entire surface of the large screen. A Fox press released declared that the new process would provide "greater flexibility, range and depth (and) a new sense of intensified audience participation."

During pre-production of *The Egyptian*, the studio gained widespread publicity with the announcement that Marlon Brando would play the title role. Brando had electrified audiences in 1951 with his performance in *A Streetcar Named Desire*. He had followed this role with equally memorable roles in *Viva Zapata*, *Julius Caesar* and *The Wild One*. And Hollywood was already abuzz with his performance in a movie he had just completed entitled *On the Waterfront*. However, after one day of rehearsal, Brando quit the project and disappeared from Hollywood. Reportedly, he didn't like his role, his director or Bella Darvi and broke his agreement to star in the film. After legal action by Darryl Zanuck, Brando had to pay half of the costs of the delay his departure had caused. He also had to agree to star in *Desiree*, playing Napoleon in a film that would prove to be uninspired, dull and far inferior to *The Egyptian*. If the entire incident proved anything, it was that the gifted actor lacked the visionary ability to see a script's potential.

Similarly, others would subsequently blind themselves to the film's quality because of the circumstances of Brando's departure. Peter Manso, in his biography entitled *Brando* (Hyperions; 1994), writes that "the script was a joke, even for as crass a commercial vehicle as this one." He is wrong on all counts, but this defense of the actor's unprofessional behavior is the fashionable view of the movie. Though most film historians feel that Brando would have brought his superior acting skills to the film, whether his decision was detrimental to *The Egyptian* is debatable. The actor who replaced Brando was not just merely adequate, as most critics claimed. In fact, he was excellent.

British-born Edmund Purdom had made his film debut in a small role in *Titanic* in 1952. He had another small role in *Julius Caesar* in 1953 and then received a big break the following year when he was chosen to replace Mario Lanza in MGM's *The Student Prince*. When Brando left *The Egyptian*, Fox needed a replacement fast. Zanuck considered having another famous actor in the title role but established stars didn't want to be viewed by the public as a second choice. Eventually, since the movie already had well-known actors for the other major roles, Zanuck decided on another tactic. Aware that MGM was building Purdom up to be a star, Zanuck selected him to play Sinuhe. Though *The Student Prince* had not yet been released, Zanuck gambled that by the time

of the release of *The Egyptian*, the musical would have hopefully established a foundation for Purdom's anticipated stardom.

Edmund Purdom did appear to have the necessary qualities for stardom. Early rushes from *The Student Prince* indicated his capabilities as a leading man. He possessed exceptionally good looks and had a cultured voice that seemed perfect for historical roles. Nevertheless, the role of Sinuhe would be quite a challenge for any actor, since the character was the central one and would occupy nearly every frame of film. Despite the high caliber of the other performers, the actor portraying Sinuhe would be the focus of attention and would have to carry the entire movie.

Screenwriters Philip Dunne and Casey Robinson painstakingly adapted the complex and lengthy novel into cinematic form while preserving its dramatic as well as historical components. Though some details of Sinuhe's lengthy journey to self-discovery are altered, the basic theme of the novel remains intact, along with the characterizations of the major players. In actuality, the narrative of the novel is rendered more cohesive and dramatically more compact. Indeed, by eliminating Sinuhe's second murder (of a Hittite warrior destined to be Baketamon's husband), Dunne and Robinson solve a major problem of the novel. That killing, unlike the poisoning of the pharaoh, was committed purely for political reasons and therefore diminished sympathy for Sinuhe.

Other changes also add to the story's impact. The transformation of Merit into a follower of Akhnaton's monotheism and the addition of the pharaoh's poignant last words to Sinuhe make his ultimate conversion to the principle of One God more logical and convincing. The screenplay also eliminates Sinuhe's romance with a Cretan bull dancer, which in the novel seemed superfluous. Sinuhe's revenge against Nefer is similarly not included in the script, though the scene from the novel in which he brings her unconscious body into the House of Death would have been horrifying. Her reappearance in the movie as a diseased woman who has lost her beauty may seem like a cliché but still is emotionally satisfying. More significantly, Sinuhe's sympathetic response to her also adds credibility to his gradual acceptance of Akhnaton's beliefs. Since the film follows the basic outline of the novel, the following summary of the script will underscore the differences.

A physician and his wife, in the city of Thebes, adopt a baby that had been cast away by his mother. They call him Sinuhe, which means "He Who is Alone" and this will be a prophetic name for him. His father, who treats only the poor, instills in him the values to which he has dedicated his life. As Sinuhe views the suffering all around him, he asks his father the simple question, "Why, Father, why?" These are the first words that Sinuhe speaks in the film and they will dictate the course of his life. He will not know the answer to that question until it is too late.

Sinuhe learns the art of medicine and intends to also dedicate his skills to the poor. But he has difficulty finding patients because even the poor doubt his capabilities, despite the help of his devoted servant Kaptah. He meets Merit, a tavern maid who falls in love with him. This, too, Sinuhe will not realize until it is too late. He also forms a close friendship with Horemheb, who has been rejected by the palace guards because he is the son of a cheesemaker. But there is emptiness in Sinuhe's life and he is not quite sure why. He only knows that he must fill that emptiness by continually searching for answers.

While on a lion hunt, Sinuhe and Horemheb save the life of the new pharaoh, Akhnaton, who believes in one god, Aton. Because of his revolutionary beliefs, everyone despises the pharaoh, except for his wife Nefertiti and their children. Akhnaton wants to appoint Sinuhe as royal physician, but Sinuhe considers it his duty to treat the poor. The pharaoh respects this decision but asks Sinuhe to be available to his family whenever needed. He also grants Horemheb's request to be a member of the palace guard. Akhnaton's mother and his sister, Baketamon, detect a resemblance in Sinuhe but do not say anything to him.

In celebration of their good fortune, Horemheb takes Sinuhe to the home of a courtesan, Nefer, who quickly seduces the naive young man and introduces him to sensuality. Obsessed with her, Sinuhe gives Nefer everything that he owns until she has no more use for him. Infuriated, Sinuhe tries to kill Nefer, but her guards brutally beat him and throw him into the street. Returning home, Sinuhe finds that his parents have committed suicide, having lost their home to Nefer. Overwhelmed with anguish and shame, Sinuhe takes their bodies to the House of Death, where he works as a slave to pay for their tombs. While he punishes himself, the pharaoh's daughter becomes ill and dies because Sinuhe could not be found to treat her.

To escape the pharaoh's death sentence, Sinuhe and Kaptah leave Egypt and spend the next 10 years traveling in foreign lands. Filled with contempt for himself and everyone else, Sinuhe becomes greedy as he amasses wealth through his skills as a physician. After he saves the life of a Hittite soldier, he accepts as payment an iron sword and uses this weapon to return to Egypt. He displays the sword to Horemheb, who realizes that Egyptian soldiers will have to acquire such weapons or they will lose the war with the Hittites. Upon learning that Sinuhe has returned, Akhenaton forgives him because of his belief in love and mercy. Sinuhe is appointed as court physician but now, greedy for more wealth, he will treat only the rich.

Meanwhile, Akhnaton's devotion to Aton has intensified and he refuses to wage war against the Hittites, who are advancing upon Egypt. Sinuhe is reunited with Merit, who has become a follower of Aton. Recognizing Merit's son as his own, Sinuhe vows to start a new life with his family. But Horemheb and the palace priests ask Sinuhe to poison the pharaoh, while Baketamon also asks Sinuhe to kill her brother. She also tells Sinuhe that he is her half-brother and rightful heir to the throne. Stunned, Sinuhe then learns that Horemheb has ordered the massacre of the pharaoh's followers and is unable to save Merit from being killed. Blaming Akhnaton, Sinuhe gives him poison but is moved by the dying man's last words of love toward everyone, even his killer. Realizing now the true meaning of life, Sinuhe begins to atone for his sins by spreading Akhnaton's message. After Horemheb exiles him, he dies alone with only the words he has written upon the scrolls left as a memento of his life.

The responsibility for bringing these intricate themes to life was entrusted to Michael Curtiz. Curtiz began his career in Germany, where he directed numerous films, including the biblical epic *Noah's Ark*, in 1926. That same year, Harry Warner of Warner Bros. brought him to Hollywood. During the next three and a half decades, he directed over 100 movies, including Westerns, swashbucklers, mysteries, thrillers, social dramas, musicals and comedies. Because Curtiz directed films in virtually every genre, some critics described him as being merely a competent studio director. However, he had a distinctive visual style and a superior ability to use his camera to tell his story in purely cinematic terms, a partial result of his early silent work.

His best-known movies during his Warner Bros. tenure include *Captain Blood* (1936), *The Adventures of Robin Hood* (1938), *The Sea Hawk* (1940), *Yankee Doodle Dandy* (1942), *Casablanca* (1943), for which he won the Academy Award, *Mildred Pierce* (1947) and *Life with Father* (1947), among many others. This is quite an impressive body of work for any director. However, even critics who praise these films tend to denigrate his films of the 1950s.

For instance, Andrew Sarris dismisses virtually all of the director's films of the 1950s. In his book *The American Cinema* (E.P. Dutton; 1968), Sarris writes that, after 1952 and the collapse of the Hollywood studio system, "his career went to the dogs." He inexplicably adds that, "if many of the early Curtiz films are hardly worth remembering, none of the later ones are even worth seeing." Ephraim Katz in *The Film Encyclopedia* (HarperCollins; 2005) writes that, "His films of the '50s, after he left the Warner mold, were considerably inferior to his earlier work (and) tended to obscure his achievements of the '30s and '40s."

In *The Casablanca Man: The Cinema of Michael Curtiz* (Routledge; 1993), author James C. Robertson provides a more objective assessment of the director's work in the 1950s. He provides praise for such films as *The Proud Rebel, The Best Things in Life Are Free, King Creole* and *The Comancheros*, which he correctly claims hold up better today than many of the more critically successful films of that era. However, even Robertson feels that *The Egyptian* represented "a commercial and critical setback" to his career. He does lavish praise upon the movie's "sheer spectacle (and) rare epic moments" and adds that its "lavishness has seldom been equaled." But he places blame for what he perceives as the film's deficiencies upon the rambling script and the fact that the novel was "too long and academic" to adapt successfully to film.

For his second movie away from Warners, Curtiz chose his property carefully. Throughout his career at Warners, Curtiz knew the importance of a first-class screenplay as a foundation for a good film, particularly on spectacles. On movies such as *The Charge of the Light Brigade* (1937), he realized that action sequences could not alone make a film successful and he subsequently demanded a solid story and characterizations to support the spectacle. He also had realized that, in films like *Dodge City* (1939), the weak script prevented the Western from being anything other than a pedestrian effort, despite his skillful action scenes. Studio head Jack Warner had gradually discovered that Curtiz required a high-quality script and story to elicit the best of his skills.

Fox's Darryl F. Zanuck shared this knowledge and also knew that spectacle alone would not ensure a film's success. Philip Dunne was one of the studio's premiere screenwriters. His previous work included *How Green was My Valley* (1941), *The Ghost and Mrs. Muir* (1947) and *David and Bathsheba* (1951). More recently, he had penned the screenplay for *The Robe* and its sequel *Demetrius and the Gladiators*. In actuality, regarding *The Robe*, Dunne always felt that he should not have received sole credit for the screenplay; the final screenplay used considerable portions from a previous adaptation by Albert Maltz but he was not given screen credit because he was one of the Hollywood Ten who went to prison. Dunne had co-founded the Committee for the First Amendment to protest the methods of HUAC (House Un-American Activities Committee) and was a character witness for another member of the Ten, Dalton Trumbo. Though a fervent anti-Communist, Dunne was an equally fervent defender of free speech.

With his prestigious résumé, Dunne was the perfect choice for *The Egyptian*. Co-scripter Casey Robinson, who had worked with Curtiz on such Warner movies as *Captain Blood* and *Passage to Marseilles* (1944), provided the first treatment of the novel in early 1953 before being succeeded by Dunne. According to James Robertson, Curtiz worked closely with Dunne and Zanuck on the final treatment of the script. The collaboration proved to be a fruitful one and an artistic foundation for the director's expertise.

Dunne would probably disagree with this. In his autobiography *Take Two: A Life in Politics and the Movies* (McGraw-Hill; 1980), he refers to *The Egyptian* as a "colossal costume picture which, although it earned a profit for the studio, shed no luster on those of us who worked on it." Thus, Dunne joins in the chorus of disapproval of the movie. Could all of these knowledgeable people be wrong? The answer is: Yes.

From the appearance of the 20th Century Fox logo on the spacious Cinemascope screen, *The Egyptian* transports audiences into another world. Unlike many historical epics in which the actors seem to be wearing strange costumes amidst bizarre settings, there is a remarkable authenticity to this film. The first scene of the elderly Sinuhe clutching his scrolls and pen conveys realism, which is aided by the fact that the face of the narrator is unrecognizable. Since the expression on his face also conveys a feeling of sadness, there is already a sense of the tragedy that is about to unfold.

The realism continues as the main narrative begins. The movie should be seen on a Cinemascope screen to be really appreciated. The magnificent cinematography by Leon Shamroy fully captures the splendor of the landscape, as well as the costumes and sets. Fox's research department reportedly spent two years amassing information that would be used to create the realistic props and furnish the magnificent sets, as well as the more humble ones. Everything, from the more obvious props, such as the clothing and the furniture, to even the less noticeable ones, such as the jewelry and even the doorknobs, seems authentic. The pharaoh's palace emanates inordinate affluence while the streets of Thebes seem to be actually inhabited by real people. Nefer's brothel reeks of garish self-indulgence while the House of Death practically exudes a foul stench.

The intelligent dialogue supplied by Dunne and Robinson complement the sets. Throughout the film, there are touches of poetry that elevate the story beyond that of most other historical epics. Sinuhe's seemingly endless quest to discover the answers to the cruelties of life is expressed through genuinely lyrical dialogue. Akhnaton's attempts to explain his radically different beliefs are beautifully articulated, particularly as they contrast with the materialism and greed of those around him, who will do anything to preserve their power.

The characterizations are not one-dimensional and are complex. Horemheb is not a totally unscrupulous person; he unselfishly tries to save Sinuhe from Nefer but is physically attacked for his efforts. The virtuous Merit sacrifices her principles to offer herself to Sinuhe, to try to make him forget Nefer, but she is rebuffed. Even Nefer warns Sinuhe to stay away from her and practically foretells his future. As a result, Sinuhe blames himself more than anyone else for his fate. As he tells Baketamon, "It is not your fault that you are warped and twisted; you were made by others. But I made the evil within myself."

There are myriad little touches throughout the movie that are memorable, from the benevolent philosophy of Sinuhe's foster-father to the pessimistic futility of life expressed by the gravedigger. All of the persons with whom Sinuhe comes in contact have an influence upon the course of his life. The tragedy of Sinuhe is that he began his life with kindness and love but gradually became corrupted by his environment and the people within it. In Sinuhe's world, partly due to his own actions, the good people suffer and die while the evil people triumph and achieve their desires.

The movie, like Waltari's novel, also manages to integrate the known facts of Akhnaton's reign into the lives of all of the main characters. The historical Akhnaton did indeed try to introduce monotheism into Egypt, but he was thwarted by political intrigues and the religious intolerance of the priests of the old religion. Horemheb eventually did become pharaoh, though only after a brief reign of Tutankhamen, whom historians believe was either Akhnaton's

son or nephew. Horemheb succeeded in destroying all traces of monotheism and restoring Egypt's ancient gods. Though the screenplay naturally condenses historical facts to some degree, it still manages to depict a considerable amount of factual data within the fictional framework.

Curtiz displays this proficiency throughout the entire film. In the spectacular sequences, regardless of the number of players involved or the grandeur depicted, he retains emphasis upon the principle characters. The massacre of the sun-worshipers is a horrifying highlight of the film, but it is Merit's participation and fate that make the sequence memorable. The pharaoh's palace is depicted in its entire lavish splendor with literally hundreds of extras in some scenes, but yet it is the manner in which Curtiz frames the gentle Akhnaton that suggests his incongruity clearly with the opulence of the position. In contrast, when Horemheb succeeds to the throne, he fits in perfectly with the surroundings and the flamboyant artifacts of decadence and corruption.

The lion hunt is also well staged and remains one of many examples of the director's creative use of composition for the wide screen. This is quite effective during the spectacular scenes and creates a feeling of wonder and excitement. His staging is equally impressive during the more intimate scenes, in which the reactions of several characters occur simultaneously. His use of colors is also used to accentuate the mood of the characters and their surroundings. The

**THE EGYPTIAN**

COLOR by DELUXE

In THE WONDER OF

**CinemaScope**

20th Century-Fox

starring Jean SIMMONS · Victor MATURE · Gene TIERNEY · Michael WILDING · Bella DARVI · Peter USTINOV and Edmund PURDOM in "THE EGYPTIAN"

Produced by DARRYL F. ZANUCK · Directed by MICHAEL CURTIZ · Screen play by PHILIP DUNNE and CASEY ROBINSON from the Novel by MIKA WALTARI

Copyright 1954 20th Century-Fox Film Corp.

54-380

garish hues of Nefer's bedroom perfectly reflect her narcissism, while the soft colors of the hut occupied by Sinuhe's foster-parents convey their gentility.

Curtiz may have had a reputation of being an ogre with actors but it should be remembered that 10 actors and actresses received Academy Award nominations under his guidance, with James Cagney and Joan Crawford bringing home the Oscar. In *The Egyptian*, he elicits memorable portrayals from all of the major performers. Michael Wilding stands out with his sensitive performance of Akhnaton, his calm expression and serene tone perfectly suggesting his character's divine vision. His death scene has a special poignancy because of the understated emotion with which he infuses his words. Gene Tierney's Baketamon is a frightening portrayal of a woman with frigid contempt for anyone that stands in the way of her ambitions. Peter Ustinov gives a scene-stealing performance as the wily Kaptah whose external ignorance masks innate wisdom. Jean Simmons as Merit strikes the right note of appeal and kindness that finally elicits some emotion from Sinuhe. And the much-maligned Bella Darvi is quite good as Nefer. Her angular features and foreign accent fit in perfectly with her role of the Babylonian courtesan. The negative comments directed at her upon the film's release were probably due more to her relationship with Darryl Zanuck than to the quality of her performance.

Deserving of considerable praise is Victor Mature as Horemheb. After over a decade as a major star, Mature had become known for starring in many biblical epics, his muscular physique and European-type features making him a perfect candidate for such roles. He was an imposing Samson in DeMille's *Samson and Delilah* (1949) and was unforgettable in that film's final scenes. In *The Robe*, his emotional portrayal of Demetrius is far more affecting and memorable than Richard Burton's Oscar-nominated performance. That movie's sequel, *Demetrius and the Gladiators*, had been released only two months before the release of *The Egyptian* and benefited greatly from Mature's persuasive portrayal of the slave who becomes a gladiator.

In all of those spectacles, Mature had played heroic or positive characters. But in *The Egyptian*, he is an opportunistic, ambitious warrior who is willing to condone murder to achieve his desires. Though the role is quite different from his Demetrius who worshiped God, he is equally convincing as a soldier who worships only power, displaying none of the dignity of his previous historical roles. However, as previously noted, Horemheb has some positive qualities, including sensitivity, and he proves his friendship and love for Sinuhe and Akhnaton in several ways. Unfortunately, like Sinuhe, he also is corrupted as much by the decadence of those around him as by his own ambitions. But unlike his friend, he does not have a moral awakening. Mature captures all of these qualities with a fine performance.

However, it is Edmund Purdom's central role as Sinuhe that is the main focus of the movie. Critics can be notoriously subjective and their criticism of Purdom indicated bias that was accentuated by their comparisons of him with Marlon Brando. At this time, Brando was the darling of many critics because he represented the antithesis of the typical Hollywood movie star. Coming from Broadway with legitimacy denied most stars, he had burst upon the film scene with a new type of method acting and monumental skills. Thus, he had the unbridled admiration of many critics. (Within a decade, the critics would turn against him with a passion.)

Purdom, on the other hand, was perceived as a typical Hollywood creation who had been given a major role not due to his talent but because two major studios—MGM and Fox—were building him up to be a star. And these critics were determined to show the studios that they were not going to be manipulated by any mogul, much less two of them (Darryl Zanuck and Dore Schary of MGM). So they attacked Purdom and ridiculed a first-rate portrayal of a complex character. Sinuhe is initially unselfish and caring but becomes bitter and cynical. Purdom conveys these opposing emotions very convincingly. When Nefer tells him that "the greatest gift a man can give a woman is his innocence, and he can give it only once," his projection of naïveté is very credible. The anger that he displays as he strangles Nefer and the shame that consumes him afterward are conveyed forcefully while the love and gentility he later exhibits are equally compelling. He suggests self-contempt and cynicism with equal conviction and even his tone reflects his change of character. When he states, "Men deserve injustice. We are vile, no more than a crawling disease on the face of the earth," he practically spits out the words. The scene is only one of many in which he fully captures the many sides of Sinuhe's personality.

Purdom got a raw deal from the critics and continues to be denigrated in reference books. However, he is in virtually every scene of the movie and he commands attention with exceptional ability. His performance is extremely moving, particularly in the final scenes when his character learns the meaning of life only after taking a life. His expression reflects illumination and remorse that is quite poignant. And the appearance of waste and regret that he displays as the frail, elderly Sinuhe lingers long after the film is over. The movie would not be the success that it is if not for Edmund Purdom's sincere and admirable performance.

Another asset is the musical score by Alfred Newman and Bernard Herrmann, two legendary composers who collaborated only this one time in their careers. Together, they created a memorable score with each composer modifying his distinctive style to accommodate the other's approach. The music splendidly complements the film's immersion into an ancient world in which intrigue and decadence wage a battle with spiritualism and martyrdom. The title theme conveys ancient Egypt, which, in predicting the course of the film, is superseded by a chorus that delineates Sinuhe's spiritual mission. Of particular interest, at least historically, is the fact that the idyllic hymn to Aton actually uses the words composed by Akhnaton. While fans of the two composers can probably differentiate between Newman's exquisite melodies and Herrmann's more vigorous contributions, the score is seamless and is a fine achievement. (Decca released a 33&1/3 rpm LP soundtrack album upon the film's release; the record was reissued on LP by MCA in 1973 and on CD by Varese Sarabande in 1990. In 1999, the Marco Polo label released a CD of a new recording of the score by William Stromberg and the Moscow Symphony Orchestra. And in 2001, Film Score Monthly released a CD of the complete original soundtrack.)

Curtiz must have had high hopes for the movie's reception by the critics and the public, since it represented his first movie to be released from a studio other than the one he had served for 28 years. But, once again, bias and prejudice were significant factors in the negative reviews the film received.

In 1953, many critics had greeted the new widescreen processes with cynicism. They tended to see Cinemascope, like Cinerama and Three Dimensional movies, as a gimmick designed to fill empty theaters. They depicted themselves as lovers of "pure cinema," which they viewed as the opposite of panoramic screens and even color. The previous year, *From Here to Eternity* had received critical acclaim as well as the major Academy Awards, while the eventual winner for 1954 would be *On the Waterfront*. Similarly, the

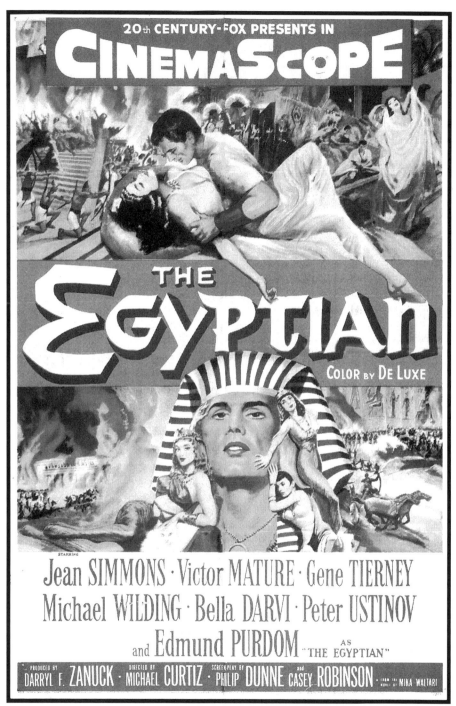

following year, *Marty* would receive acclaim and awards. These are all very good films but they had a critical advantage by being in black and white and

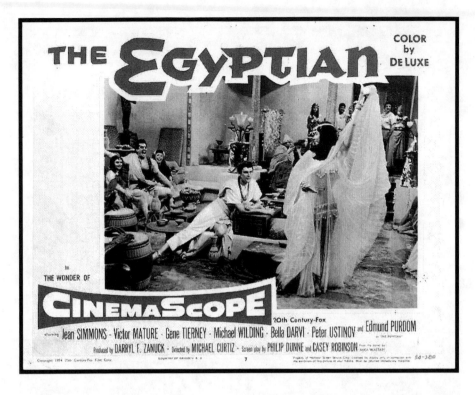

THE **EGYPTIAN**

COLOR by DE LUXE

In THE WONDER OF

**CinemaScope**

20th Century-Fox

starring Jean SIMMONS · Victor MATURE · Gene TIERNEY · Michael WILDING · Bella DARVI · Peter USTINOV and Edmund PURDOM

Produced by DARRYL F. ZANUCK · Directed by MICHAEL CURTIZ · Screen play by PHILIP DUNNE and CASEY ROBINSON

presented on normal-sized screens. Cinemascope and creativity, in the minds of snooty critics, just didn't jell. And, in their minds, expensive historical epics were representative of Hollywood's extravagance and lack of artistry.

Because of this, *The Egyptian* was handicapped from the beginning and didn't stand a chance with critics whose negative reviews impacted its box-office performance. In *Variety*'s 1954 list of Top-Grossing Films, *The Egyptian* earned $4.25 million in domestic theatrical rentals to be the 15th highest grossing movie of the year. While this figure is not comparable to the $17 million earned by *The Robe*, it was equal to the figures for *Demetrius and the Gladiators* and just below *Desiree*'s $4.5 million. And it was very popular in foreign markets. However, such figures were definitely disappointing. (Two years later, Cecil B. DeMille's *The Ten Commandments*, for which Paramount purchased Fox's props from *The Egyptian*, would earn $34 million.)

Interestingly, the highest-grossing movie of 1954 was *White Christmas*, which Curtiz had directed prior to *The Egyptian*, though it was released two months afterward. The Paramount movie earned over $12 million in domestic rentals to become the most successful musical to date, eclipsing Curtiz's own *This is the Army* of 1943. Curtiz had additional commercial successes throughout the 1950s with such films as *We're No Angels* (1955), which reunited him with Peter Ustinov, and *King Creole* (1958), one of Elvis Presley's best movies. His career ended on a high note with the enjoyable Western, *The Comancheros* (1961), which star John Wayne partially directed due to the director's illness. Curtiz died in 1962, leaving a legacy of many outstanding motion pictures, one of the best of which is *The Egyptian.*

Edmund Purdom's career had started with a disadvantage. His first two major roles were eleventh-hour replacements for the original actors and this unfairly typed him as a proxy for genuine stars. After *The Egyptian*, he made the musical *Athena* (1954) before starring in the biblical epic *The Prodigal* (1955) and the swashbuckler *The King's Thief* (1956), all for MGM. (In the latter film, he was once again a last-minute replacement for another star, this time Stewart Granger.) His last MGM film was *Strange Intruder* (1956), a modest programmer that ended his Hollywood career. He then settled in Rome where he starred in numerous sword-and-sandal melodramas before settling into character parts. He worked steadily for four decades, acting and dubbing Italian movies into English. His death in January 2009 unjustly attracted little attention, except for a perceptive tribute by Camille Paglia who praised *The Egyptian* and Purdom's "reserved but intense (and) extraordinary performance" in a Salon.com tribute. However, though stardom eluded him, he will always deserve acclaim for his superb portrayal of Sinuhe.

Incidentally, one of his Italian movies deserves mention only because of its subject matter. In 1961, Purdom starred in *Nefertiti, Regina del Nilo* (U.S. title: *Queen of the Nile.*) This movie is set within the same period as *The Egyptian* and features some of the same characters. Purdom plays the sculptor Tumos, who is in love with Tanit, but Tanit's father arranges for her marriage to Amenophis, who will be the next pharaoh. Tanit is crowned Queen Nefertiti and assumes command of the kingdom after the mentally deranged Amenophis commits suicide, leaving Nefertiti free to reunite with Tumos. Despite the presence of Jeanne Crain and Vincent Price, the movie is a typical example of the shoddily-made Italian sword-and-sandal programmers that flooded the market in the early 1960s. It is totally forgettable. (Historically, Amenophis later changed his name to Akhnaton to honor his belief in Aton. The sculptor Thutmose created the famous bust of Nefertiti. Nothing else in the movie has any relation to history. Actually, Anetra Stevens, who played Nefertiti in *The Egyptian*, resembles the bust far more closely than Crain.)

*The Egyptian* is a perfect example of the kind of movie that simply cannot be made anymore. In 1954, the spectacle was genuine, not an artificially created computerized effect. More significantly, the human drama reflected the emotions and feelings of believable characters, not cardboard creations. The main character's battle was internal and, though it reflected the chaos surrounding him, required audiences to think, not merely watch. It is a rare movie, indeed, that challenges and pleases the eyes, the minds and the hearts of viewers. *The Egyptian* does just this.

One indication of a movie's quality is its ability to remain in the memory long after it has been seen. There are many such scenes in *The Egyptian* that have such power. However, perhaps none is as hauntingly memorable as the last one, in which the almost-lifeless Sinhue places his scrolls down, stares sadly into space and slowly rests his head to one side as his life ends.

CREDITS: Producer: Darryl F. Zanuck; Director: Michael Curtiz; Screenplay: Philip Dunne, Casey Robinson, Based Upon the Novel by Mika Waltari; Cinematographer: Leon Shamroy; Editor: Barbara McLean; Music: Alfred Newman, Bernard Herrmann

CAST: Edmund Purdom (Sinuhe); Jean Simmons (Merit); Victor Mature (Horemheb); Gene Tierney (Bakeneton); Michael Wilding (Akhnaton); Bella Darvi (Nefer); Peter Ustinov (Kaptah); Judith Evelyn (Taia, Queen Mother); Henry Daniell (Mikeri, High Priest); John Carradine (Grave Robber); Carl Benton Reid (Senmut, Sinuhe's Father); Tommy Rettig (Thoth, Sinuhe's Son) Anetra Stevens (Nefertiti); Angela Clarke (Kipa, Sinuhe's Mother); Peter Reynolds (Sinuhe, age 10); Michael Ansara (Hittite Commander); Leo Gordon (Egyptian Soldier); Mike Mazurki (Foreman, House of Death); Mimi Gibson (Princess); Ian MacDonald (Ship's Captain); [Note: the voices for characters actors Leo Gordon and Mike Mazurki were dubbed.]

# THE LAST HUNT

The frozen, lifeless face stares menacingly ahead. Ice covers the skin, sharpening the features as if to emphasize the expression of hatred. Lower, an arm extends outward, the hand still clutching a gun which seems grafted onto the body. It is an appropriate end for a man whose only desire in life was to kill. It is also ironic that the body is encased within a buffalo hide which resembles a death shroud, seemingly extracting revenge against the man who had killed so many of its kind.

The image is haunting and unforgettable. It is the closing scene from the 1956 film, *The Last Hunt*. Upon its release, the movie was neglected by critics and ignored by the public. This may have been due in part to the fact that the motion picture marketplace in 1956 was virtually inundated with Westerns.

In that year alone, over 50 Westerns were released. They included a John Wayne classic (*The Searchers*) as well as films with Clark Gable (*The King and Four Queens*), Robert Mitchum (*Bandido*), James Cagney (*Tribute to a Bad Man*) and Glenn Ford (*Jubal*). Other respected actors starring in Westerns were Richard Widmark (*The Last Wagon*), Robert Ryan (*The Proud Ones*), Dana Andrews (*Comanche*) and Anthony Quinn (*The Man from Del Rio*), while Jeff Chandler (*The Spoilers*), Robert Stack (*Great Day in the Morning*), John Payne (*Rebel in Town*) and Tony Curtis (*The Rawhide Years*) appeared in programmers. Barbara Stanwyck (*The Maverick Queen*) and Greer Garson (*Strange Lady in Town*) represented the women. Two singing idols of different generations appeared in Westerns: Elvis Presley made his film debut (*Love Me Tender*) and Frank Sinatra starred in his only serious oater (*Johnny Concho*). Dean Martin and Jerry Lewis found laughs on horseback (*Pardners*), while Guy Madison battled a dinosaur out West (*The Beast of Hollow Mountain*). And B

M·G·M Presents The Mighty Drama of The Last Buffalo Hunt in CINEMASCOPE and COLOR

THE LAST HUNT

STARRING

ROBERT TAYLOR
STEWART GRANGER

LLOYD NOLAN · DEBRA PAGET · RUSS TAMBLYN

RICHARD BROOKS   EASTMAN COLOR   RICHARD BROOKS   DORE SCHARY

Westerns were still plentiful with such stalwarts as Rory Calhoun (*Red Sundown*), Dale Robertson (*Dakota Incident*) and George Montgomery (*Canyon River*). Of course, Audie Murphy (*Walk the Proud Land*), Joel McCrae (*The First Texan*) and Randolph Scott (*Seven Men from Now*) were represented. And there were many, many more.

*The Last Hunt* was released in the midst of this abundance. The novel by Milton Lott (Houghton-Mifflin; 1954) became the basis for the MGM release. Lott's novel chronicles the experiences of two buffalo hunters, Charley Gilson and Sandy McKenzie, in the 1880s on the Montana range. Through finely delineated portraits of the two men, the novel is also an exploration of the reasons for the slaughter of millions of buffalo and the near-genocide of the American Indian.

Charley and Sandy are totally different personalities. Charley is skilled with a gun, likes to kill and wants to make a fortune from buffalo hides, while Sandy has grown tired of the killing and has begun to question the worth of his fame as a buffalo hunter. Beneath Charley's bravado is insecurity as well as fear, which he conceals with brutality and contempt for others, particularly Indians. He also has a need for friendship and for the respect of Sandy who, in turn, is repelled by Charley's lust for killing. As the buffalo herds are slowly exterminated over the course of three years, each man is brought closer to an awareness of his relationship to nature.

Through an Indian girl whom Charley enslaves, Sandy is provided with a means for atoning for his past. He learns humility after almost being killed and then risks his life to bring food to a tribe of starving Indians. With the end of the buffalo herds, Charley is reduced to a pitiful figure whose last attempt to regain his former glory results in humiliation. Becoming lost in a blizzard after tracking a lone buffalo, he is further shamed. Wrapping himself in the hide of his prey, he is soon trapped and dies after finding inner peace.

Though literary critics today hold Lott's novel in high esteem, original reviews were mixed. Some reviewers were critical of the author's preoccupation with the mechanics of the hunting trade, while others appreciated the rich detail and authenticity of the story. Regardless of critical opinion, Hollywood studios were not rushing to buy the novel. While the pro-Indian theme had been the subject of many films in the early 1950s, the environmental message of a need to commune with nature would not translate easily to the film medium. Furthermore, there appeared to be some dramatic deficiencies. Since the two main characters have a near-fatal confrontation long before the end of the novel and then go their separate ways, the rest of the novel seemed anti-climactic, which suggested that the author had sacrificed his story to his message. Thus, a film version did not seem too likely. However, such a view did not take into account four talented people in Hollywood who would come together to convert a good novel into a superior film.

Two decades before the publication of Lott's novel, Dore Schary, Richard Brooks, Robert Taylor and Stewart Granger were just beginning their careers in different parts of the world. In 1933, after some minor success writing plays for a New Jersey community theater, Dore Schary, age 28, signed a contract with Columbia pictures and for the next two years co-wrote scripts for such forgettable movies as *Fury of the Jungle* (1934) and *Chinatown Squad* (1935). Also in 1933, Spangler Arlington Brugh, age 22, graduated from Pomona College and, having enjoyed acting in school plays, started taking drama classes. This brought him to the attention of an MGM drama coach and, due to his exceptionally handsome features, was signed to a contract with MGM for $35 a week. After his name was changed to Robert Taylor, he was loaned to Fox where he was given his first role in a Will Rogers vehicle called *Handy Andy*. He then landed small roles in a number of movies that highlighted his looks. Meanwhile, in Philadelphia, Richard Brooks, age 21, was beginning a journalistic career at a local newspaper. And in England, James Lablanche Stewart, age 20, started earning a living as an extra in movies, receiving no credit for his first movie, something called *A Southern Maid*.

During the 1930s, Dore Schary wrote and co-produced numerous films for various studios. The success of *Boys' Town* (1938), for which he won an Academy Award for Best Original Story, led to a writing position at MGM, which at the time was the film capital's most prestigious studio. By this time, one of the studio's biggest stars was Robert Taylor, who had been catapulted to stardom in 1936 when he was loaned to Universal for the sentimental drama *Magnificent Obsession*. The following year, his status as a matinee idol was certified when he co-starred with Greta Garbo in the famous love story *Camille*. Despite convincing performances, he was still considered more of a movie star than an actor, even by his own studio. Meanwhile, Richard Brooks worked on newspapers and radio stations and started to direct regional theater. James Stewart was also working regularly in British repertory theaters and, in 1938, earned his first prominent film role in *So This is London*. To avoid

Stewart Granger stops Robert Taylor from shooting Lloyd Nolan because he recklessly wrecked their supply wagon.

M-G-M presents "**THE LAST HUNT**" In CinemaScope and Color

confusion with the American actor of the same name, he changed his name to Stewart Granger. However, World War II and his enlistment in the service interrupted his movie career.

In 1941, Dore Schary was named executive in charge of low-budget movies at MGM. He then produced numerous B movies, but was the uncredited executive producer on some A movies including *Bataan* (1943), which starred Robert Taylor, who remained one of the studio's most popular stars. Schary left MGM because studio president Louis Mayer disapproved of Schary's desire to make socially conscious films. Schary then accepted a position with David O. Selznick's Vanguard Productions. Taylor's rugged performance as the cynical sergeant in *Bataan* had been another step in the actor's successful attempts to shed his pretty-boy image and followed equally fine performances as the enamored Army officer in *Waterloo Bridge* (1940), the sensitive yet brutal *Billy the Kid* (1941), his first Western, and the ruthless gangster *Johnny Eager* (1942). Richard Brooks, after writing daily radio scripts for a Hollywood station, started his film career by collaborating on screenplays for pulp movies such as *Sin Town* (1942) and *White Savage* (1943). After fulfilling their film commitments, Brooks and Taylor enlisted in the service. Taylor's last movie before becoming a Navy fighter pilot was *Song of Russia*, which he did not want to make because of its pro-Communist sentiments, but Louis B. Mayer and an envoy from the OWI (Office of War Information) persuaded him to star in the film due to the government's desire to strengthen positive feelings toward the Soviet Union. Across the pond, Stewart Granger had been medically discharged from the service due to an injury. Returning to the British film industry, he signed a contract with J. Arthur Rank. After a flashy supporting role in the costume melodrama, *The Man in Grey* (1943), his popularity rose and he graduated to leading roles.

When the war ended, Dore Schary left Selznick and became Vice President at RKO. Robert Taylor returned to MGM to find that the studio had lost some of its luster, while his career had subsided to some degree. His portrayal of the disturbed veteran in *The High Wall* (1947) was an indication of his ongoing desire to expand his range. Also in 1947, Taylor was compelled to appear as a friendly witness at the HUAC hearings due to his appearance in *Song of Russia*; another friendly witness was Louis Mayer, who confirmed that Taylor had not wanted to make the film. Schary was also called as a friendly witness, though the committee treated him with hostility due to his liberal views. He subsequently incurred the wrath of both sides of the conflict. Initially, he stated that he would hire Communists until it could be proven that CPUSA was advocating forceful overthrow of the country. After taking some heat for this view, he co-wrote "The Waldorf Conference Statement," which supported the firing of Communists and subversives but ensured the protection of innocents and free speech. He quickly found out that neither the extreme right nor the extreme left would tolerate any deviance from its rigid stance.

Upon Richard Brooks' discharge from the service, he graduated to major films and wrote the screenplay for the hard-hitting prison drama, *Brute Force* (1947). He also wrote his first novel, *The Brick Foxhole*, which appealed to the liberal beliefs of Dore Schary, who purchased it for production. It was filmed as *Crossfire* (1947), though the murder victim of the novel was changed from a homosexual to a Jew. In 1948, Schary left RKO to accept Louis Mayer's offer to be Vice-President in Charge of Production at MGM. Among the newly signed writers at the studio was Brooks, who had agreed to come to MGM upon condition that he also direct. Meanwhile, in Britain, after films such as *Madonna of the Seven Moons* (1946) and *Captain Boycott* (1947), Stewart Granger became one of Britain's most popular romantic leads in swashbucklers, which brought him to the attention of Mayer. In 1949, Granger was signed by MGM to star in *King Solomon's Mines*, that would begin his Hollywood career.

In 1950, Dore Schary was intent on not only restoring MGM to its former glory but also on making socially conscious films, while Robert Taylor continued to ask for more challenging roles. *The Devil's Doorway* (1950) satisfied the requirements of both men. Schary believed in the film's message about the mistreatment suffered by the American Indians and Taylor gave a terrific performance as a Shoshone, who encounters prejudice upon his return home from the Civil War. Despite its quality, the movie was a failure at the box office, which was a personal disappointment for Taylor. However, *King Solomon's Mines* was a huge hit and resulted in an MGM contract for Stewart Granger. Also in 1950, Richard Brooks directed his first movie, *Crisis*, but the political thriller with Cary Grant was not successful.

In 1951, Dore Schary succeeded Louis Mayer as the new president and head of production at MGM. The studio's biggest film of the year was the historical epic *Quo Vadis*, which was an immense financial hit. Stewart Granger had tested for the lead role of the Roman officer, but it was given to Robert Taylor and the film's success restored him to his pre-war level of popularity. When Granger refused to do his next assignment, *Scaramouche*, because of the proposed director's intention to make it as a comedy, Schary agreed not to suspend him if he would star in Richard Brooks' second film, *The Light Touch*. Granger had an unpleasant working relationship with Brooks and the lightweight movie disappeared quickly, failing to make a dent at the box office.

In 1952, at Dore Schary's request, Robert Taylor played the title role of the Saxon knight in *Ivanhoe*, which was another huge commercial success. Taylor followed it with *Above and Beyond* and gave a sterling performance as the Army Air Corps officer in command of the atomic bombing of Japan; Lawrence Quirk, author of *The Films of Robert Taylor* (Citadel; 1975), feels that this role should have earned him an Academy Award nomination. Also in 1952, Richard Brooks achieved his first success as director at 20th Century Fox with *Deadline U.S.A.* with Humphrey Bogart. That same year, Stewart Granger became the screen's premiere swashbuckler with two successive hits, *Scaramouche*, which was filmed the way he wanted, and the remake of *The Prisoner of Zenda*. However, Taylor maintained his position as the quintessential medieval hero with his portrayal of Sir Lancelot in the studio's first Cinemascope production, *Knights of the Round Table* (1953), one of the year's top-grossing movies.

In 1953, Robert Taylor and Stewart Granger co-starred for the first time in *All the Brothers Were Valiant*. According to Lawrence Quirk, Taylor wasn't particularly fond of Granger during production and found him "stuffy," though the actors made a good screen team in the mediocre adventure film. In Granger's autobiography, *Sparks Fly Upward* (Putnam; 1981), he expresses admiration for Taylor's abilities and annoyance due to his co-star's agreement of the studio's image of him. "He was convinced he was not really a good actor," Granger writes, "and his calm acceptance of this infuriated me." The evidence that the studio and Taylor were both wrong about his abilities increased the following year when he gave a performance as a corrupt police officer in *Rogue Cop* that even Bosley Crowther in *The New York Times* wrote was "very well acted." Ironically, Granger belittles his own work, including

**Robert Taylor, Debra Paget and Stewart Granger relax during filming.**

excellent performances as the British dandy in *Beau Brummel* (1954) and a smuggler in *Moonfleet* (1955), two highly underrated films. Also in 1955, Richard Brooks adapted and directed his most commercially successful film to date, *Blackboard Jungle*, which was criticized for its depiction of delinquency in an urban high school, but was a film that Dore Schary felt should be made.

Now it was time for the paths for these four artists to come together on a project that would benefit from the talents of each man. Of the over 300 movies released by MGM during Dore Schary's eight-year reign, he personally produced only 10, one of which is *The Last Hunt*. Schary was probably attracted to the novel because it reflected issues that fit in with his agenda. His choice of Richard Brooks to write and direct the film version is also understandable, in view of Brooks' desire to make movies that integrated social comment with entertainment. The casting of Robert Taylor to play Charley Gilson was a masterstroke, though readers of the novel probably never imagined him in the role. Although he had previously displayed the dark side of his screen persona in selected films, Taylor must have relished the opportunity to play such a despicable character, particularly since he had just finished playing the title role in another entertaining costume epic, *Quentin Durward*. To play opposite Taylor, Schary chose Stewart Granger who had had just finished starring in *Bhowani Junction*. In his autobiography, Granger relates how Brooks visited him in London with his script and a request from Schary to play the film's hero, Sandy McKenzie. Granger welcomed the opportunity to make a Western and looked forward to again working with Taylor, though he doesn't comment about his feelings about again working with Brooks.

The main titles of *The Last Hunt* are set against paintings of Frederic Remington, which establishes a mood of both nostalgia and realism. The first part of the movie follows the novel fairly closely. Former buffalo hunter Sandy McKenzie loses the herd of cattle with which he had hoped to start a new life and meets Charley Gilson, who persuades him to form a partnership to kill buffalo. The differences between the two men are quickly established. "Killing is natural," Charley says, "the war taught me that." Sandy replies, "I was in the war, same side you were on; I didn't learn that." To prepare for the hunt, the new partners ride to the nearby town where they hire two skinners, the one-legged Woodfoot and the young half-breed, Jimmy.

Sandy accepts the two skinners as equals but Charley merely tolerates Woodfoot and treats Jimmy contemptuously, because of his ancestry. The characterizations are further established as the four men sit around a campfire. While Sandy and the skinners reminisce about good times in the past, Charley can only make bullets as he eagerly anticipates the killing. Charley cannot understand the longing Sandy has for a more innocent past when hunting was mainly for food. For Charley, there is only the present when killing brings wealth as well as suffering to others, specifically Indians. Charley considers Indians less than human and thus can feel superior to them. His skill with a gun heightens his feelings of superiority. But before the last hunt is over, it will be revealed that Charley's self-image is fragile and conceals a bitter loneliness.

When a small group of destitute Indians steals their pack mules for food, Sandy is content to simply get the animals back, but Charley uses the theft as an excuse to hunt the Indians. Tracking the small band, he ambushes the men and women as they try to flee. He is disappointed to find that an Indian girl (as in the novel, she is deliberately not given a name) has survived with a child but, because of her attractiveness, he takes her back to the camp.

The next day, the killing of the buffalos begins. As dozens of majestic animals, pummeled by bullets, fall to the ground, Sandy is sickened but Charley becomes increasingly excited. Andy hesitates when he sights a fabled white buffalo, but Charley quickly kills it, knowing the hide will bring a fortune. Following the slaughter, the two men walk among the scores of carcasses and Sandy is disgusted by Charley's ecstasy. Sandy's shame is increased when the Indian girl tells him of the religious significance of the white buffalo to her tribe. The slaughter has awakened Sandy's conscience, and the presence of the Indian girl will be the catalyst that will eventually force him to try to make amends for his past.

Sandy's conscience will not allow him to rest. A wandering Indian tries to bargain for the white hide but Charley will only duel for it and promptly guns him down. When the Indian doesn't immediately die, Sandy defies Charley to try to save his life but his death averts a confrontation. Charley's continuing abuse of the Indian girl further alienates Sandy. Though Charley initially treats her like a slave, he eventually becomes annoyed at her lack of response to him. He knows that he may possess her physically but not emotionally and he is further upset to notice the affection developing between her and Sandy. However, Sandy is reluctant to acknowledge his feelings since he is torn between conflicting loyalties. He feels indebted to Charley for saving his life when they first met, but he also feels obligated to help the girl because of his part in destroying her culture. Divided between his past and his present, Sandy leaves the camp and goes to town to try to wash away the scent of death, but finds that the scent, like his shame, is internal. He returns to camp knowing that he must help the girl, for her sake as well as his own.

However, Charley has also been affected by his experiences. Though he has always been a loner without friends, the warmth enjoyed between the others in the camp has made him aware of his need for human companionship and especially for Sandy's friendship. He is overjoyed to see Sandy return and is hurt by Sandy's distant attitude toward him. Sandy, in turn, feels guilty because he knows that he must betray Charley if he is to regain his self-respect. He also knows that Charley's lust to kill is due as much to ignorance as maliciousness. "I don't hate him," he tells Woodfoot, "I feel sorry for him." But Charley is aware of Sandy's rejection of his friendship, while also noticing Sandy's closeness to Woodfoot, Jimmy and the Indian girl as well. Not knowing why he is the only one in the camp that Sandy has rejected, he can only react with anger.

Woodfoot, aware of Sandy's dilemma, schemes to help him by getting Charley drunk. "Ain't our company good enough for you?" Woodfoot slyly asks Charley, sensing Charley's desire to be a part of the group. "The best in the world," Charley replies. Charley's response is a pitiful one for it indicates his dire need to be accepted and liked by others. The fragility of his false superiority has been fully exposed. Charley's pathos is further underscored when he excitedly believes that that the sound of thunder is the sound of buffalo herds. "I told you the buffalo would be back," he eagerly says, then adds, "It'll be like old times, huh, Sandy?" His motivation for wanting to kill more buffalo is now more complicated than greed or racism, for only through the slaughter can he hope to retain Sandy's companionship.

Upon awakening the next morning, Charley is furious to find that Sandy has taken the Indian girl away. From his viewpoint, Sandy has not only taken his property but more significantly, has rejected his friendship. He starts tracking the pair immediately and, when Woodfoot tries to delay him, he realizes that the old man took advantage of his loneliness and kills him. Jimmy tearfully tells him that Woodfoot's gun was empty and Charley hastily blames Sandy for provoking the killing by taking the Indian girl. It is important to Charley that Jimmy accepts Sandy's responsibility, because now he has no one left but Jimmy. But Jimmy knows that Charley and no one else is responsible for his own actions.

In town, Charley tries to beat Jimmy into submission, but Jimmy refuses and stumbles out of the bar. This violent scene is followed immediately by an emotionally painful revelation for Charley, as he realizes his mistake and becomes aware that his brutality is one cause of the emptiness of his life. He races after Jimmy to apologize and pathetically pleads, "Don't leave me now, boy; I'm lonely." But even Jimmy, whom he had previously considered beneath him, rejects him. "Lonely, Mr. Charley?" Jimmy replies, "I'm just an Indian." Charley's prejudices have now come back to haunt him. He now knows that his image as an independent, superior man has been totally shattered.

Alone and aware that his superficial façade has been destroyed, Charley replaces his desperate and unfulfilled need for companionship with hatred. Upon hearing that Sandy is in town, he becomes so consumed with hatred that he discards the money for his hides and rushes out to kill the man whose friendship he needed the most. He tracks Sandy and the Indian girl through a blizzard and traps them inside a cave. His craving for vengeance is so strong that he refuses to seek shelter and wraps himself in the hide of a buffalo to keep warm. He stares malevolently at the cave, gun in hand, as the freezing snow pelts his face. The next morning, Sandy reluctantly emerges from the cave to fight but is shocked to find Charley's frozen body. As Sandy and the Indian girl ride away to start a new life, Charley's lifeless eyes stare after them, his hatred sealed within a coffin of ice.

Richard Brooks' screenplay for *The Last Hunt* is a textbook example of how to adapt a complex novel to the screen. Although the script condenses the time of the story and eliminates some characters and events, it still maintains

the integrity of the story and fully captures its themes and characterizations. While the two main characters pursue different courses than they do in the novel, their actions remain consistent with those of their counterparts, and their fates remain essentially the same, albeit under different circumstances. The motivating forces behind each character's behavior are conveyed through the dialogue, some of which is taken verbatim from the novel. When Brooks departs from the novel, he improves upon the original story. For instance, in the novel, after Woodfoot tricks Charley into drunkenness, Sandy helps the Indian girl to escape but remains in camp. At this point in the novel it is Sandy and not Woodfoot who tries to delay Charley in his pursuit and who is shot by Charley, though he doesn't die. Sandy's refusal to defend himself seems somewhat foolish, despite his feelings of guilt.

The novel also strains credibility by having Woodfoot and Jimmy remain with Charley after they believe he has killed Sandy. Also, after a long period of physical and spiritual rehabilitation, Sandy emerges as almost too saintly. More detrimental, the relationship between Sandy and Charley is basically over. The screenplay, instead of having Charley and Sandy go separate ways, keeps the focus on their relationship until the final confrontation. In the novel, Charley eventually kills Woodfoot but by accident after the old man has played a trick on him. In the film, Woodfoot is allowed a more heroic death that is dramatically more coherent since it advances the main plot. Brooks also wisely eliminates

the subplot of Jimmy's romance and maturation, two threads that would have been superfluous to the film. The intelligent script is evidence of why Brooks subsequently became one of the foremost adapters of literary works to film.

Brooks' direction is equally praiseworthy. The director captures the horror of the slaughter of the buffalos vividly by filming the annual thinning of the herds by sharpshooters in South Dakota's Custer State Park and interpolating the footage into the film. As a result, the killing of the buffalos is quite disturbing and demonstrates the effect of the slaughter upon Sandy and Charley. Through the depiction of the townspeople as well as of Charlie, Brooks also efficiently conveys the frontier racism that stimulated the extermination of the great herds. The violence that men commit upon one another, epitomized by Charley, is equated with the wholesale slaughter and is equally disturbing. However, though the action scenes are brutally realistic, they are not allowed to dominate the emotion of the story or the intimacy of the characterizations. The film's message and its demythologization of its characters are never intrusive and emanate naturally from the story. Though this uncompromising and provocative movie doesn't have the reputation of many of the director's other films, it is one of Richard Brooks' most accomplished works.

The first-rate cast is a definite asset to the movie. As Woodfoot, Lloyd Nolan is quite compelling. In a career that spanned 50 years, Nolan appeared in only a few Westerns, being more of a modern type, but he brings his usual reliability to the role. Beneath the scruffy exterior, his suggestion of innate wisdom evident from his expressions makes his later actions believable. Equally fine is Russ Tamblyn, who turns in a sensitive portrait as Jimmy. As the Indian girl, Debra Paget is convincing in a role begun by Anne Bancroft until an injury forced her replacement.

Stewart Granger is not usually associated with Westerns, though he comfortably fits into the genre with this film, which was his first Western (excluding the Canadian wilderness setting of *The Wild North* in 1952, in which he played a French-Canadian trapper). He is quite compelling as Sandy McKenzie, giving a restrained performance that indicates insightful awareness of his character. Sandy is a flawed hero. He allows himself to be coaxed back into killing buffalo, despite his distaste of the trade, and he is reluctant to help the Indian girl until internal and external pressures make such action necessary. Granger is especially moving in the key scene in which he breaks down in tears after killing scores of buffalo. In this difficult scene, as well as in the later barroom scene, he conveys Sandy's self-loathing perfectly, which fully explains his subsequent behavior. Since Sandy is the antithesis of Charley, Granger underplays and projects his character's gradual development of honor through suggestions of quiet strength. In critical scenes, his expressions and tone project an inner decency that foreshadows his moral decision. The role was a departure for Granger from his usual swashbuckling or romantic roles and allowed him to play a more subdued and emotional hero, which he does quite admirably.

However, Robert Taylor's performance is the film's centerpiece. The role of Charley Gilson is the most complex one of his career and he plays it with exceptional skill. He also proves to be a very humble actor, who was willing to play a character that is despised and shunned, as well as patronized and humiliated, before being subjected to a pitiable death. On the surface, Taylor chillingly projects his character's pathological sadism. His expressions during critical scenes indicate complete immersion into his role. The pleasure he displays as he prepares to kill and the ecstasy he projects as his victims die is frightening. One memorable scene is typical of the character's malevolence. Knowing that Sandy and the Indian girl are growing fond of one another, Charley lies down in camp and pretends to fall asleep. Sandy, seeing Charley's eyes close, exchanges a warm smile with the girl. Then Charley opens his eyes and grins wickedly until Sandy glances his way and is shocked to see Charley awake. Smiling learingly, Charley stands and leads the girl into the cave. Taylor splendidly communicates unmitigated evil.

Yet he was also aware of Charley's inner needs and he succeeds in making his character quite pathetic by imparting an urgent sense of loneliness and despair beneath the brutality. His child-like joy as he greets Sandy upon his return to camp, followed by his quick conversion to confusion and anger, is painfully believable. Equally pitiful is the desperate expression on his face when he almost begs Jimmy not to leave him alone, lowering his voice so the men in the bar will not witness his vulnerability. Similarly, when he drunkenly tries to play with the child who cries to leave his arms, his puzzled and anguished expression evokes both pity and disgust. Taylor makes Charley Gilson as much a victim of his times as the Indians and buffalos he so mercilessly kills. It is a superlative performance.

Preceding its release, *The Last Hunt* received a positive review by "Gene" in *Variety* who called it "grim, fierce, raw-boned and strikingly vivid." He added that the film "is somewhat off the beaten path for Westerns, having strong story values and well-defined characters. (It) will likely stir revulsion among the sensitive and score with he-men of the audience. Taylor hits the nadir in ruthlessness and Granger is of gentle stock, but they act out their parts with believability." When the movie was subsequently released, Gene's review would prove to be one of few favorable ones, if not the only one.

In fact, critics castigated *The Last Hunt*. The reviewer for *Time* called it "a bloodstained Western" and attacked producer Schary for exploiting the slaughter of the buffalo herds, somehow missing the obvious point of the movie. *Newsweek*'s reviewer called the movie "noble but shaggy," whatever that was supposed to mean. The critic of *The New Yorker* was condescending toward the film and toward Taylor's performance, writing that, "I had no idea Taylor would ever develop sinister characteristics in a movie, but he does so here and we'll just have to face it." The reviewer for *The New York Times* acclaimed the recording of the killing of the buffalo and the film's message but disapproved of the surrounding story as slow moving, concluding that "that's the way sermons sometimes go."

*The Last Hunt* did not score at the box office. On *Variety*'s list of Top-Grossing Films for 1956, over 100 movies earned more than the $1 million required to make the list. At the top of the list and in a league of their own are the costly spectacles *The Ten Commandments* with $34 million and *Around the World in 80 Days* with $23 million, followed by the modern-day Texas saga *Giant* with $14 million. *The Last Hunt* ranked 57th on the list with domestic theatrical rentals of $1.7 million. This places it in the same range as the juvenile oaters, Disney's *The Littlest Outlaw* and the big-screen version of the television series *The Lone Ranger*, both of which earned $1.6 million. The highest-grossing Westerns of the year are *The Searchers* with $4.8 million and *Love Me Tender* with $4.2 million. The Civil War drama *Friendly Persuasion* was also a hit with $4 million (this film has the distinction of having no screenplay credit because its writer had been blacklisted). *The Fastest Gun Alive* earned $2.2 million, while *Johnny Concho* made $1.9 million.

The rejection by the public of *The Last Hunt* may have been due to the large number of Westerns released during the year, as well as the number of adult Westerns on prime-time television. It should have attracted a larger audience but negative reviews and a lack of effective promotion helped to kill its chances. The movie did not last long in theaters and quickly disappeared. But that's the luck of the draw in Hollywood and the four artists who contributed so much time and effort into this fine movie went on with their careers, while the result of their collaborative effort was all too quickly forgotten.

Robert Taylor starred in several more Westerns but was always the hero. His contract with MGM expired in 1958, following another neglected but excellent performance as a crooked lawyer in Nicholas Ray's *Party Girl*. Most of his subsequent movies are undistinguished. *The Detectives Starring Robert*

**Director Richard Brooks (center) discusses a scene with Lloyd Nolan and Robert Taylor.**

*Taylor* was the official title of a television series that ran from 1959 to 1962 and he also was the host of *Death Valley Days*, a Western anthology series, from 1966 to 1968. He died the following year. He was a major motion picture star for over two decades but was never regarded as a great actor. Yet very few actors could convincingly play such diverse roles as a romantic lover, a heroic knight, a ruthless gangster, a Western outlaw and a sadistic killer. Robert Taylor did it all plus more; his artistry as an actor was evident in many of his films, most assuredly in *The Last Hunt*.

Stewart Granger also left MGM when his contract ended in 1957. He then freelanced, displaying a surprising flair for comedy co-starring with John Wayne in *North to Alaska* (1960). In the 1960s, he starred in numerous European movies that were all standard or sub-standard programmers and included three German Westerns. In 1970, he starred for one season in a Western television series, *The Men from Shiloh*, and subsequently worked regularly in television. In 1989, he co-starred on Broadway in a revival of Somerset Maugham's *The Circle* and, at age 76, won The Theater World Special Award for Outstanding Broadway Debut. He died in 1993. Like Taylor, he also was unjustly underrated as an actor but yet he made swashbuckling look easy, something not many actors can do. And, when his characterizations required more dimension, as in *The Last Hunt*, he brought considerable emotion and depth to the role.

Richard Brooks subsequently received five Academy Award nominations for writing and three for directing. He adapted and directed films based upon the works of such writers as Robert Ruark (*Something of Value* in 1957), Fyodor Dostoyevsky (*The Brothers Karamazov* in 1958), Tennessee Williams (*Cat On a Hot Tin Roof* in 1958 and *Sweet Bird of Youth* in 1962), Joseph Conrad (*Lord Jim* in 1965) and Truman Capote (*In Cold Blood* in 1966). In 1960, he received an Academy Award for his screenplay of the Sinclair Lewis novel, *Elmer Gantry*. He directed two more Westerns: *The Professionals* (1966) received acclaim and a Best Director Academy Award nomination, but *Bite the Bullet* (1975) was disappointing and pretentious. In 1966, he received the Laurel Award for Achievement from The Writers' Guild. When he died in 1992, obituaries didn't mention *The Last Hunt*, though *The BFI Companion to the Western* edited by Edward Buscombe (Atheneum; 1988) calls it "one of Brooks' very finest works."

Dore Schary left MGM in 1957 and subsequently received acclaim on Broadway for his play *Sunrise at Campobello*. He died in 1980. In his autobiography, *Heyday* (Little Brown; 1979), he writes about his lengthy career as writer, producer, director and studio executive but does not mention *The Last Hunt*, despite his personal involvement in the film. In the encyclopedic book, *The Western* (William Morrow; 1983), author Phil Hardy writes that the movie "was first eagerly promoted by (Schary) and then mutilated when it became clear that Brooks' savage indictment of the wasteful slaughter of the buffalo spelt disaster at the box office." Possibly, the film was the victim of the bitter internal disputes that led to Schary's departure.

Nevertheless, *The Last Hunt* is an artistic triumph and one of the great Westerns.

CREDITS: Producer: Dore Schary; Director: Richard Brooks; Screenplay: Richard Brooks, based upon the novel by Milton Lott; Cinematographer: Russell Harlan; Editor: Ben Lewis; Music: Daniele Amfitheatrof

CAST: Robert Taylor (Charley Gilson); Stewart Granger (Sandy McKenzie); Lloyd Nolan (Woodfoot); Debra Paget (Indian Girl); Russ Tamblyn (Jimmy); Constance Ford (Peg); Joe De Santis (Ed Black); Ainslie Pryor (First Buffalo Hunter); Ralph Moody (Indian Agent); Fred Graham (Bartender); Ed Lonehill (Spotted Hand)

# THE SINGER NOT THE SONG

Disaster was written all over this movie even before it was made. Its director didn't want to do the film before the fact and despised it after the fact. It was filmed amidst hostility and tension. Its star subsequently boasted that he intentionally sabotaged it during filming. It has been called a "camp classic" and a "homosexual howl" and those may be the kindest descriptions.

The movie is entitled *The Singer Not the Song*. It is a British production filmed in Spain in 1960. Though it contains gunfights and murders, it is primarily about moral and psychological conflicts. It is also a character study that explores the personalities of the two antagonists and their evolving relationship. And it is a spiritual drama about the fight between good and evil.

The basis of the movie is a novel of the same title by Audrey Erskine Lindop (Appleton-Century-Crofts; 1953). The setting is a Mexican town in the 1930s. Anacleto is a bandit leader that controls the town through terror and violence. Father Keogh has been sent to the town to replace the ineffectual Father Gomez. Years before, when Anacleto was a child, Gomez had a sexual relationship with the bandit's mother. As a result, Anacleto developed a hatred for the Catholic Church and all of its priests. He also became an outlaw to oppose what he considered the Church's hypocrisy. However, Keogh believes that all men can be redeemed. His allies include American expatriate Sam Frankenson and Locha, the 13-year-old daughter of a wealthy family.

In the past, the murders of innocent citizens by Anacleto's gang terrified the people. As Keogh earns the respect of the people, Anacleto knows that killing him will make him a martyr. Due to a quirk of fate, he is forced to save Keogh's life but is imprisoned as a consequence. But incarceration and weekly visits from Keogh only increase his resolve to destroy the priest. After his release, Anacleto learns that

The Rank Organisation Presents A Roy Baker Production

THE SINGER NOT THE SONG

Starring

**DIRK BOGARDE · JOHN MILLS · MYLENE DEMONGEO**

A Cinemascope Picture                          In color

From the novel by Audrey Erskine Lindop
Screenplay by Nigel Balchin
Produced and Directed by Roy Baker
Associate Producer Jack Hanbury

This film is made under licence from
Twentieth Century-Fox Film Corporation
the registered proprietor
of the trade mark "Cinemascope"

Locha is in love with Keogh and plans to use this knowledge to entrap the priest. Meanwhile, Locha tries to deny her forbidden love by becoming engaged to another man. The psychological battle escalates steadily and culminates in a violent gunfight in a darkened hut.

The novel's storyline and characters retain interest but the narrative drags when Anacleto is imprisoned for five years, seemingly only to enable Locha to mature into a woman. The novel's ending is also unsatisfying. Anacleto is shot accidentally by one of his own men, who also shoots Keogh. When Keogh pleads for Anacleto to signify his contrition, Anacleto complies but then tries to shoot the priest before being killed by Frankenson. Frankenson's conversion is supposed to vindicate Keogh but his character is superfluous. It also seems too contrived that Locha suddenly realizes that she can now love her fiancé and leaves with him for wedded bliss.

London-born Lindop was also a playwright and screenwriter but was known primarily as a novelist. *The Singer Not the Song* was a Literary Guild Selection in the United States and sold moderately well. But it would be a long and rocky road from novel to motion picture. Fortunately, the film version would benefit from some of the British film industry's finest talents.

Roy Baker started his film career as an assistant director in 1934 and directed documentaries during World War II. After the war, he directed his first theatrical movie *The October Man* (1947), an effective suspense drama with John Mills. Baker's fourth movie, *Morning Departure* (1949), also starred Mills and was his first for The Rank Organization. Soon afterward, Hollywood called and Baker signed a contract with 20th Century Fox. He directed four movies at Fox, including *Don't Bother to Knock* (1952), which featured Marilyn Monroe. He also was responsible for *Inferno*, one of the best 3-D movies, featuring a terrific performance by Robert Ryan as a man left to die in the desert.

After three productive years, Baker returned to England and Rank. In 1957, Baker directed a surprise winner called *The One That Got Away*, based upon a true story about a German prisoner of war who repeatedly escapes his English captors. *A Night to Remember* followed in 1958 and was a worldwide success that won plaudits for Baker. It remains to this day the best film about the sinking of the Titanic and vaulted him into the ranks of one of England's top directors.

Prior to World War II, Dirk Bogarde had some minor stage roles. After the war, he was signed by Rank and started to build his film career. In 1950, he had his breakthrough role as a killer in *The Blue Lamp* for director Basil Deardon. In 1954, he made *The Sleeping Tiger* for American director Joseph Losey (who worked under a pseudonym due to blacklisting in Hollywood). Throughout the 1950s, he appeared in several successful movies, including *Doctor in the House* (1954) and *A Tale of Two Cities* (1958), which made him one of England's most popular actors. In fact, he was voted the Number One Star in the *Motion Picture Herald*'s poll of British cinema managers and distributors.

Despite his popularity, Bogarde was considered by critics to be a lightweight actor (due primarily to his role as Simon Sparrow in the *Doctor* series) and this image stuck to him in spite of some fine performances. Inevitably, his fame in his home country attracted the attention of Hollywood. After rejecting several roles from the film capital during the 1950s, he accepted a lucrative offer at the end of the decade to make his first American film, *Song Without End*, in which he played composer Franz Liszt.

In *Dirk Bogarde: the Authorised Biography* by John Coldstream (Weidenfeld & Nicolson; 2004), the author writes that Bogarde was first asked by Rank producer John Stafford in 1958 to consider *The Singer Not the Song* as his next film project. At the time, Bogarde was considered for the role of the priest. But Ken Annakin, who was slated to direct, wanted Marlon Brando and Peter Finch for the two main roles. Annakin eventually dropped out and Roy Baker was then asked to take over.

In his autobiography *The Director's Cut* (Reynolds & Hearn; 2000), Roy Baker writes that the head of production at Rank, Earl St. John, gave him Lindop's novel to read in 1959, but the story didn't appeal to Baker. He wanted to film Alan Sillitoe's novel *Saturday Night and Sunday Morning* but couldn't convince St. John because the coarse subject matter was not suitable for Rank's image of a family-friendly studio. Over a year later, St. John again asked him to direct Lindop's novel and he felt compelled to accept. Baker was also asked to speak to Dirk Bogarde, who had one more film to do on his Rank contract. Since the studio was anxious to keep the actor, he was given his choice of which role to play.

Baker met with Bogarde in Hollywood and the actor agreed to play the role of the bandit chief. Baker hoped to get Richard Burton for the role of Father Keogh but Burton preferred to play the bandit and was not interested in playing the priest. Montgomery Clift was considered a good candidate for the role, but he was unavailable. Other American stars declined because they felt that the film might not get released in the United States due to its controversial theme. Some months later, Baker again met with Bogarde in Spain where he was making another film. Baker now wanted Paul Scofield for the priest but Earl St. John preferred John Mills, an actor Baker respected based on their two previous films together.

In *John Mills and British Cinema* (Edinburgh University Press; 2006), author Gill Plain calls the actor "the archetypal Englishman (with) the talent for demonstrating the qualities of English decency." More than any other actor, Plain postulates, Mills "took on the burden of national representation (and) represented a newly democratic masculine ideal." He could convincingly play a working-class everyman or a member of the upper class establishment. In all of his characterizations, he projected dignity, civility and a quiet strength that could assert itself when the need arose. In brief, he projected all of the qualities that the English believed represented their country.

Mills appeared in his first movie in 1932. As the decade progressed, he gradually landed more significant roles and by the 1940s had developed into a dependable and popular actor. His memorable role in *Great Expectations* in 1947, the first of several for David Lean, brought him international renown. He frequently played heroic military characters and in the 1950s appeared in such films as *The Colditz Story* (1955) and *Dunkirk* (1958). He looked forward to working for the third time with Roy Baker on *The Singer Not the Song*. He also had no qualms about working again with Dirk Bogarde, who had become a major star since they had first acted together eight years earlier in *The Gentle Gunman*.

**Publicity shot of Dirk Bogarde in his infamous leather trousers.**

Unbeknownst to Mills, Dirk Bogarde stated emphatically that he did not want John Mills to play Keogh for reasons that he chose not to explain. Baker reports in his book that he was puzzled by Bogarde's resistance and equally puzzled by St. John's insistence on signing Mills, since the studio chief had initially stated that he wanted to make Bogarde happy so he would re-sign with Rank. Regardless, Mills signed on and Bogarde was livid. He told Baker that "I will make life miserable for everyone concerned." Baker adds that Bogarde proved to be a man of his word.

John Coldstream suggests that Bogarde's hostility may have been due to the story's alleged homoerotic undertone. Bogarde interpreted the script to be about not one but two forbidden loves. While the relationship between Locha and Keogh is a major plot device, Bogarde detected a suggestion of suppressed sexual desire between Anacleto and Keogh. In view of this, he could not envision John Mills as the object of Anacleto's interest.

Problems increased as filming progressed. John Mills provides his own reasons for Bogarde's attitude in the revised edition of his autobiography *Up in the Clouds, Gentlemen, Please* (Orion Books; 2001). "I was playing the priest and Marlon Brando was supposed to play the gunslinger but he backed out," Mills writes. "Dirk Bogarde was cast and he was not keen to do it, because he knew he was miscast." Furthermore, on the set one day, one of the workers said that Mills was going to steal the picture with his performance. "Dirk heard him and it caused a great rumpus," Mills writes. "He wouldn't speak to me off the set. I was very unhappy about it."

Mills divulged more secrets as time passed. The above anecdote was not in his first edition of his book, which had been published in 1980. A few years after publication of his revised edition, he provided more information to John Coldstream. In the Bogarde biography, Coldstream writes that Mills told him that Dirk's hostility was due in part to another incident that occurred during production, which involved the young son of Dirk's close friend and manager, Anthony Forwood. Forwood's ex-wife Glynis Johns was concerned about her son's possible drinking when in the company of Dirk and Tony. Mills reportedly confirmed some misbehavior to Johns, which she related to Forwood. Consequently, Bogarde refused to ever speak to Mills again.

Suffice to say, it was not a happy set, either on location in Spain or in Pinewood Studios in London. In his study of the director entitled *Roy Ward Baker* (Manchester University Press; 2004), author Geoff Mayer reports that Baker told him in a personal interview that Bogarde "acted outrageously and upset everybody on the film." Mills writes that, "In my 77 years of acting, Dirk was the only actor who I had any trouble with." Baker writes in his own book that, "As we went struggling on, I became more and more convinced that this picture would be a turkey."

In defense of Bogarde, this was a difficult period for him. In *Dirk Bogarde: Rank Outsider* (Bloomsbury; 1996), Sheridan Morley writes that Dirk was uncertain about his future in his homeland due to the emergence of the 1960s' social-realism films. Bogarde is quoted as saying, "(Albert) Finney and (Peter) O'Toole had come along and I knew I'd worn myself out over here." Prior to this time, his efforts to change his image had been repeatedly stymied by executives at Rank.

In one of his autobiographical volumes *Snakes and Ladders* (Chatto & Windus; 1978), Bogarde writes of his frustration at not being given roles of more substance. He had been overjoyed in 1957 when Rank had signed him to play Lawrence of Arabia in a screenplay by Terence Rattigan. However, Rank suddenly cancelled the production at the last moment and this proved to be the "bitterest disappointment" of his entire career. (Rattigan later turned his film script into a play titled *Ross* that was a success in London with Alec Guinness. When this play opened on Broadway in December 1961, John Mills played the title role. Possibly this may have been another reason for Dirk's hostility toward Mills the following year.)

Other efforts to change his image similarly failed. He had an opportunity to star in Paul Osborne's *Look Back in Anger* but Earl St. John rejected the project. He asked St. John to obtain rights to the novel *Saturday Night and Sunday Morning* for him but was unsuccessful. (Ironically, this was the same property that Roy Baker had wanted to direct. If St. John had been more amenable, Bogarde and Baker would have collaborated on a movie they both wanted to do instead of one they both didn't want to do.)

Thus, Dirk remained identified with the kind leading man that was rapidly becoming out of fashion in the early 1960s. He sensed that his Hollywood debut *Song Without End* was going to flop, which it did. Concern for his future most likely had an effect upon his state of mind during the filming of *The Singer Not the Song*. In *Snakes and Ladders*, incidentally, he doesn't even mention the title of the movie

**Anacleto (Dirk Bogarde) and his men humiliate Father Gomez (Leslie French).**

but dismisses it rather derisively. "I was sent off to Spain to play a Mexican bandit sheathed in black leather, riding a white horse, carrying a white cat, and belting everyone in sight with a silver-topped riding crop," he writes, concluding that, "it wasn't much fun."

Bogarde's expressed preference of Paul Newman for the role of Keogh indicates how he envisioned the characterization. Director Baker's choice of Richard Burton also emphasizes the sexual appeal of the priest, specifically as it pertains to his relationship with Locha. Geoff Mayer feels that Bogarde was probably correct, even without the homoerotic element. He points out that Mills was too old to be a convincing object of lust for a woman who is supposed to be in her late teens. Even in his younger years, Mills was not perceived as a romantic leading man and his image of a typical English gentleman devoid of passion did make his casting as Keogh problematic.

Gill Plain expands on this, writing that the type of character epitomized by Mills was no longer a figure of respect. He proposes that his role of an emotionally brittle officer in *Tunes of Glory* (1960) was the first of many that symbolized the fall from grace of the type of character previously glorified by Mills. By the 1960s, Plain writes, this type of English hero gradually came to be seen at best as an anachronism and at worst as "redundant, phony and ineffectual." He believes that *The Singer Not the Song* "set the traditional English masculinity of Mills against Bogarde's modernity. The dissonant clash of acting styles exposed the archetypally repressed Englishman as a powerless and absurd figure, unable to identify, let alone articulate his desires."

Baker became increasingly pessimistic about the film during production. His fears were realized upon the film's release by Rank in England in January 1961. "They threw the book at the film and at me," Baker writes of the reviews. "They tore the picture to pieces. They all had a go at Dirk for wearing

**Locha (Mylene Demongeot) does not trust Anacleto.**

tight-fitting black leather trousers. It never struck me that there was anything special about those trousers." William Whitebait in *The New Statesman* called it "the year's wackiest film." An anonymous reviewer, apparently John Russell Taylor, wrote in *The Times* that Bogarde "enters with some enthusiasm into the slightly lunatic mood of the piece; there is in particular an hallucinatory moment when he appears, tightly sheathed in black leather and carrying a white Persian kitten, for all the world like a latter-day Queen Kelly."

In the United States, Warner Bros. released *The Singer Not the Song* the following year with very little publicity. The studio may have been discouraged by the review by "Rich" in *Variety*. Rich praised Mills for giving "an honest and intelligent performance" and wrote that Bogarde "is cool, cynical and impressive in a role that might have been hammed up badly." (The latter point should be remembered in view of Bogarde's later claims.) But Rich forecast larger problems. "The Roman Catholic angle may make this one a difficult selling proposition in many markets, obviously in the United States" and the moral of the story, praising the man over the religion "is bound to cause controversy." This may explain why the movie played smaller venues before it appeared in larger markets. For instance, it opened in Providence Rhode Island in January 1962 but didn't appear in New York City until four months later. It received little advertising and had only one play date at the Lyric Theater on West 42nd Street.

The movie received a generally unfavorable review in *The New York Times*. "This curiously ambivalent drama bites off more than it can chew," Howard Thompson wrote. "The first half simmers promisingly (but) what follows is pretentious, oblique and none too convincing," adding that "although the film never specifies, the plain obvious crux of the matter is a psychological triangle of the most delicate nature." (Thompson, like Bogarde, apparently perceived the same homoerotic sub-theme.) Philip T. Hartung in *Commonweal* also expressed disappointment in the film, writing that "the movie establishes a conflict between good and evil and then fails to follow the argument to its logical conclusion." Hartung concludes that the movie "tries so hard at such great length that the viewer has a right to expect more than its vaguely existential finale." Neither *Time* nor *Newsweek* bothered to review it. The controversy predicted by *Variety* never developed, possibly because the movie disappeared from theaters rather quickly.

On *Variety*'s chart of Top-Grossing Films for 1962, *The Singer Not the Song* did not earn the minimum amount of $1 million in domestic theatrical rentals to make the list, which is quite sad since such movies as *Hey Let's Twist* and *The Three Stooges Meet Hercules* earned places at the bottom of the list. It apparently was not a hit in England either. However, it was reportedly very popular in other countries, especially Roman Catholic ones throughout South America. Baker writes: "A further irony was (the fact that the movie) has taken over four times as much money overseas as it did in the UK. After 23 years on release it came into profit and is still paying royalties after 36 years." But Baker never changed his opinion of the movie and refused to introduce it at the 1993 Dinard film festival in tribute to his body of work.

It has become a part of cinema legend that Bogarde deliberately gave a frivolous performance to sabotage the film. In *The Cinema of Dirk Bogarde* (A.S. Barnes; 1974), by Margaret Hinxman and Susan d'Arcy, Bogarde is quoted as saying, "I played the bandit like Gloria Swanson's Queen Kelly; it was a great joke." Bogarde further adds: "Only John Russell Taylor got the point where he likened my portrayal to that of a male Queen Kelly, white cat and all." Hinxman and d'Arcy write that, "To Bogarde, it was pure camp, but the studio didn't get the message." The actor seemed anxious to make certain everyone accepted this version. Over a decade after its release, Bogarde told an audience at the National Film Theater, "I had a great love affair with me." He added that, "Can you believe that not one single person in that bloody organization knew what I was up to?"

However, there are indications that Dirk was not being entirely truthful. He never made the "Queen Kelly" reference until after it was written in *The Times*. The derisive content of this review and others must have been a source of humiliation for Bogarde and it is probable that he subsequently claimed to be camping it up to deflect the cruel barbs. By creating the impression that he was deliberately not giving a serious performance, he could revise history and expunge the terrible reviews from the official record. There is another interesting incident that supports this. John Coldstream reports that, on one occasion during filming, Bogarde was found crying uncontrollably in his car because he thought that Roy Baker was grooming a young South African actor to take over the part of Anacleto. This negates his assertion that he was playing the role for pure camp and supports the belief that he was serious about providing a good performance.

Today, just as the negative reviews are immaterial, so too are the opinions of both Baker and Bogarde who were both too close to the film to view it objectively. The movie itself can be now judged apart from all of the controversial aspects that preceded, permeated and pursued the production. *The Singer Not the Song* is not campy except for those who consider themselves too chic to accept its message. It is not a howl of any sexual kind except for those who get a thrill out of seeing Bogarde in leather pants. It is a spiritual movie but it is not a traditional religious movie. As implied by the title, it is not the religion that softens the soul of the outlaw but the man representing it. This major theme was transferred intact from novel to film, thanks to a very intuitive screenwriter.

Nigel Balchin was a critically acclaimed British novelist whose background in scientific research and psychology provided considerable material for his books. Among his more famous novels are *Mine Own Executioner* (1947) and *The Small Back Room* (1949). Besides writing 16 novels, he also wrote several screenplays, including *Mandy* (1955) and *The Man Who Never Was* (1956), for which he won the BAFTA Award for Best British Screenplay. Most of his scripts, like his novels, illustrate psychologically complex personal relationships. *The Singer Not the Song* is no exception.

Balchin's adaptation of Lindop's novel successfully translates the plot and major characters to the screen. But there are differences. The period of the story has been moved up to the 1950s. Father Gomez's liaison with Anacleto's mother is not in the film, nor is Sam Frankenson. The script eliminates Anacelto's five-year imprisonment, which allows the relationship between the two adversaries to build steadily from beginning to end. Since Locha is a woman at the beginning of the film, her romantic feelings develop almost immediately. Unlike the novel in which Keogh always sees Locha as a child, his reaction to her love is quite different. Finally, the climactic gunfight takes place outdoors instead of in a darkened room. That makes it more exciting and cinematic. The ending, though similar regarding Keogh's attempt to save Anacleto's soul, is more dramatically satisfying as well as more distressing due to subtle differences that Balchin injects into the sequence. All of these changes result in a vastly improved story.

The movie begins with Father Keogh's arrival in the town of Quantana, which is under the tyrannical rule of the bandit chief Anacleto. The first person he meets is Locha, a young woman who is one of the few villagers who does not view him with contempt. He visits Father Gomez, who has been defeated by Anacleto because he couldn't tolerate the deaths of innocent men and, as a result, capitulated and became a broken man. When Keogh escorts Gomez out of town, Anacleto and his men humiliate him even further. But Keogh shows that he is a man of physical force by throwing Vito, one of Anacleto's men, off his horse and putting Gomez in his place. This act appears to elicit some admiration from Anacleto, who has never seen a priest like this one.

Keogh's visits to the town's mayor and police captain offer him no help. The mayor defends Anacleto to conceal his own corruption, while the police captain expresses his frustration because he has never been able to get any direct evidence of crimes committed by the bandits. Keogh then visits Locha's father, the wealthiest landowner in the town, who admits that he pays Anacleto protection money and will not risk angering the bandit chief. To do so, he admits, could result in danger for his wife and daughter.

Despite attempts on his own life, Keogh persuades the villagers to attend church. As his influence over the people grows, Vito wants to kill the priest, but Anacleto again orders the killing of villagers. This leads to a dilemma for Keogh, who is not afraid for his own life but does not want others to die because of him. Then Anacleto's loyal friend, Old Uncle, inadvertently confesses Anacleto's guilt to Keogh in a moment of drunken stupor. Realizing his mistake, he tries to murder Keogh but Anacleto saves the priest's life by killing Old Uncle. Keogh gives his word to Anacleto that he will not divulge Old Uncle's confession to the police. When the police arrive, Keogh defends Anacleto, thus earning Anacleto's respect.

However, the incident gives the police captain a reason to banish Anacleto and his men from the village. Some time later, Anacleto returns alone, apparently repentant, and asks Keogh to teach him about his faith. He projects the image of a beaten man who has lost his friends and his power. Keogh, believing that he now has an opportunity to save the bandit's soul, accepts the challenge and allows Anacleto to live in his home. Keogh believes completely in the power of good to defeat evil. And Anacleto begins to show some signs of atonement, though his lack of sincerity will soon be evident.

Locha's mother, meanwhile, has found Locha's secret love letters but believes they are for Anacleto. When she gives the letters to Keogh, neither of them know that Keogh is the object of Locha's love. But Anacleto deduces that she loves the priest. This knowledge, he explains to his men whom he meets in the hills, will enable him to regain his control of the town. However, Locha is angered by Keogh's apparent indifference to her and leaves the village to visit

**Father Keogh (John Mills) is dismayed by the condition of the town's only church.**

an American, Philip Brown, whom her parents want her to marry. When she returns, Anacleto learns that she has become engaged and knows that he must stop the marriage if his plan to trap Keogh is going to succeed.

On Locha's wedding day, Anacleto provides an opportunity for her to escape with him. Knowing that she cannot allow the man she loves to perform her marriage ceremony, Locha leaves Philip on the altar and flees with the bandit. After attempts to locate her are unsuccessful, Anacleto tells Keogh of Locha's love for him. Keogh knows now that Anacleto was only pretending to be repentant but blames himself for failing in his mission. Anacleto promises that he will not harm Locha if Keogh will publicly admit in church that he has misjudged the bandit. He gives his word to Anacleto that he will praise him to the villagers if he is allowed to see Locha. Anacleto takes him to Locha, who confesses her love for him. Keogh reluctantly admits his own love for her, though he knows that it is wrong. But Anacleto smiles in satisfaction.

When Keogh addresses the parishioners at mass, Anacleto and his men are in the church to witness the priest's endorsement of the bandit. But Keogh has informed the police of Locha's hiding place and, in the midst of mass, he sees that she is safe. Now knowing that she cannot be harmed, Keogh unleashes his fury upon Anacleto, who has noticed that the police have surrounded the church. Stunned by the betrayal, Anacleto responds furiously. He states that he never believed in God or the Church but he did believe in the goodness of Keogh, which has now been proven to be as fraudulent as his Church. The police take Anacleto away but Keogh is devastated. He knows that Anacleto's words are justified and that he deserves the bandit's contempt.

As the police lead Anacleto away from the church, his men are waiting and open fire. When Anacleto is shot by the police, Keogh realizes that he only has moments to save Anacleto's soul and runs to him. Kneeling beside the fallen bandit, he tries to help the dying man but is shot by Vito. Falling next to the bandit, Keogh struggles to say an act of contrition for Anacleto and pleads with him to ask for God's mercy. But the bandit remains obstinate. Dying and unable to hear, Keogh implores Anacleto to squeeze his hand to signify his plea for forgiveness from God. Anacleto does squeeze his hand and Keogh dies happily, believing that he has saved the bandit's soul. However, Anacleto's dying words reveal that he was only responding to the man and not his message.

*The Singer Not the Song* isn't just a conventional battle of wills between two opposing antagonists. In *A Mirror for England* (Faber & Faber; 1970), Raymond Durgnat asserts that the film's theme is "the hidden complicity, and love, between good and evil." He writes, "behind the obvious antithesis, the inner complicity of the two adversaries clearly emerges." Just as Keogh is devoted fervently to his faith, "Anacleto, too, is a champion of a creed, that of cruelty and a love of evil. It is important to him that good be challenged on its own terms." Anacleto must spiritually destroy Keogh, just as he destroyed Gomez and thereby expose the fallibility of his devotion.

Anacleto believes that the Church, which was aligned with the corrupt government before the revolution, is equally corrupt. When Keogh explains that his vocation fills him with joy, Anacleto replies that his vocation is to prove that the Church is fraudulent and that priests are charlatans. After Anacleto orders the murder of a seven-year-old boy, Keogh's faith is tested and his violent outburst of rage indicates that he might capitulate just as Gomez did. He must decide if a man who could order such a terrible act is worthy of redemption. But then fate, or God, intervenes and brings him Old Uncle's confession, which precipitates the change in the relationship between Keogh and Anacleto.

Upon his return from banishment, Anacleto appears to be a changed man and his ruse is not easily apparent since his humility appears sincere. Even his clothing is different since he no longer wears black, though the wardrobe will return when it is no longer necessary to continue the deception. And yet, there is the definite suggestion in his manner and his expressions that he is slowly being affected by the sincerity of his adversary. It is a very subtle transformation because his character tries to resist such changes. It also soon becomes apparent that the basis of his depravity is his isolation, despite the fact that men surround him.

When Anacleto tells Keogh that he understands Locha, he adds that it is because he knows something of loneliness. Anacleto says these words in a hesitant manner, as though embarrassed to admit his feelings to the priest. This explains his unexpected tenderness with Locha. It is revealing that he apologizes to Locha for kissing her, displaying concern for her and disappointment as well, since she doesn't respond to his embrace. It is also meaningful that, when he brings Locha and Keogh together and watches them embrace, he averts his eyes. He knows that both of them have something he does not have. Since he cannot fill his emptiness with love, he can only fill it with power, which is why he is so intent on getting it back. Even though he has learned to respect Keogh's goodness, he nevertheless must control his adversary.

Similarly, Keogh must control—or convert—Anacleto. However, the priest is eventually forced to realize that his usual means of conversion has been futile and that he must use dishonesty to win the battle. When Keogh gave Anacleto his word for the first time, he kept it and thereby won the bandit's trust. But when he gives his word a second time, he breaks it. In doing so, he saves the town but destroys himself. "If you break your word to me," Anacleto told him, "you will cease to exist—as a priest and as a man." His words prove to be prophetic. Keogh's spirit has been broken, like his predecessor's, and he is filled with self-contempt.

In contrast, Anacleto now invites some degree of sympathy because his hatred of priests has been validated. Consequently, as the police officer waits sadistically for Anacleto to emerge from hiding, this police action appears unjust despite the bandit's crimes. Anacleto gives the appearance of a trapped animal as he prepares to run for his horse. But he is shot, not just once but a second time as he helplessly struggles to rise. Keogh, knowing that he is responsible, risks his life to save Anacleto's soul and his own as well. He dies believing that he has succeeded, that he has atoned for his sin. In actuality, Anacleto's rejection of the Christian song would appear to indicate that Keogh has failed.

This ending can be interpreted to reflect the triumph of evil. Raymond Durgnat writes: "When Keogh betrays Anacleto to the law, thus breaking his given word, Anacleto is doomed. But he has won. Good has revealed its helplessness, its dependence on lies, on evil." Thus, in the film's denouement, Keogh has been corrupted by the evil he tried to destroy. Anacleto, in some respects, has become the victim. It is ironical that Anacleto's two Christian acts lead to his destruction. Just as he had earlier been banished from the town as a result of saving Keogh's life, he is now killed because he believed in the priest's goodness. Thus, the ending of the film appears quite depressing. Keogh dies believing a lie, Anacleto dies rejecting God and Locha walks away alone and in tears.

But it can also be argued that Anacleto has absorbed some of the good that the priest exemplified. Accordingly, the fact that Anacleto squeezes Keogh's

**Father Keogh desperately tries to save Anacleto's soul—as well as his own.**

hand and thereby embraces the singer could be interpreted as remorse. Despite the evil epitomized by Anacleto, the spirituality personified by Keogh has made an impact upon the bandit. Keogh's belief that Anacleto is asking God for forgiveness may be erroneous but Anacleto, in his dying moments, exhibits compassion for the man who betrayed him. As he stares impassively upward, he doesn't care that he is dying but regrets the priest's death. It is ironic that Keogh has had to resort to treachery to win and thereby loses. But Anacleto displays the mercy and forgiveness preached by the religion he despises.

Roy Baker's skill is manifested throughout the entire movie. He displays an assured visual style, evident from the beginning as Keogh walks through the town amidst stares, some curious and others disapproving, while the camera captures the flavor of the town and the various citizens who will be affected by his arrival. For some of the more intimate scenes, intense close-ups are selectively used to establish the suppressed feelings within the three principal characters. Many of the scenes between Anacleto and Keogh are propelled by an edgy intensity. A sense of electric tension is always present primarily because of the multi-layered conflict between the two men.

Regardless of his later claims, Dirk Bogarde provides a charismatic portrayal that is not campy, despite the infamous wardrobe and white cat. It was the actor's idea, incidentally, to wear black leather pants and Baker had no objection. Though photos of the actor clad in black leather quickly achieved iconic status, such a wardrobe fits in with his characterization of

Anacleto. He controls the town not only through terror but magnetism as well. While the villagers may fear him, his men are willing to die for him. Bogarde provides a brazen charm that makes his character attractive as well as evil. His performance also suggests authority. The strength he displays is quiet when he is extorting money from a farmer, but brutal when he angrily lashes out at his men.

Bogarde's multi-faceted performance is most evident during the sequence in which he kills Old Uncle. His expression as he pulls the trigger is masked with pain. Directly afterward, he almost breaks down in tears but quickly catches himself. When Keogh maintains his silence about Old Uncle's confession, he looks at the priest with newfound respect. "How irritating it must be," he says to the priest, "how fascinating it must be to be a really good man." This heartfelt statement indicates why his reaction to Keogh's eventual treachery is filled with both rage and disillusionment. The fury in his voice indicates that he wanted to believe in Keogh even while he was intent on destroying him. Bogarde conveys all of these conflicting emotions.

John Mills provides a heartrending portrayal and submerges himself totally in his role. Though he initially may seem to be too old to be a romantic interest for Locha, he provides such warmth to his character that it is appears possible that a young, sheltered woman could respond to such tenderness. Mills convincingly displays the range of emotions that exist beneath Keogh's superficial composure. Initially projecting sincerity, decency and unselfishness, he gradually becomes consumed by self-doubt, confusion, rage and, ultimately, despair. His expression of frenzied desperation in the climactic sequence is truly distressing. He conveys the distinct impression that the meaning of his entire life as well as his own redemption depends upon his ability to convince Anacleto to repent. His expression of relief upon dying is exceptionally poignant.

Discussion of the two main actors and their interpretations of their roles naturally lead to the often-cited homosexual theme of the story. In the novel, there is no suggestion of such an idea and the only romance is between Keogh and Locha. When the two dying adversaries clutch hands at the end it is purely a spiritual bonding. In the film, the sexual theme is suggested by subtle ambiguities injected into the dialogue by screenwriter Balchin. It is also significant that Balchin eliminates Anacleto's two mistresses, Maria and the mayor's wife, from the film. As a result, Anacleto's sexuality is a mystery in the film, though it isn't in the novel.

There are two key scenes in the film regarding the nature of Anacleto's relationship with Keogh. The first scene is the one in which Anacleto saves Keogh's life. Old Uncle has come to kill Keogh because he feels that he has betrayed Anacleto, whom he states he loves as his son. Upon finding Anacleto with the priest, Old Uncle is consumed with not only anger but perhaps jealousy. "So you love this priest so much you will put yourself between him and me?" he asks furiously. When Anacleto doesn't answer, Old Uncle shouts, "Well I love you so much I will put myself between you and him." This leads to Anacleto being forced to shoot his closest friend.

Old Uncle's age and appearance clearly indicate that his love is a paternal one. But his reference to Anacleto's love for the priest could be interpreted either way, if not for the casting of Mills. It can perhaps be assumed from Bogarde's resentment of Mills that he initially preferred the homosexual premise but, once his co-star was signed, he appears to have rejected the theme. Both Mills and Laurence Naismith, who plays Old Uncle, were 52-years old during filming while Bogarde was 39-years old. But Anacleto is stated in the film to be 29 years old. Bogarde convincingly plays a man 10 years younger than himself while both Mills and Naismith look their actual ages, so the disparity is obvious. Thematically, it is also significant that it has been noted earlier in the film that Anacleto's father deserted his mother, whom he never married. Obviously, Old Uncle is jealous that Anacleto is replacing him with Keogh as a new father figure.

The second key scene is the one in which Anacleto confronts Locha with her love for Keogh. "I'm very sorry," he says to her, "it must be heartbreaking to fall in love with a man you can never have." He then adds, "I understand this." There does not seem to be anything ambiguous about this line, at least on the surface. But it is Bogarde's recitation of the line that is most revealing. He doesn't instill any passion in the line and, in fact, divests the line of any suggestion of fervor. And this goes back to his opposition to Mills in the role. If a younger actor had been cast, he most likely would have injected the line with emotion. Instead, his dry recitation of the line clearly implies that his feeling is only for Locha because of their shared loneliness.

Thus, the casting is crucial to the understanding of the dialogue. As far as Bogarde's initial interpretation of the relationship, then Paul Newman or Richard Burton, who were both four years younger than Bogarde, would have been preferable. Casting Montgomery Clift, who was one year older than Dirk, would also have allowed other interpretations. This perhaps explains Earl St. John's insistence on casting the older Mills. The Rank Organisation was known for making films for family audiences and J. Arthur Rank was known for having strict Methodist views. Thus, a decision may have been made in the upper echelon of the studio that the theme of a love between the priest and a woman was daring enough without adding a homosexual element. It then makes sense that St. John, faced with the choice of alienating Bogarde or the audience, chose the former.

As a result, Bogarde replaced the sexual interpretation with a filial one which fits in with his lack of passion during such scenes. Since he could not envision Mills as a romantic interest, he eliminated such feelings from his

**Locha struggles with her forbidden love.**

characterization. So, in effect, the casting of Mills negates the homosexual theme not only because his presence caused Bogarde to deliberately remove such implications but also because Keogh, as portrayed by Mills, doesn't project an awareness of such an attraction. Even Keogh's love scene with Locha is not very passionate since he appears to kiss her with a minimum of feeling.

This is not a criticism of Mills who conveys the impression that he is suppressing his desire for Locha, as though he doesn't want to admit his love for her, and that his interest in Anacleto is purely in saving his soul. This spiritual theme from the novel remains intact and the story is powerful enough without any hidden subtext. Accordingly, it is Keogh's essential goodness, not sublimated sexual desire, which earns Anacleto's respect and affection. And it is when Keogh's goodness is shown to be flawed that Anacleto responds with vehemence. Mills is actually perfect casting for such a characterization and Bogarde accommodates the change skillfully, despite his personal feelings.

In the pivotal role of Locha, French actress Mylene Demongeot was perhaps miscast. Someone less overtly attractive and capable of projecting a shy, reserved manner would have made her character's attraction to Keogh more credible. Nevertheless, she delivers a sincere portrayal. More deserving of criticism is Philip Green's inadequate score which is too shrill during the action scenes and doesn't effectively convey the emotionalism of the story.

But neither of these deficits offsets the effectiveness of the film. Unfortunately, the director didn't quite see it that way.

Roy Baker blames the movie for almost ruining his career. He writes that, "My self-confidence was dented and it took me four years to get myself back on an even keel. I have never to this day fully regained the professional status I had at the time." This rather extreme assessment was probably the result of the terrible reviews. It is ironic that, because of Baker's initial predisposition toward the film as well as all of the problems during production, he believed the negative reviews.

Baker's next movie for Rank starred John Mills in *Flame in the Streets* (1961), a brutally honest movie on the subject of interracial marriage. Since Rank ceased to produce motion pictures around this time, Baker's next two movies were freelance assignments. *The Valiant* (1962), again with Mills, and *Two Left Feet* (1963) both bombed and these failures were probably responsible for his decision to take a leave from motion pictures. He subsequently worked extensively in television on shows such as *The Saint* and *The Avengers*. In 1967, he returned to films billed as Roy Ward Baker with *Quatermass and the Pit*, an excellent science-fiction film which began his association with Hammer Films, for which he would make seven movies.

John Mills continued to provide superb performances in movies and on television throughout his career which would encompass more than 70 years. Over the next decade, he would provide flawless portrayals in films such as *The Family Way* (1966), the little-seen but excellent *Run Wild Run Free* (1969) and *Ryan's Daughter* (1970). He also worked extensively in television for the rest of his career. It is probably not coincidental that Mills, who had starred in Roy Baker's first movie, also starred in the director's last movie. He plays Dr. Watson to Peter Cushing's Sherlock Holmes in the made-for-television *The Masks of Death* (1984). Among numerous honors, he was nominated twice for Best Actor by BAFTA. In 2002, he received the Fellowship Award for his contributions to cinema throughout his career, the highest accolade given by BAFTA.

Dirk Bogarde's next film was *Victim* (1962), for Basil Deardon. Perhaps due to his missed opportunity in the previous movie, he agreed to play the part of a married man who is blackmailed for his homosexual past. With this film, he shattered his image and this paved the way for more challenging roles. He reunited with Joseph Losey for several movies which brought him recognition that had previously been denied him. He also made many European films which expanded his international acclaim. He was nominated five times by BAFTA for Best Actor and won twice. Toward the end of his life, Bogarde may have preferred that he would be chiefly remembered for such roles as Barrett from *The Servant* (1963) or Robert from *Darling* (1965) or Von Aschenbach from *Death in Venice* (1971). However, it is Anacleto that gives him screen immortality.

Bogarde was obviously capable of changing his opinion, especially with the passage of time. John Coldstream reports that, some years after the release of *The Singer Not the Song*, Dirk sent a letter to Roy Baker in which he wrote, "I have always thought of *Singer* as one of my preferred movies. It was way ahead of its time and the unforgivable casting of JM all but ruined it. But it holds up jolly well." Hopefully, he also accepted the fact that his performance is both sincere and terrific. Perhaps, during his last days, he even had second thoughts about his co-star, particularly after a fortuitous telephone call.

In 1999, John Mills heard that Bogarde was ill and decided to phone him, even though he was told that Dirk probably wouldn't speak to him. But Mills persevered: "I screwed up the courage and made the call." Dirk answered the phone and Mills complimented him on his latest book which led to a pleasant conversation. "We talked for the next couple of minutes, so we got it right before he had gone," Mills wrote, "and I am always glad I made that phone call." Symbolically, it was almost like squeezing one another's hand. Bogarde died shortly thereafter. Mills died in 2005.

*The Singer Not the Song* is a memorable movie that is entertaining and profound, provocative and compelling. It will never appeal to people with preconceived agendas, but it will emotionally touch people who appreciate proficient filmmaking and beautiful stories expertly told.

CREDITS: Producer/Director: Roy Ward Baker; Screenplay: Nigel Balchin, From the Novel by Audrey Erskine Lindop; Cinematographer: Otto Heller; Editor: Roger Cherrill; Music: Philip Green

CAST: Dirk Bogarde (Anacleto Comachi); John Mills (Father Michael Keogh); Mylene Demongeot (Locha De Cortinez); Laurence Naismith (Old Uncle); John Bentley (Police Captain); Leslie French (Father Gomez); Eric Pohlmann (The Mayor); Nyall Florenz (Vito); Selma Vaz Dias (Chela); Laurence Payne (Pablo); Roger Delgado (De Cortinez); Jaqueline Evans (Marian De Cortinez); Lee Montague (Pepe); Philip Gilbert (Phil Brown); Serafina Di Leo (Jasefa)

# THE LAST SUNSET

In 1961, Universal-International released a Western entitled *The Last Sunset*, starring Rock Hudson and Kirk Douglas. Like two other movies starring Douglas, the epic *Spartacus* of the preceding year and the contemporary Western *Lonely Are the Brave* of the following year, *The Last Sunset* was written by Dalton Trumbo and was produced by Douglas through either his Bryna or Joel companies. But the Western lacks the esteem accorded the other two films and is generally disregarded in assessments of the careers of the creative people involved in its production. Indeed, some people involved in its production have expressed contempt for the movie as well as for one another.

The first review of *The Last Sunset* by "Tube" in *Variety* forecast limited box-office potential, calling it "a tricky story burdened with serious unlikelihoods; the artificial strain is compounded by a number of key scenes that have a distractingly postured appearance, a shortcoming for which the director must take the rap." Regarding the performances, Tube had praise only for Joseph Cotton, who plays his supporting role "with a vigor and abandon that opens up a brand new vista of character parts for him." But he wrote that Douglas "gives his characteristically intense portrayal" while Hudson and lead actress Dorothy Malone "are a bit wooden." As it turned out, this rather dismal review would be one of the kindest ones the movie received.

Bosley Crowther in *The New York Times* called the movie, "exceedingly conventional (and) a routine combination of Hollywood actors and Western film clichés; considering what's free on television, it's not worth paying a lot of money to see." He concluded by writing that, "The actors go through their assignments as if they were weary and bored. After one hour's exposure to them, we were weary and bored, too." The reviewer for *Newsweek* seemed intent on impressing the reader with his wit, calling the movie "not so much an adult Western as a smiling Western," concluding predictably with the remark that everyone was smiling except the audience. The reviewer for *Cue* wrote that the film contains "every cliché in the gun-and-gallop plot grab bag." In *Commonweal*, Philip Hartung called the movie "pretentious, contrived and mediocre," adding that "since moviegoers expect a Western to be filled with action and gunplay, a Western that delves into psychology and grandiose ideas has to be doubly good; this one isn't." He also disclosed to his readers the entire story, including the surprise revelation and the denouement, which probably kept many potential ticket buyers away.

Furthermore, since both the writer and director of the film have since expressed their disdain for it, the movie's status has not improved. Director Robert Aldrich did not like the film. In a 1962 interview, reprinted in *Robert Aldrich Interviews* (University of Mississippi; 2003), he stated that, "You have to take assignments like this to make money to eat." He was exaggerating but perhaps not by much. Reportedly, the director was on the verge of bankruptcy at the time due to a period of inactivity as well as a drawn-out battle with Columbia studio honcho Harry Cohn. Aldrich also feels that writer Trumbo's absence from the set for an extended period of time hurt the film. And in a 1968 interview, he stated that filming the movie was an unpleasant experience that "started badly and ended up badly." He praised Rock Hudson but criticized Douglas, other actors and the writer for not having the same dedication.

But Kirk Douglas, in his autobiography *The Ragman's Son* (Simon & Schuster; 1988), reprints a 1959 letter from Aldrich asking to direct the picture and promising to make it better than any of the actor's previous films. Douglas hired him but when Aldrich appeared on the set in Mexico, he came with several writers who were working on other projects for the director. Consequently, Douglas had to tell the director to send the writers home and concentrate on *The Last Sunset*. Aldrich did as he was told, but Douglas states that the relationship was subsequently very cool. Perhaps Aldrich's subsequent scorn for the movie was his way of striking back at Douglas.

Trumbo—one of the original Hollywood Ten—is even harsher on the film. In *Additional Dialogue: Letters of Dalton Trumbo* (M. Evans; 1970), Trumbo writes: "I have a film in current release called *The Last Sunset* which scarcely qualifies me to rebuke anyone for monetary inefficiency. If by some misfortune, you should blunder into a theater playing it, you will understand at once why my mood is so forgiving." In another letter, he states that, "Even that abomination *The Last Sunset* will not lose money as it deserves; it won't make (money) but it won't lose." There seems to be a bit of hypocrisy in Trumbo's words. He was more than willing to take the money to write the script but then went to great lengths to disparage it, as though a mere Western lacked the prestige of his other films. It also seems to smack of ingratitude for Trumbo to be so critical of a Kirk Douglas film since Douglas was the first producer to give him screen credit—on *Spartacus*—after he was blacklisted for over a decade.

*The Last Sunset* did not fail at the box office but its grosses were disappointing, particularly considering Rock Hudson's immense popularity during this period. Quigley's Annual List of Box Office Champions, as printed in the Motion Picture Almanac, was based upon information from theater exhibitors on which stars generated the most box-office revenue. Hudson had been Number One in 1959 and was Number Two for the next three years, including 1961, the year this film was released. But yet his fans did not patronize this movie in very large numbers, particularly compared to his other films of the period.

On *Variety*'s list of Top-Grossing Films of the Year, *The Last Sunset* is 37$^{th}$ with domestic theatrical rentals of $3 million. By comparison, the top film on the list is *The Guns of Navarone* with $12.5 million, while the top Westerns on the list are two John Wayne movies that had been released late in 1960: *The Alamo* with $8 million and *North to Alaska* with $5 million. Marlon Brando's only film as director, *One-Eyed Jacks*, scored with $4.3 million. Two other Rock Hudson films released that year were far more successful: *Come September* earned $5.8 million, while *Lover Come Back*, released at the end of the year, earned $7.6 million. And Douglas's production of *Spartacus*, which was in general release in 1961, finished its theatrical run with $11 million.

The poor critical reception of *The Last Sunset* may be due in part to the fact that it imputes subjects and characterizations of classic works of literature, including Greek tragedy and Shakespearian drama, to the Western genre. The year 1961 was in the midst of a period when movies were beginning to present themes that had previously been prohibited on the screen. Critics usually welcomed such subjects, especially if they were presented in a film based upon a Broadway play or a prestigious novel. But many of these same critics were unwilling to accept such themes in a Western. Some were biased against Westerns in general and particularly those that they perceived as having literary pretensions. However, almost half a century after its release, the movie can now be viewed more objectively.

*The Last Sunset* is based on the novel *Sundown at Crazy Horse* by Vechel Howard, which was published in 1957 as an original paperback by Fawcett Gold Medal Books. Vechel Howard is the pseudonym of Howard Rigsby, who was a playwright and poet as well as the author of many Western and mystery novels. The main character of the novel is Carolus Cassidy, a gunfighter who agrees to help rancher John Breakenridge drive his herd of cattle from Texas to Wyoming. Breakenridge, whose fondness for liquor hides his shameful past, has two children, Oliver and Susan, and a young wife, Belle, with whom

Cassidy has fallen in love. Weary of being a gunman, Cassidy longs for a family of his own and delights Belle and the children with his songs and stories. In pursuit of Cassidy, however, is Dana Stribling, whose brother Cassidy has killed. Stribling recognizes the family's need for help and joins the drive after agreeing with Cassidy that they will have a showdown at their destination, the town of Crazy Horse. The drive is fraught with peril, including rustlers and Indian attacks, which matures Oliver but reveals Breakenridge's cowardice. At the end of the trail, Cassidy realizes that Belle has fallen in love with Stribling. Knowing that she was his only chance of starting a new life, he faces the sun in the final duel, having lost the will to live.

Dalton Trumbo's adaptation owes a large amount to the novel but he also makes considerable changes. He converts the two children into one daughter. Breakenridge's death occurs earlier and more pathetically than in the novel. Most significantly, Cassidy evolves into Brendan O'Malley, a poetic and philosophical gunman whose external facade as a callous killer masks an emotionally tortured soul. There are scenes in the film that not only expand upon his and other characterizations but deepen the emotional intensity of the relationships. Other scenes indicate knowledge of Western lore that adds to the film's tone of authenticity. The dialogue is at times gritty and at other times attains a level of sheer poetry. Trumbo also adds a theme that is quite unusual for a Western. The novel is basically a conventional paperback Western but the movie is more complex and gradually develops into a morality tale of guilt and salvation.

In *The Last Sunset*, Dana Stribling, a lawman who hates his quarry for personal reasons, pursues fugitive Brendan O'Malley into Mexico. O'Malley doesn't appear worried and seems amused by Stribling's pursuit. He is not really running from Stribling as much as he is running to his childhood sweetheart Belle Breakenridge, whose whereabouts he has only recently learned. As he approaches Belle's ranch, Belle's expression indicates that she is not pleased to see him, perhaps because she has a husband, John, and a teenage daughter Melissa, called Missy. When O'Malley learns that Belle's husband needs drovers to take his herd to Texas, he hires on and amusingly offers Stribling's services as trail boss. Stribling arrives and agrees to join the drive only to get O'Malley back across the border. Stribling quickly realizes O'Malley's true motives, since O'Malley doesn't hide from anyone (including her husband) the fact that he wants Belle. The death of Belle's husband allows O'Malley to once again court her but, during the course of the drive, Belle falls in love with Stribling. Embittered, O'Malley responds to the love of Missy only to be informed by Belle of a shocking revelation. The climactic gunfight between O'Malley and Stribling is similar to that of the novel.

From the opening sequence, the wardrobe of the main characters is designed to showcase O'Malley as the center of the film. He is dressed

**O'Malley (Kirk Douglas) dances happily with Missy (Carol Lynley), unaware of who she really is.**

completely in black, the usual garb of a villain, but yet his appearance and demeanor exudes charisma. He is as charming as he is deadly, as much a poet as a killer. In contrast, nominal hero Stribling is dressed in drab colors and is initially austere and not especially likeable. It will become clear that he is an avenging angel whose purpose is to make O'Malley pay for his transgressions. At this point, however, O'Malley is not even aware of the extent of his sins. He appears initially to be totally self-centered with little respect for human life, his list of victims including Stribling's brother-in-law and, indirectly, Stribling's sister. Yet it gradually becomes clear, from his emotional responses to a series of critical events, that his face is a mask that hides his true emotions.

When Stribling tells him of his sister's suicide, O'Malley turns away without showing any emotion, but the audience sees his expression reveals his pain. When he sees Belle in Stribling's arms, the fury of the rainstorm that surrounds him is no match for the rage in his eyes.

But O'Malley's emotional turmoil is best revealed in a vivid confrontation with the herd dog. After Stribling insults him in front of Belle, O'Malley leaves the cabin and struggles to control his temper for Belle's sake, but the hatred within him needs an outlet. In the open air, he sits angrily as the dog approaches. They stare intensely at one another, the animal sensing O'Malley's killer instincts. Suddenly, the dog lunges at O'Malley, ready to tear him to pieces, but O'Malley instead almost strangles the animal with his bare hands. But the rage within him subsides and he releases the dog who limps away. When we next see the dog, it is following O'Malley meekly, obviously knowing who the master is.

While O'Malley's violent side is reflected by his external actions, his sensitive side is revealed when he is near someone he loves. In the company of Belle or Missy, he is able to see the beauty in a bird's nest or in the reflection of the stars upon the horns of the cattle. Missy sees only his sensitive side, while Belle has seen both sides of his nature. When he tells Belle that he loves her, she wants to believe him, but his words reveal his true desires. "A hundred years from now," he tells her, referring to a fateful dance they shared as teenagers, "I could still see a pretty little girl in a yellow dress." With these words, Belle understands that he is in love with a vision of the past. When she tries to tell him that she is no longer an innocent girl, he only kisses her hand in response, preventing any further discussion that might pierce his idealized fantasy.

O'Malley is searching for the childhood sweetheart he loved so many years before because she represents not only her own youth and innocence but his as well. Belle correctly perceives his refusal to accept the truth and responds to Stribling, who loves her for herself. But she doesn't understand that O'Malley must deny reality because it is within the real world that his violent nature exists, the same violence that ripped flowers off her yellow dress and crushed her innocence. Obsessed with memories of a seemingly happy past, he is seeking to erase the pain that his subsequent life of brutality has caused to so many people, including the girl he loved. He has created a fantasy world out of the past to counter the despair of his present.

While Belle's words cannot penetrate his fantasy, the sight of her in Stribling's arms stuns O'Malley. He becomes despondent and withdrawn because, in his idealized world, Belle can love no one but him. His fantasy is in danger of collapsing which would threaten his only reason for living. While in such a precarious emotional state, he is susceptible to anything that will validate his dream. The next evening, as they celebrate their last night in Mexico, as Belle and Stribling dance, Missy appears out of the darkness, wearing her mother's yellow dress, looking like the perfect realization of his dream. O'Malley stares unbelievingly at Missy as she approaches him. When she remarks that the dress is torn, Belle tells her that a jealous boy once ripped primroses off it, reminding him of his violent nature. But O'Malley has eyes only for Missy and tells her simply that someday he will give those primroses back to her. It is a promise that he intends to keep, to Missy and to her mother, for in his mind, Missy is already transformed into the young Belle.

O'Malley takes Missy into his arms to dance and softly sing the song that symbolizes his dream, "Pretty Little Girl in a Yellow Dress." The emotion on Belle's face as she watches them illuminates her for reasons that will later become clear. Even Stribling is affected by the tenderness shared by O'Malley and Missy. But in the midst of the music, the foreman interrupts to call O'Malley to his watch for the night. The foreman's actions seem harsh but yet the music had to be cut short because the beauty of the scene was based upon deception and fantasy. Belle's pleasure at seeing O'Malley dance with Missy is tinged with guilt because she cannot disclose her secret. Stribling knows that he and O'Malley will have to duel the next day. Missy has no idea that the man with whom she is enchanted is in love with an image of her mother. And for O'Malley, all the years of pain and emptiness are disappearing as his fantasy becomes reality.

That night, as O'Malley stands watch over the herd, Missy appears, still wearing the yellow dress, and confesses her love for him. He only half-heartedly tries to dissuade her, his expression indicating that he desperately wants to be loved by her. His self-control eventually crumbles and he takes her in his arms. "Oh, Missy, I've loved you all my life," he happily tells her, his words revealing that he is once again holding the young Belle. For O'Malley, the present has now disappeared and he is once again an innocent teenager with no blood on his hands and with his first and only love in his arms. He has found what he has been searching for and he has been given a chance to re-live his life.

The next day, as they cross the border, O'Malley and Stribling know that the time has arrived for their showdown, but it is apparent that, as they agree to meet at sundown, neither man wants to kill the other. Stribling has been cleansed of his hatred by his love for Belle and the reluctant affection he has developed for O'Malley. Since O'Malley has returned to a time that predates his life of violence, he can no longer kill. Also, because of his feelings for Belle, which are blurred in his mind with his feelings for Missy, he does not want to kill the man she loves. Belle has tried to avoid telling O'Malley about Missy but when she becomes aware of their romantic attachment she knows that she must reveal the truth. O'Malley initially misunderstands her urgent pleas as concern for her daughter's youth. He attempts to comfort her by telling her

**O'Malley displays to Belle (Dorothy Malone) the rage that destroyed their love.**

how deeply he and Missy love one another, adding that he loves Missy more than his life. Seeing that it is hopeless to plead with him and realizing that she must reveal the truth, she frantically tells him that Missy is his daughter.

The shock of her words stuns O'Malley. His face fills with disbelief and shock, then to fury and hatred as he calls her a liar, repeating the words, his rage increasing as he tries to force her to take back her words. When she doesn't, he strikes her, once again reverting to brutality as a way of denying the truth. When she stares defiantly at him in response, he turns slowly and walks away. As shock gives way to acceptance, his face loses all hope and already achieves a pallor of death. For O'Malley, truth has finally destroyed his fantasy and knowing this, he wants only to die. When he again sees Missy, he stares at her as if seeing her for the first time and realizes that she indeed is his daughter. Now no longer thinking only of himself, no longer obsessed with the past, he is only concerned with Missy and her future. To prepare her for his death, he tells her gently that if something were to happen to him she would have to learn to love again. She repeatedly resists the thought of loving anyone else but he assures her that this is what he would want. Then he stands, prepared to die. Anxious now due to his fatalistic words, Missy pleads with him to come back to her and he promises to return with the sunset.

When Stribling sees O'Malley walking toward him, he hesitates and then reluctantly starts walking. The two men draw and one shot shatters the silence.

From different directions Missy and Belle rush to the scene to find O'Malley lying lifeless on the ground. Stribling picks up O'Malley's gun and is stunned to find it empty. As Missy cradles O'Malley in her arms, never to know that he was her father, the foreman brings her the primroses that O'Malley had left with him to give to her. As he promised, he returned with the sunset. In replacing the flowers he had torn from Belle's dress so many years before, he is atoning for his first sin and for his entire life. Lying in his daughter's arms, O'Malley has finally achieved his dream.

*The Last Sunset* is a mesmerizing study of an obsession that is as romantic as it is irrational. Though flawed, Dalton Trumbo's elegiac script provides a solid foundation for the film, regardless of what he would later say about it. This was Trumbo's third filmed screenplay under his own name after his return from anonymity following his imprisonment (for contempt of Congress following his refusal to testify at the HUAC hearings) and blacklisting in 1947. Trumbo is usually considered the most gifted of the screenwriters that composed the Hollywood Ten. He was also an unapologetic member of the American Communist Party. During World War II, he was one of the highest-paid screenwriters in Hollywood (which is ironic in view of his anti-capitalist sentiments). He wrote two of the most patriotic films of the war period, *A Guy Named Joe* (1943) and *Thirty Seconds Over Tokyo* (1944), but that was when Russia was an ally.

After moving to Mexico, Trumbo continued to write scripts with "fronts" taking screen credit and sharing payment. Two of these scripts won Academy Awards, though the Academy did not realize that Trumbo had actually written them. Upon the end of the blacklist, Trumbo returned to Hollywood and resumed his career. After *The Last Sunset*, Kirk Douglas hired him a third time to write the script for *Lonely Are the Brave*, which is one of his finest. Though Trumbo would write a fourth script for Douglas, it would never be filmed. Subsequent assignments included tripe such as *The Sandpiper* (1965) and prestigious films like *Hawaii* (1965) and *Papillon* (1973), as well as *Executive Action* (1973), a perceptive film about the assassination of President Kennedy.

Despite his publicly stated opinion of the film, Trumbo must have put considerable effort into the script for *The Last Sunset* and, particularly, his creation of Brendan O'Malley, who is brought vividly to life by rhythmical dialogue that dramatizes the depth of his feelings poignantly. His personality is skillfully depicted through several scenes that highlight his dual nature and the battle being waged within him. There are also distinctive touches to Dana Stribling's characterization that make him more than a standard lawman. In one scene, when a baby calf loses its mother, he shows Missy how its sense of smell will attach itself to her as a substitute mother. Actually, this scene would have been more consistent with O'Malley's characterization and it is possible that it may originally have been written for him but switched to Stribling to give him more depth. Quite possibly, Rock Hudson may have requested this change for fear of his character being completely overshadowed by his rival.

Though the script has its share of the genre's expected scenes, including rustlers and the threat of an Indian attack, the offbeat characterizations and narrative compensate for the familiarity of such situations. Other plot elements, however, strain credibility. When O'Malley tells Breakenridge that he will take his herd to Texas in exchange for his wife, Breakenridge drunkenly and laughingly accepts, but it seems doubtful that he wouldn't mention it once sober. Stribling also too readily agrees to act as trail boss, though the fact that he has no legal status in Mexico helps to make up for this. It also helps that these contrivances create the foundation of the main plot that soon takes precedence. More distracting is the appearance of three obviously troublesome cowboys to help on the drive. Since their motives are suspect from their initial appearance, it seems unlikely that they would have been hired. Though taken from the novel, they seem to have been retained for the film to provide a pretext for some customary action scenes.

*The Last Sunset* represents the only collaboration between Dalton Trumbo and Robert Aldrich, which is perhaps not surprising in view of their similar opinion of the film. The script's plot flaws are, to a large degree, concealed by the film's rapid pace, due to the efficient direction of Aldrich who keeps the emphasis on the relationships between the four main characters. As the story unfolds, it becomes apparent that the external forces that have brought these characters together, though contrived, are not as important as their internal stresses. O'Malley, like innumerable figures in classical literature, has been brought to this setting by fate to meet his destiny, and the director focuses on this appointment in Samarra.

Aldrich was an ideal choice to direct the film, regardless of his later judgment of it. His previous films had revealed a skill at developing alienated characters within familiar genres. In 1954, *Apache* and *Vera Cruz* presented Western heroes and themes that departed from conventional traditions. *Kiss Me Deadly* (1955) and *Attack* (1956) also feature unstable protagonists within, respectively, the private detective and war film genres. Following *The Last Sunset*, similar outsiders would be the focus of such films as *Whatever Happened to Baby Jane?* (1963), *Hush... Hush, Sweet Charlotte* (1964) and *The Flight of the Phoenix* (1965). *The Dirty Dozen* (1967) features a group of such individuals and was his biggest commercial success, though it now seems predictable and contrived. In contrast, such underrated and excellent films as *The Grissom Gang* (1971), *Ulzana's Raid* (1972), his last Western, and *Twilight's Last Gleaming* (1977)—all focusing on ostracized characters—were commercial failures.

*The Last Sunset* is the only movie in which Aldrich worked with Kirk Douglas, who shares a similar flair for bringing angst-ridden characters to life believably. (In contrast, he directed Kirk's frequent partner Burt Lancaster in four films.) Despite the strained relationship between star and director, their mutual interest is undoubtedly a factor in the successful realization of O'Malley who emerges as a three-dimensional character with complexities that gradually become comprehensible. During the course of the story, it becomes apparent that O'Malley's alienation is based upon a longing for an ideal that can never be attained in part because his own bestial nature condemns him to constantly destroy that ideal. His quest for the innocence of youth is also a quest for his own cleansing, thus making him ultimately a sympathetic character. Furthermore, Aldrich and cinematographer Ernest Laszlo romanticize O'Malley and his fantasy in lush, almost sensual images, enhancing empathy for him and his ultimately futile dream.

Douglas seems so credible as a Westerner in this movie that it might be surprising to realize that he once seemed like a fish out of water in the genre. When he began his film career in 1946, his screen image was not compatible with Westerns but was more suitable for crime films and modern dramas. Also, the passion he brought to his performances seemed out of place in the wide open spaces. Indeed, when he starred in his first oater, *Along the Great Divide* in 1951, he looked like a tenderfoot pretending to be a cowboy. It was perhaps fortunate timing that the adult Westerns of the 1950s added a psychological depth to characters that was more suitable for his trademark intensity. While this trend was developing, he must have been honing his skills with horses and six-guns because, by the time he starred in King Vidor's terrific *Man Without a Star* in 1955, he looked like he was home on the range

**Frank Hobbs (Neville Brand) knocks Milton Wing (Regis Toomey) unconscious before stealing the cattle.**

*The Last Sunset* was Kirk's sixth Western and his exceptional performance as Brendan O'Malley dominates the film, conveying both sides of his dual nature as well as his raging internal conflict. He is totally believable as a poet and a killer, a dreamer and a destroyer. He is equally convincing at projecting gentility and brutality. His manner of speaking and walking are noticeably different when he is with Missy or Belle and yet his body, his expression and the tone of his voice become frightening and threatening when away from the source of his love. This is one of the actor's many roles in which he seems to fully inhabit his character, and it is a very powerful portrayal. Douglas has the distinction of creating two of the most memorable characters in the Western film genre—Dempsey Rae in *Man Without a Star* and Brendan O'Malley. Though he would make five more Westerns (plus two comedy Westerns), he would never again create such an unforgettable character.

Rock Hudson's role as Dana Stribling is handicapped by the relative drabness of his character—compared to O'Malley—but the actor projects the right qualities to make him a worthy physical adversary. Like Douglas, Hudson also had a shaky beginning in horse operas. After making his film debut in 1948, his first two appearances out West were in small parts in *Winchester '73* (1950), in which he played an Indian, and *Tomahawk* (1951). *Bend of the River* (1953) provided him with his first major role in a Western and he was not convincing, his performance lacking self-confidence. But five subsequent Westerns in the 1950s gradually decreased his unease, while his capabilities as an actor improved. When he made *The Last Sunset*, he had not appeared in a Western for seven years (excluding the modern-day *Giant* in 1956), but he projects total credibility as a vengeance-seeking lawman. He commendably underplays, conveying quiet strength and sincerity to complement O'Malley's extroverted presence. But he is also capable of uncontrollable ferocity when he and his adversary engage in a vicious brawl. He definitely holds his own against his co-star's more colorful portrayal. Though Aldrich expressed his admiration for Rock's work ethic, the two would never make another film together. Hudson would only make two more Westerns and this remains his best.

Douglas and Hudson make a good team. It is regrettable that Douglas' plan to produce and star as Cortez in a proposed film entitled *Montezuma* from a Dalton Trumbo script, with Hudson in the title role, never materialized. The roles of the Spanish conquistador and the Aztec emperor seemed tailor-made for the two actors and, though Trumbo's script has been called his finest unrealized one, historical spectacles in the early 1960s were not as successful as they had been the previous decade, and Universal cancelled the project. In his autobiography, incidentally, Douglas writes that he had a problem working with Hudson, who consistently avoided personal contact; he adds that, though he tried to make Rock feel comfortable, it remained difficult to get close to his co-star who remained, though not unfriendly, distant during filming. Nevertheless, Kirk was desirous of working with him again but his attempts to secure funding for *Montezuma* at other studios were unsuccessful.

Dorothy Malone is effective as Belle, succeeding in a role that is difficult because she must impart conflicting emotions through expressions that become clear only with her climactic revelation. (Douglas writes in his autobiography that he first offered the role to Lauren Bacall, who rejected it angrily; he doesn't report why she was so irate but it could have been the revelatory plot point.) This was Malone's third role opposite Hudson in five years and they appear to enjoy each other's company, making their eventual union credible. It is probably not coincidental that Malone's previous pairings with Rock were in two deceptively complex Douglas Sirk melodramas (*Written On the Wind* in 1956 and *The Tarnished Angels* in 1958), both of which are noted for the type of passionate emotional conflicts included in this movie.

As Missy, Carol Lynley projects an appealing innocence and is quite touching in the final sequence. Lynley and Malone appear to be daughter and mother quite convincingly and this contributes to the sorrow of the unfolding tragedy. Though his role is brief, Joseph Cotton provides his usual impressive performance. After two decades as a lead actor and appearing frequently on television in the 1950s, this was the second film in which he played a supporting role. He is splendid as John Breckenridge and creates a successful portrait of a man who is living a lie that no one believes but himself; the scene in which

his cowardice is exposed is painful to watch due to his expertise at projecting pitiable vulnerability. Cotten would make two more films with Aldrich (*Hush... Hush, Sweet Charlotte* in 1965 and *Twilight's Last Gleaming* in 1977). Familiar villains Neville Brand and Jack Elam utilize their screen presences to make their superfluous roles as rustlers and kidnappers convincingly menacing, while Rad Fulton (later to be billed as James Westmoreland) is suitably creepy as the third member of the trio.

Another major distinction is a notable score by Ernest Gold. During the main titles, the composer establishes the relationship between the two antagonists by alternating a foreboding theme for O'Malley with a heroic one for Stribling. As the film progresses, O'Malley's theme takes precedence and sets the mood for the film's air of impending doom. Gold gently underscores some scenes but enhances the dramatic pitch of others, particularly the climactic sequences. He also makes judicious use of the film's romantic ballad "Pretty Little Girl in a Yellow Dress," which was written by Dimitri Tiomkin and Ned Washington. Tiomkin composed many fine scores for Westerns and his beautiful melody for this film adds a further dimension to O'Malley's dream. (Recordings of the song were released by Mike Clifford on Columbia and Carl Dobkins, Jr. on Decca; Dobkins' version is included on a Bear Family CD entitled *Rio Bravo and Other Western Movie and TV Themes*, released in 2000.)

There are some indications that the movie is finally getting some overdue recognition for its merits. While some current reviews still denounce it, others are more perceptive. Phil Hardy in *The Western* (William Morrow; 1983) calls it "a powerful essay in sexual neurosis" and "the most lyrical of Aldrich's films." *The Motion Picture Guide* by Jay Robert Nash and Stanley Ralph Ross (Cinebooks; 1986) calls it "an underrated, superbly cast picture that draws Aldrich's dark side into the public eye." Adrian Turner in the annual *Time Out Film Guide* writes that "the movie is more lyrical than Aldrich's usual macho posturings and the script is abrim with classical allusions." *The BFI Companion to the Western*, edited by Edward Buscombe (Atheneum; 1988), agrees, noting that "this is one of the director's least harsh films (and) contains a number of characteristic tours de force, such as the death of Breckenridge, Stribling swallowed by the marsh, Missy's appearance at the festival and O'Malley's flamboyant suicide." The review also notes that the outdoor shots "are much enhanced by Ernst Laszlo's lyrical photography." The fact that more than one critic uses the adjective "lyrical" to describe the movie clearly indicates that the filmmakers succeeded in creating a Western that must be viewed on different levels to be fully appreciated. Indeed, as an indication of just how many critics at the time of the film's release just didn't understand it, the song that O'Malley sings was included to certify the lyricism at the heart of the movie and not to generate a possible hit tune, as many of them suggested. Undoubtedly, with the passing of more time, the film's admirers are certain to multiply.

*The Last Sunset* is not the first Western to share themes and characterizations with the ancient classics. And Brendan O'Malley is not the first emotionally unstable protagonist to inhabit a Western. But the addition of such themes as incest and suicide establish more distinctly the association with classical tragedy. As a result of his own transgressions, Brendan O'Malley can no longer endure the torment of his life. The pain that he has caused others is visited back upon him with such intensity that he can only find relief by ending his life. It is only with his death that the object of his love can be free to find true happiness. And when that happens, as he expresses it so poetically and so fatefully, he will hear the angels in heaven shouting for joy and he will be able to sleep in peace.

*The Last Sunset* is a unique and haunting Western. Its flaws may be due to the intrusion of conventional elements into what is primarily an unconventional story. Nevertheless, it attempts something different and, for the most part, succeeds. While the complexity of its themes may be disturbing, it remains an absorbing and unforgettable study of sin and redemption in the Old West.

CREDITS: Producers: Eugene Frenke, Edward Lewis; Director: Robert Aldrich; Screenplay: Dalton Trumbo, Based Upon a Novel by Vechel Howard; Cinematographer: Ernest Laszlow; Editor: Edward Mann; Music: Ernest Gold

CAST: Rock Hudson (Dana Stribling); Kirk Douglas (Brendan O'Malley); Dorothy Malone (Belle Breckenridge); Joseph Cotten (John Breckenridge); Carol Lynley (Missy Breckenridge); Regis Toomey (Milton Wing); Neville Brand (Frank Hobbs); Rad Fulton (Julesberg Kid); Adam Williams (Bowman); Jack Elam (Ed Hobbs); John Shay (Calverton); Margarito De Luna (Jose); Jose Torvay (Rosario)

# CAPE FEAR

In the first scene of the film, beneath the main titles and accompanied by a sinister musical score, a large and imposing figure walks decisively through the center of a small southern town, his manner and expression conveying a sense of determination and anger. Upon entering a building that by its structure conveys official and legal authority, he becomes increasingly insolent. He brushes past a woman on a stairway, knocking some of her books to the floor, and keeps walking. He challenges a passerby, who dares to glance at him, with a look of contempt. After insulting an elderly janitor, he enters a courtroom and his eyes light up with pleasure as he sights the object of his hatred.

This is the beginning of a terrifying motion picture with a truly exceptional performance by a durable and popular actor. At the time of the film's release, he had been a star for over two decades. Excluding one role seven years earlier, he had not been known for playing villainous characters and, in his 15 films prior to this one, he had played conventional heroes in Westerns and war movies, as well as the lead in dramas and even a couple of comedies. However, in this movie, he would create one of the most thoroughly despicable and dangerous characters ever to appear on screen. The actor is Robert Mitchum. The character is Max Cady. The movie is *Cape Fear*.

Released by Universal-International in 1962, *Cape Fear* features two major stars, Gregory Peck and Robert Mitchum, acting together for the first time. Though both actors had always been associated with quality productions, the film was widely viewed as an innately unpleasant one due to its plot. The mere thought of a sadistic ex-convict planning his revenge upon the man he holds responsible for his imprisonment by sexually assaulting his wife and young daughter was considered extremely repugnant. In less able hands, the movie could have been a sleazy piece of exploitation. Though it is definitely a deeply disturbing movie, it is the work of talented artists who painstakingly avoid prurience to create a superb study in terror. Yet the theme sparked outrage in some critics and uneasiness in audiences who stayed away. In the year 1962, the public was not ready for such a movie, even one made as brilliantly as this one.

*Cape Fear* is almost two hours of unrelenting suspense and tension. Although its primary purpose is to entertain while it shocks, it also contains some valid points on the nature of humanity versus bestiality and civilization versus savagery. It begins on a sunny day in a peaceful town with its immaculately dressed hero practicing law in a courtroom, the symbol of civilization. Sam Bowden represents not only civilized society and the law but all the qualities that are indicative of a successful life. He is admired as a leading citizen in his hometown and is respected as a skillful attorney of integrity. His personal

A TERRIFYING WAR OF NERVES UNPARALLELED IN SUSPENSE!!!

GREGORY PECK · ROBERT MITCHUM · POLLY BERGEN

"CAPE FEAR"

LORI MARTIN · MARTIN BALSAM · JACK KRUSCHEN · TELLY SAVALAS AND BARRIE CHASE
Screenplay by JAMES R WEBB · Directed by J. LEE THOMPSON · Produced by Sy BARTLETT · A Melville-Talbot Production · A Universal-International Release

life is equally successful and probably means more to him than his profession. He is married to an attractive and loving wife, has a 13-year-old daughter who is the epitome of innocence and even has a dog that is cherished by the entire family. But by the end of the film, this symbol of legal authority and family devotion will be covered in mud and slime as he claws and grunts and struggles with every ounce of his strength to destroy his enemy with his bare hands.

This enemy is his exact opposite in many ways, mocking the values that he cherishes and using brute force to satisfy his desires. Max Cady is the embodiment of evil, bestial essence in human form, without a trace of morality. He enjoys hurting people and he intends to make Sam Bowden suffer for each day of his incarceration. Eight years earlier, Sam had testified against Cady after having witnessed a brutal rape while on business in Baltimore, and it was this testimony that convicted Cady. Following his release, Cady appears in Sam's hometown in Georgia and begins to execute his sadistic plan of vengeance. His intrusion into the peaceful world of the Bowdens is the worst kind of nightmare for Sam and Peggy Bowden and their daughter Nancy. A good citizen and a firm believer in the law, Sam seems to be above the kind of degradation that Cady exudes. At the beginning of the film, he is so self-assured and complacent that he doesn't even notice the hate-filled Cady glowering at him from the rear of the courtroom.

When Cady follows Sam into the parking lot and then reaches into Sam's car to take his keys, Cady symbolically forces himself into Sam's world and his life. Sam is surprised to see Cady and initially only annoyed. But he becomes more concerned that evening at the bowling center when he sees Cady glaring at his family like a rattlesnake stalking his prey. This is only the beginning of Cady's campaign of terror. With each carefully planned act, he strikes deeper into Sam's orderly life as his mere presence and manner brings the threat of harm increasingly closer to Peggy and Nancy. He violates the sanctity of the Bowden home by poisoning Nancy's dog, sending a clear message to Sam that his family is equally vulnerable. He appears at a dock where the family is trying to enjoy a pleasant outing and provokes Sam into an assault by making lewd remarks about both Peggy and Nancy. Then he arrives at Nancy's school, smiling monstrously as his presence sends the frightened child into the path of a car. Yet he is clever enough to refrain from making himself culpable to any overt illegality, preferring to watch patiently as Sam and his family disintegrate under the strain.

Initially, Sam's response to Cady is legal as he seeks help from the Chief of Police and then from a private detective. But Cady outwits him repeatedly, displaying the ability to use the law for his own purposes. Becoming increasingly unraveled, Sam offers money to Cady who makes it clear that he wants blood, not just from Sam, but from his family. This motivates Sam's descent into criminality and, at one point, only Peggy's hysterical pleas prevent him from resorting to murder to protect his family. Instead, he hires three thugs to give Cady a beating, but Cady again emerges triumphant and presses charges against Sam immediately. His career in ruins, Sam is forced to use his wife and daughter as bait in an intricate plan to ensnare Cady into committing a criminal act. But Cady is too smart to fall into any kind of trap and seems to be one step ahead of Sam all the way. By the time of the climactic duel to the death in the swamps of Cape Fear, Sam has been dragged down to Cady's level but it is the only arena in which he has any chance of defeating him.

Sam Bowden is a sympathetic figure as well as a heroic one, clearly the antithesis of Cady, but as the film progresses some similarities between the two antagonists emerge. Though Sam's cause is righteous, he nevertheless becomes willing to twist and break the law in the same manner as Cady. Because of the inadequacy of official law, he sees no alternative to violating his principles and surviving by the law of the jungle, which is clearly Cady's only law. Sam feels justified in his actions because of fears for his family, but Cady feels equally justified in his actions because of the loss of his family. Though the fact that he was a rapist is an indication of what kind of husband and father he was, he still sees himself as a victim. In his view, women are only getting what they deserve when beaten or raped. His perception of women is established throughout the movie by his frequent statements, including a casual remark about a woman passing by Sam's car or a cruel insult to a friendly waitress. His hatred of women is even more evident from the vicious beating he gives to a young drifter whom he picks up in a bar. Cady believes that rape is justified and that Sam was wrong in preventing it. Similarly, Cady feels that his former wife was equally wrong in divorcing him while he was in prison, and he delights in telling Sam of his revenge upon her.

Cady enjoys seeing Sam squirm. But he fails to realize that his tactics will eventually bring out the ferocious animal hidden deep within Sam's cultured veneer. That veneer finally cracks when Cady brutalizes Peggy and then closes in on Nancy. Pushed to the breaking point by Cady's unrelenting

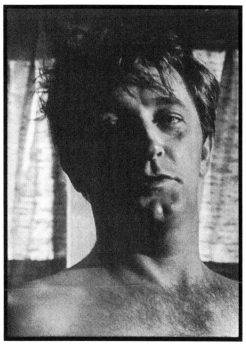

**Max Cady (Robert Mitchum) exudes pure evil.**

viciousness, Sam has only one desire in the Cape Fear River and that is to crush the life out of Cady, who is equally intent on killing Sam. It is a brutal fight to the death that Sam and Cady engage in, and no trace of civilization exists in either man as they viciously seek to kill one another. When Sam overpowers Cady and doesn't pull the trigger of his gun, it is not out of mercy or respect for the law, but out of a desire to make Cady rot in a cell and suffer for the rest of his life. In this respect, Sam has become Cady.

The film deliberately offers little insight into Max Cady's character. He exists merely as evil, a human beast in a clean suit and Panama hat. The superiority of his brute force is evident early in the film. When Sam uses his friendship with Chief Dutton to bring Cady in for questioning, Cady readily agrees to all of the official requests, including a strip search. Shedding his clothing and standing nearly naked in the presence of Sam and Dutton, he doesn't react with embarrassment or humiliation as most suspects would. Instead, his muscular frame challenges them as much as his sarcasm and he isn't even slightly intimidated. The impotence of official law in the presence of raw degeneracy is strikingly clear. Yet while he is cunning enough to use cultured society's law to his advantage, he is more at home in the swamp, sliding in and out of the water like a reptile, crushing the life out of a deputy with the force of a python.

Cady belongs in the jungle and he knows it, behaving like a vicious animal whenever he can, whether out of innate malevolence or for the sheer enjoyment. In contrast, Sam had always believed that he was fully civilized, never realizing that he was only repressing his animal instincts. After all of the defenses of his enlightened society have failed, it is those primitive instincts that will defeat Cady, though at a cost. Sam will never feel secure or self-righteous again and his family will never feel safe again. In the last scene of the movie, beneath the end titles, Sam, Peggy and Nancy are being taken out of the swamp. They are all solemn and silent, their expressions grim. They know that their lives have been changed forever. Physically they are leaving the swamp but psychologically the swamp and Max Cady will always be with them.

*Cape Fear* is based upon John D. MacDonald's novel *The Executioners*, published in 1957 by Fawcett Gold Medal Books. Though the story and characterizations are similar, significant differences exist between the novel and the film. In the novel, the setting is a small town in Florida and Sam and Carol Bowden are the parents of three children. Sam, a junior partner in a law firm, is noted for his integrity. He is also an ex-Army officer who, during World War II in Australia, interrupted the rape of a teenager by Sergeant Max Cady. As

a result of Sam's testimony at the court-martial, Cady received a life sentence at hard labor. Released after 13 years, Cady tracks down Sam and begins his plan of revenge with Nancy, the eldest child, as the main target. After poisoning the family dog, he tries to kill the middle child by shooting him and causes an automobile accident that almost kills Carol and two of the children. Finding the law powerless to prevent further tragedy, Sam and Carol plot to kill Cady and, with the help of the police, set a trap in their home. Though the trap doesn't work as planned, Cady takes the bait and is killed but almost by accident with the family then returning to its peaceful existence.

Readers of the novel learn more about Cady than viewers

of the film. Born into a backwoods hill family of a feeble-minded mother and brutish father, Cady and his brothers have been in trouble all of their lives. Given a choice of joining the Army or going to prison, Cady enlists and after some combat experiences is sent to Australia with fatigue. Being a psychopath with a hatred for authority, Cady assumes no responsibility for his vicious assault of the teenager and blames Sam for his imprisonment, not only because of his testimony but because he was an officer.

The novel is fairly interesting but moves slowly and contains many illogical incidents. MacDonald tends to preach at selected intervals and hammers his message into the reader in a patronizing manner. As in many of his novels, the author's philosophical thoughts are voiced intrusively through his main character and interrupt the flow of the story. The ending is unsatisfying and contains a minimum of suspense, due to the author's obvious attempt to create a finale that is different than what might be expected. As a result, the long-awaited confrontation between Sam and Cady never occurs.

The filmmakers converted a conventional paperback thriller into a superior motion picture and many artists share the credit. *Cape Fear* is a co-production of Gregory Peck's Melville Productions and Robert Mitchum's Talbot Productions, but the project originated with Peck, whose company had purchased film rights to the book. After considering other actors—including Jack Palance and Rod Steiger—for the role of Cady, Peck then aggressively sought Mitchum to be his co-star. As reported in the biography by Lynn Haney, *Gregory Peck: A Charmed Life* (Carroll & Graf; 2004), Peck states, "I thought of Mitchum because I remembered *The Night of the Hunter* and I knew what Bob was capable of doing with a good part." Greg's instincts proved to be absolutely correct and would result in an unforgettable performance from Robert Mitchum that no other actor could have equaled.

Peck also felt comfortable working with talents behind the camera, who had previously been associated with him on several films. Producer Sy Bartlett began his film career as a writer in 1933, learning his trade on everything from programmers to comedies and thrillers. In 1949, Bartlett and Beirne Lay, Jr. wrote the screenplay for *12 O'Clock High*, based on their novel and presented Gregory Peck with one of his most memorable roles. In the following decade, he co-wrote *The Big Country* (1958) and *Beloved Infidel* (1959), both of which starred Peck. In 1959, he produced *Pork Chop Hill* for Melville Productions, in which he and Peck were partners, with Peck starring. Their next film together was *Cape Fear*.

James Webb, who wrote the screenplay for *Cape Fear*, began his screenwriting career in 1941 and wrote many low-budget Westerns, graduating to A Westerns and other major productions in the 1950s. He was one of the co-writers with Bartlett on *The Big Country* and scripted *Pork Chop Hill* for Melville. His tight, compact script for *Cape Fear* eliminates all of the faults of the novel, including several superfluous characters and implausible incidents. Gone are two of Sam's children, as well as Nancy's boy friend, who exists in the book as an excuse for the author to express his views on the younger generation. Sam's partner is relegated to an insignificant role as junior associate. Cady's two attacks upon family members are also wisely left out of the script.

Sam Bowden emerges as a more admirable and empathetic character than his counterpart in the novel. The script emphasizes his role as husband and father with his profession becoming almost irrelevant to him. When he is threatened with disbarment, a likely possibility in view of his illegal actions, he shows no emotion since his only concern is for his wife and daughter. In the climax of the film, he is not the bungler of the novel, but instead is as vicious and cunning as Cady.

While Webb fleshes out Sam's character, he reduces the characterization of Max Cady by eliminating most of his history. Without the psychological and social explanations for his behavior, Cady becomes more loathsome and frightening since he seems to exist only for the purpose of inflicting harm upon innocent people, particularly a defenseless child. Webb doesn't allow any trace of sympathy for Cady, deliberately excluding his son's death while he was in prison, an incident in the novel that provided a partial reason for his revenge upon his wife. In the film, Cady only refers to his still-living son casually and is obviously disinterested in him, though he subjects his former wife to the same brutal fate as in the novel.

Webb retains the character of Chief of Police Dutton who becomes Sam's close friend, a relationship that allows the script to imply some cogent points about the misuse of the law that such a friendship would permit. Charley Sievers, the private detective, functions as he did in the book but is around longer and becomes an integral part of the final trap. Two new characters are created for the film and add to the effectiveness of the story. Dave Grafton, a shady lawyer whom Cady hires, illustrates ironically how the law that Sam unsuccessfully tried to utilize to shield the innocent can be used cleverly to protect the guilty. The second new character is Diane Taylor, the young drifter that Cady picks up and brutalizes. Diane is a substitute for the blowsy tramp Blanche in the novel, and she is a more prominent character.

The climax of the film is far more effective than that of the novel in which Cady's actions simply lack credibility. Placing the trap away from the Bowden home and using extreme measures to convince Cady that Peggy and Nancy are defenseless become more credible plot developments. The setting of the Cape Fear River, besides being visually symbolic of Cady's nature, not only provides the opportunity for more genuine suspense but thematically is more valid since it reverses the set-up at the beginning of the film. The setting now brings Sam into Cady's world. Since civilized law has proven to be so ineffective, only the law of the jungle and the survival of the fittest can determine the victor.

142

Cady's proficiency at triumphing in such a setting is unequivocal, as an unfortunate deputy soon discovers. In the novel, Cady falls too easily into an obvious trap and his killing of the deputy becomes unwise, since his guilt for the crime will be easily determined. In the film, he is aware that Sam and the police may be laying a trap for him and he double-checks everything. Even when he realizes from the deputy's presence that a trap has indeed been set for him, he takes great care not to leave a mark on his victim and then proceeds to wreak his vengeance on Nancy, knowing that she will never testify against him. The entire climactic sequence is a series of emotional shocks as Cady draws closer to his prey, outsmarting Sam and smashing everything that stands in his way, including Peggy. And the extremely vicious fight between Sam and Cady, missing from the novel, is far more dramatically satisfying.

Webb's masterful screenplay is brilliantly complemented by J. Lee Thompson's direction. Thompson started out in the film industry in England as an actor in 1934, became a screenwriter in 1937 and started directing in 1951. After several programmers, he displayed notable skill with the anti-death penalty drama *Yield to the Night* (1956), which was nominated for a BAFTA award for Best Film. More acclaim was bestowed upon him for one of the first so-called "kitchen-sink" dramas, *Woman in a Dressing Gown* (1957). He received still more praise for the gripping war movie *Ice Cold in Alex* (1958), which earned another BAFTA nomination for Best Film and should be avoided in its truncated U.S. version, *Desert Attack*. Two 1959 releases, the suspenseful yet poignant *Tiger Bay* and the superb adventure movie *Northwest Frontier* (U.S. title: *Flame Over India*), brought—within the same year— two additional BAFTA nominations for Best Film and certified his status as one of England's most gifted directors—as well as one of the most versatile, as indicated by the range of genres which his work encompassed. However, Steve Chibnall demonstrates in his definitive book on the director, *J. Lee Thompson* (Manchester University Press; 2002), that all of these films, despite the genre, scrutinized social problems and presented his characters with moral dilemmas. These shared themes would be present in many of his future films.

In 1961, shortly after *The Guns of Navarone* had started filming, Thompson replaced the original director (Alexander Mackendrick) and helmed the movie that became a worldwide commercial success; it received an Academy Award nomination for Best Picture and earned him a nomination for Best Director. (The absence of a BAFTA nomination is generally considered to be due to the fact that Thompson had also directed a biography of Wernher von Braun entitled *I Aim at the Stars* in 1960. Since von Braun had developed the V-2 rockets which had bombed London during the war, the film infuriated many Britishers.) While directing *Navarone*, its star Gregory Peck asked him to come to the United States and direct his next movie, *Cape Fear*, for his own production company. This film would be quite different from the color and widescreen World War II adventure film.

In *Cape Fear*, Thompson's direction is gritty and methodical, stylish and innovative. Filmed in black and white to accentuate the film noir aspects of the story, Thompson brings a striking visual sense to the movie that contributes immensely to individual scenes as well as the overall effect of the film. A rapidly paced intensity propels the story along at a dizzying speed. His attention to every aspect of the film, from camera angles and movement to light and shading, is obvious. From the opening shot of Cady cutting a swath through the quiet town, Thompson creates a vision of evil and unwholesomeness lurking on the outskirts of refined society. As the film steadily progresses, a definite sense prevails that there is only a thin curtain separating society from the jungle, civilization from savagery

Of the many scenes that highlight the director's visual ingenuity, the entire Diane Taylor sequence is notable. In her introduction, the naïve but self-confident drifter and the psychopathic Cady eye one another across the floor of a crowded nightclub. The scene is punctuated by the threat of violence between Cady and the police that foreshadows how the relationship will end. Later, as they drive to her room, Diane insults Cady patronizingly, foolishly secure in her sense of superiority, smugly unaware of the danger enveloping as suggested by the claustrophobic feeling within the car. One of the most riveting scenes in the film follows. Lying in bed, as Cady encircles her like a

GREGORY PECK, ROBERT MITCHUM POLLY BERGEN

Cape Fear

LORI MARTIN
MARTIN BALSAM
JACK KRUSCHEN
TELLY SAVALAS
AND
BARRIE CHASE

Screenplay by JAMES R. WEBB
Directed by J. LEE THOMPSON
Produced by SY BARTLETT
A Melville-Talbot Production
A Universal-International Release

beast of prey about to pounce, the awakening of terror upon Diane's face is too late to save her. Devoid of any dialogue, the scene is a stunning example of Thompson's skill, conveying the extent of Cady's sadism without showing any actual violence.

Thompson exercises similar restraint in the waterfront scene in which Cady's fight with the three hired thugs is brief and shown from a distance, ending with a closer shot of Cady as he wrenches a chain from an assailant and charges him. Though there is an undercurrent of brutality throughout the entire film, very little violence is actually depicted until the climactic sequence, which is exceedingly discomforting as well as suspenseful. Cady's detection of the deputy, whose fate is sealed by a mosquito, is one of the film's many unforgettable moments. His subsequent terrifying encounters with Peggy and Nancy are deliberately distressing, but the director doesn't allow the film to become unsavory and knows the extent to which he can depict Nancy's jeopardy. The final battle between Cady and Sam is savagely realistic and ultimately an emotional catharsis. *Cape Fear* is a splendid example of Thompson's expertise and a distinctive accomplishment.

All of the film's production values are first-rate. George Tomasini edited the film briskly. His numerous film credits include editing all of Alfred Hitchcock's films since *Rear Window* in 1954. The dark and somber photography, particularly impressive in the nighttime scenes, is by Samuel Leavitt, who previously worked on *Pork Chop Hill*. Art Directors Alexander

GREGORY PECK, ROBERT MITCHUM POLLY BERGEN

CAPE FEAR

LORI MARTIN
MARTIN BALSAM
JACK KRUSCHEN
TELLY SAVALAS
AND
BARRIE CHASE

Screenplay by JAMES R. WEBB
Directed by J. LEE THOMPSON
Produced by SY BARTLETT
A Melville-Talbot Production
A Universal-International Release

Golitzen and Robert Boyle also contribute effectively to the tone and mood of the film.

Bernard Herrmann's score is another of the composer's memorable contributions to film music. In 1962, Herrmann was in the midst of his Hitchcock collaborative years, and his music for *Cape Fear*, though not as rich as his score for *Vertigo* or as chillingly identifiable as *Psycho*, is nevertheless equally evocative. The opening credits are accompanied by an ominous four-note motif, highlighted by French horns, which clearly suggest the appearance of unadulterated evil as Max Cady propels himself through the peaceful town. This refrain is used in variations throughout the film, heightening the images of Cady's increasing sadism. As the violence of the film steadily escalates, the music also becomes more discordant and upsetting. The brutality of the climactic fight is especially enhanced by the orchestration that conveys the impression that various instruments are engaging in their own fierce battle to the death. Throughout the film, the music entwines seamlessly with the images onscreen and is an integral part of the film's harrowing impact.

The acting is uniformly superb. Gregory Peck is solid and compelling as Sam Bowden. Peck is a strong enough screen personality to play against his co-star's overpowering portrayal and he convincingly projects moral strength and sincerity to balance the interaction. It is a very controlled performance with his quiet intensity visibly reflecting his increasingly irrepressible emotions. As his character gradually loses his struggle to contain his baser instincts, he displays the steady escalation of his inner anguish and rage through his progressively more pained expressions and the strained tone of his voice. He also provides an added dimension to the role by making Sam Bowden initially appear just a bit pompous, suggesting a belief that a pervert like Max Cady could never penetrate his secure world. This implication tends to make Sam's metamorphosis more emotionally gripping. Though generously aware that his co-star is the centerpiece of the movie, Peck's less noticeable performance is still an excellent one.

In support, Polly Bergen is very good as Peggy, initially displaying a logical and poised reaction to Cady's threat as though believing someone like him could never penetrate her home and security. By the end of the film, her self-assurance is completely disintegrated and she is reduced to hysterical terror. As Nancy, Lori Martin is equally fine, projecting innocence and vulnerability that eventually turns to paralytic fear. Reportedly, director Thompson has sought Hayley Mills, whom he had discovered for *Tiger Bay*, for the role, but she was unavailable. This was fortunate since Lori seems so exceptionally vulnerable and fragile, particularly when Nancy is being manhandled by Cady; in addition, from a purely physical perspective, Lori actually looks like she could be the daughter of Peck and Bergen. Martin Balsam as Chief Dutton and Jack Kruschen as Dave Grafton perform ably, while Telly Savalas, who had tested for the role of Cady before Mitchum was signed, is effective in the role of Charley Sievers. Particular praise has to be given to Barrie Chase, daughter of noted screenwriter Borden Chase, who gives a standout performance as Diane Taylor. She is extremely affecting as the former prom queen who is both self-assured and self-contemptuous until her fateful encounter with Max Cady leaves her a cowering, defeated shell of fear and pain.

However, the movie belongs to Robert Mitchum, who provides an impeccable portrait of evil. Taken for granted as a leading man, his talents were often wasted in mediocre films and unappreciated in more prestigious roles. In 1955, he surprised critics with a superior portrayal of the maniacal preacher in Charles Laughton's *The Night of the Hunter*, but the film attracted meager audiences. Over the next seven years he played more conventional roles while turning in two admirable performances in *Home from the Hill* (1959) and *The Sundowners* (1960).

Nevertheless, nothing in Mitchum's career prepared audiences for his portrayal of Max Cady. It is not just the powerful and overt expressions of brute force and amorality he displays, but the subtle mannerisms and gestures that add significantly to the characterization. His swagger and sneer project contempt for everything that is decent. The look in his eyes and the tone of his voice combined with the way he wears his Panama hat and chews his cigar all convey an unforgettable impression of unmitigated degeneracy. The scene in the police station in which Cady allows his attorney to charge Sam and Chief Dutton with persecution is just one of the many examples of the actor's skill. Throughout most of the scene, while the others often exchange heated words, he doesn't say a single word but yet he still dominates the scene with his posture and expressions. From the malignant arrogance in his introduction to his final scene in which the rage and terror on his face evoke the image of a trapped wild beast, Mitchum creates a nightmarish portrait of human depravity.

Incidentally, his co-star concurred. In *The Films of Gregory Peck* by John Griggs (Citadel; 1984), Peck is quoted as saying, "It's Bob's picture; the best performance he ever gave."

*Cape Fear* received some very good reviews. *Variety* called the movie "a forthright exercise in cumulative terror." Bosley Crowther in *The New York Times* wrote that it was "a pitiless shocker," adding that "a cold-blooded calculated build-up of sadistic menace and shivering dread is accomplished with frightening adroitness." Arthur Knight in *The Saturday Review* wrote that the movie is "an old-fashioned suspenseful melodrama (that) has no purpose beyond scaring the daylights out of you." Paul Beckley in *The New York Herald Tribune* called it "a tour de force (and) a study in terror that verges on the horror genre." However, it also received some negative reviews. Brendan Gill in *The New Yorker* wrote that "everyone concerned with this repellent attempt to make a great deal of money out of a clumsy plunge into sexual pathology should be ashamed of himself." In later decades, such an endorsement would have filled theaters but, in 1962, it was perhaps discomforting for some potential patrons.

*Cape Fear* was a box-office failure. On *Variety*'s list of Top-Grossing Films for 1962, it was a dismal Number 47 with only $1.6 million in domestic theatrical rentals, which placed it alongside the cheap horror film *Tales of Terror* and just below a dismal comedy called *The Pigeon That Took Rome*. Other suspense/thriller films had diverse results at the box office. *Experiment in Terror*, which lived up to its title, should have reached a much wider audience but also bombed at Number 54 with $1.4 million. In the hit category, *Whatever Happened to Baby Jane* scored with over $4 million to earn 12th place on the list and *The Manchurian Candidate* was in 25th position with $3.3 million. *Cape Fear* did much better business in England, possibly due to the controversy over six minutes of cuts demanded by the British censors, but the film still ended in the red for producer Peck. The financial losses of *Cape Fear* ended Melville Productions.

It wasn't just the negative reviews that impacted upon the movie's commercial failure. Only a couple of years before, Hitchcock's *Psycho* had been a huge commercial success, despite many negative reviews. But Norman Bates stayed in his motel and only preyed upon women who came into contact with him unluckily, while "Mother" remained in her home. Max Cady forcibly intruded into the comfortable world of middle-class values, and not only preyed upon women but upon young, innocent schoolgirls. And while *Psycho* had its intentional moments of humor, there was absolutely no humor in *Cape Fear*. Filmgoers in 1962 had queasiness about the subject of the film and were reluctant to admit that someone like Max Cady could puncture the comfortable and secure bubble erected around their lives and homes.

Three decades later, everything had changed. In 1991, a terrible remake of *Cape Fear* was released. Directed by Martin Scorsese with Robert De Niro as Cady and Nick Nolte as Sam, this repulsive movie contains explicit violence and unsavory dialogue. In keeping with the times, the family is dysfunctional. Sam is a dishonest adulterer, his wife is a disagreeable shrew and the daughter is an obnoxious tease. Cady is justified in seeking his revenge because Sam's suppression of evidence resulted in his conviction. The movie is filled with pretentious moralizing and spurious symbolism.

De Niro plays Cady with a complete lack of subtlety that fits in with the film's tone. The scene in which Cady bites a chunk of flesh out of the cheek of Sam's law clerk is typical. Also, the members of the Bowden family are so unlikable that it is difficult to care what happens to them. Furthermore, the absurdities of the plot make the story unbelievable. For instance, this Cady ties himself to the driveshaft of Sam's car for the journey to Cape Fear, which is too incredible to sustain belief. And in the contrived climax, Cady's frequent reappearances are reminiscent of the teenage slasher movies in which the killer repeatedly seems to be dead but keeps coming back for encores.

The remake received some very negative reviews. Terrence Rafferty in *The New Yorker* called the movie "a disgrace (and) an ugly, incoherent, dishonest piece of work." David Denby in *New York Magazine* called it a "nasty" film, which Scorsese "wildly over-directs as if to make up for something hollow at the core." Mark Goodrich in *People Weekly* wrote that the movie is "simply a disintegrating exercise in gratuitous violence in which Scorsese paints himself into a dark corner and then covers his mistakes with buckets of blood."

However, graphic bloodshed had become profitable among younger audiences. The remake was a box-office success and De Niro received an Academy Award nomination, which reflects the ignorance of Academy members. As Terrence Raffery wrote, "De Niro's frenetic but thoroughly uninteresting performance is emblematic of the movie's inadequacy. He's covered with tattooed messages but he doesn't seem to have a body. We could feel Mitchum's evil in all its slimy physicality; De Niro's is an evil that we merely read."

Bernard Herrmann's score is reused while Gregory Peck (as the shyster lawyer), Robert Mitchum (as the detective) and Martin Balsam (as the judge) play small roles. Mitchum originally refused to appear in the remake, but Peck convinced him to do it. He shouldn't have. Scorsese may have stated that he included the two legendary stars in his film to show that his version was intended as a tribute to the original, but this rings hollow. It is not a tribute; it is debasement. Though it certainly couldn't have been Scorsese's intention, the presence of the original stars tends to remind viewers of the pitiable quality of the remake, which Leonard Maltin calls "a *Cape Fear* for the Freddy Krueger generation." At least, one benefit from the remake was that Peck, as owner of the rights to the original property, finally profited financially from his original investment.

The commercial failure of the original *Cape Fear* in 1962 must have been discouraging to the stars and director but they at least had the satisfaction of knowing they had made a superb movie. But, of course, the movie was just one stage of their respective careers and they would all go on to other projects.

For his next film, *To Kill a Mockingbird*, Gregory Peck won an Academy Award for in essence playing a variation of his own persona. In actuality, he deserved far more praise for *Cape Fear*, in which he expanded his range and unleashed the primitive beast lurking beneath Sam Bowden's reputable façade. (Peck agreed, stating in the Griggs book that his role in *Mockingbird* was his "easiest," adding that "I feel that I've done better acting in more unsuccessful pictures.") Highlights of Peck's subsequent career include fine performances in the superb Western *The Stalking Moon* (1968), the horror thriller *The Omen* (1976) and the title role in *MacArthur* (1977).

Robert Mitchum also was fortunate enough to have opportunities, far too infrequently, to showcase his skill, providing wonderful performances in *El Dorado* (1967) and *Farewell My Lovely* (1975). His surprising versatility was displayed with his portrayal against type of the gentle schoolteacher in *Ryan's Daughter* (1970), though the film itself was overblown and tedious. But he never received official recognition in the form of an Academy Award for his exceptional talent. Undoubtedly, Max Cady remains his most outstanding performance.

J. Lee Thompson's ensuing career included virtually every genre, including historical epics (*Taras Bulba* in 1962), mysteries (*Return From the Ashes* in 1965), horror (*Eye of the Devil* in 1966) and musicals (*Huckleberry Finn* in 1974), all of which presented his characters with the type of moral dilemmas that typified his earlier films. But the disparate quality of these films prompted some British critics to claim that, after settling in Hollywood, he sacrificed his individuality for commercialism. In the Chibnall book, Thompson admits that there is some truth to this since he wanted to stay in Hollywood and therefore accepted many projects that he later regretted. These probably include *What a Way to Go* (1964), a laborious comedy which featured Mitchum among many stars, as well as *The Ambassador* (1984), a muddled political thriller which was his last film with Mitchum. Indeed, his filmography does seem to indicate that he simply went through the motions on such terrible films as *The Greek Tycoon* (1978), *Happy Birthday to Me* (1981), *Firewalker* (1986) and *Death Wish 4: the Crackdown* (1987).

Nevertheless, many of Thompson's Hollywood films reveal that his proficiency surfaced periodically. *Kings of the Sun* (1963) is unique in its presentation of a culture clash between Mayans and Indians. *Mackenna's Gold* (1969) with Peck—and with Telly Savalas again in a supporting role—was cut prior to release and is considered a disaster but an entertaining Western adventure film. *The Chairman* (1969), his third and last film with Peck, is a suspenseful espionage thriller. *Conquest of the Planet of the Apes* (1972) is the best of the *Apes* sequels, especially in its original version. *The White*

*Buffalo* (1977), the second of nine movies he made with Charles Bronson, was denounced by critics who misunderstood its surreal sequences. It remains a haunting film.

In reviewing his career to Steve Chibnall, Thompson states quite frankly, "*Cape Fear* was like my old style and I think it is probably the best American film I made, which is regrettable, since it was my first American film. That was in the style of my early British films and I

**Diane Taylor (Barrie Chase) is unaware of the fate that Cady has planned for her.**

shouldn't have relinquished that style." It is definitely his best American film but it established such a high standard that it is not surprising that he never surpassed it.

*Cape Fear* stands as a testament to the talents of all of the personnel who were involved in its production. Almost five decades since its release, it retains its power to shock and horrify. It is a masterpiece of terror and a genuine film classic.

CREDITS: Producer: Sy Bartlett; Director: J. Lee Thompson; Screenplay: James R. Webb, Based on the Novel *The Executioners* by John D. Macdonald; Cinematographer: Sam Leavitt; Editor: George Tomasini; Art Directors: Alexander Golitzen, Robert Boyle; Music: Bernard Herrmann

CAST: Gregory Peck (Sam Bowden); Robert Mitchum (Max Cady); Polly Bergen (Peggy Bowden); Lori Martin (Nancy Bowden); Martin Balsam (Chief Dutton); Jack Kruschen (Dave Grafton); Telly Savalas (Charley Sievers); Barrie Chase (Diane Taylor); Paul Comi (Garner); John McKee (Officer Marconi); Page Slattery (Deputy Kersek); Ward Ramsey (Officer Brown); Edward Platt (Judge); Will Wright (Dr. Pearsall); Joan Staley (Waitress); Norma Yost (Ticket Clerk); Mack Williams (Dr. Lowney); Thomas Newman (Lt. Gervasi); Alan Reynolds (Vernon); Herb Armstrong (Waiter); Bunny Rhea (Pianist); Carol Sydes (Betty); Paul Levitt (Police Operator); Alan Wells (Young Blade); Allen Ray (Young Blade)

# FIRST MEN IN THE MOON

"Poor Cavor. He did have such a terrible cold."

One indication of a memorable movie is a great ending. It may be a line of dialogue, or it may be an image displayed on the screen. Or it could be both. In *First Men in the Moon*, it is the line of dialogue quoted above, spoken with relish and perhaps a bit of sadistic delight by an aged and frail old man, who starts to chuckle as he recites those profound words. It is a somewhat bleak ending, perhaps even a bit cruel, though simultaneously satisfactory and rewarding.

Columbia Pictures released *First Men in the Moon* in 1964. Filmed in color and Panavision, the movie features special effects by the legendary Ray Harryhausen, master of stop-motion animation and creator of many amazingly life-like monsters, aliens and mythological creatures that inhabit so many of his memorable films within the fantasy and science fiction genres. Ray's colleague Charles H. Schneer is the producer, a position he would occupy on most of Harryhausen's films. Ray, who also served as Associate Producer, had provided the genesis of the film and also participated in the development of the script, as he did on most of his films. But unlike many of the duo's other movies in which the special effects are the main reason to see the film, this one has the distinction of being a terrific movie even without the effects, due to the source material by H.G. Wells and a great script by Nigel Kneale and Jan Read.

**Ray Harryhausen's mooncalf is struck by a Selenite's stun gun.**

Such a statement is not intended to diminish Harryhausen's other films, but his movies of the 1950s in particular are burdened with unimaginative scripts. His first two films are "monster movies" which were produced after the successful reissue of the 1933 *King Kong* and were patterned after that classic film. But while *Kong* is exciting from beginning to end, the only interesting aspect about *The Beast from 20,000 Fathoms* (1953) is the beast. *It Came from Beneath the Sea* (1955), which began his partnership with Schneer, is also boring when the octopus is not on screen. For his next movie, the popularity of outer space movies inspired Harryhausen to venture into the field of science fiction. *Earth vs. the Flying Saucers* (1956) is mildly entertaining but is basically a poor imitation of the superior *The War of the Worlds* (1953). The mediocrity of the first two Schneer-Harryhausen collaborations, effects notwithstanding, is undoubtedly due to their limited budgets, not surprising since they were executive-produced by shlock-king Sam Katzman. Happily, Katzman was not involved with their next foray into the science fiction genre. As a result, *20 Million Miles to Earth* (1957) is an improvement; it has a good monster from Venus and benefits from Italian location footage but, regrettably, the lengthy scenes without the monster are still tedious.

After monsters and science fiction, Harryhausen decided to enter the fantasy field and it is easy to see the reason for this decision. Dinosaurs did actually exist at one time, while extraterrestrial life was speculative but possible. However, creatures of fantasy exist only in the imagination and therefore would be perfect subject matter for Ray's skills. Due to the success of the earlier inexpensive films, he was given a bigger budget for his first fantasy film, *The 7ᵗʰ Voyage of Sinbad* (1958), which proved to be his biggest success to date. It has some marvelous creatures and is a delight to see, especially since it is his first movie in color, but the juvenile storyline and characters make it just a great children's movie. It also benefited from being filmed mostly in Spain and not on cheap Hollywood studio sets, which unavoidably had given his previous projects the stigma of B movies. This move away from Hollywood would prove to be the pattern for Ray's future films and the decision to film on foreign locations with bigger budgets would be an auspicious one. Consequently, the films of the 1960s—and thereafter—look more expensive and professional than the films of the previous decade.

The 1960s also witnessed a noticeable improvement in the scripts for Harryhausen's movies, which resulted in a steady rise in quality. *The Three Worlds of Gulliver* (1960) is based upon Johnathan Swift's classic novel and is totally enjoyable. *Mysterious Island* (1961), directed by blacklisted director Cy Endfield, is an exciting adventure-fantasy based on Jules Verne's novel and is the best of the several versions that have been filmed. *Jason and the Argonauts* (1963), based upon Greek mythology, combines truly fantastic special effects with a literate script, making it one of the best fantasies ever brought to the motion picture screen.

For his next movie, Harryhausen revisited the science fiction genre. *First Men in the Moon* is not as well known as *Jason* but is of equal quality. However, it isn't usually on anyone's list of favorite science fiction movies and, in summaries of Ray's career, it is often given short thrift. Possibly because of its commercial failure, Ray returned to monsters and fantasy. He functioned as a hired hand for his next movie, *One Million Years B.C.* (1966), for Hammer Films. He returned to Schneer for *The Valley of Gwangi* (1968), *The Golden Voyage of Sinbad* (1974), *Sinbad and the Eye of the Tiger* (1977) and *Clash of the Titans* (1981), his last movie. Though he never made another science fiction movie, his last foray into the genre remains a highpoint of his career.

*First Men in the Moon* is based upon the novel (originally published in 1901) of the same name by H.G. Wells. Mr. Bedford, an indebted businessman who retreats to a cottage to write a play, narrates the novel. He befriends a neighbor, Mr. Cavor, a research scientist who has developed an anti-gravity paste that he calls Cavorite. Bedford perceives possibilities for wealth from Cavorite, but Cavor is not interested in riches and instead builds a sphere which he intends to use to travel to the moon. After some doubts and fears, Bedford decides to accompany Cavor on his journey. Once they land on the moon, they find the surface to be breathable but uninhabitable. During the day, it has an atmosphere that freezes each night into a solid mass, only to thaw out the next morning and allow wild vegetation to flourish anew each day.

The two men explore the moon but soon are lost, having no idea where the sphere is. They sight a strange creature that they later learn is called a mooncalf. Then moon inhabitants capture the human visitors. Called Selenites, these moon inhabitants are about five feet high, with cylindrical bodies and tentacles. Cavor and Bedford are chained and taken beneath the surface, where they discover an advanced civilization. Cavor recognizes that the Selenites are intelligent creatures and wants to communicate with them, but Bedford fears that, as they are led deeper and deeper below the surface of the moon, they will never be able to get back to the sphere.

Eventually, Bedford breaks free of his chains and escapes with Cavor reluctantly following behind him. While trying to find their way to the surface, they discover that gold is very plentiful within the moon. After several fights with the Selenites, the two men find their way to the surface and separate to search for the sphere. Bedford luckily stumbles upon the sphere and returns to get Cavor but finds a bloodstained note that indicates his capture by the Selenites. He manages to pilot the sphere back to earth, bringing with him two bars of gold. His plans to return to the moon with an expedition are thwarted when the sphere is accidentally unleashed into space. Some time later, after publishing a novel based upon his experiences, he receives a message from a Dutch electrician who has been sending electro-magnetic messages into space and been receiving communications from Cavor.

Cavor's messages reveal a highly structured society of creatures living within the moon in which the division of labor has reached its ultimate expression. This society is divided into several groups, according to intellectual and employment capabilities. At the top of the social ladder is the Grand Lunar, a large-brained dictatorial ruler who presides over the society. Below him are various levels of classes, including intellectuals who have to be transported in cots due to their exorbitant mass of brain tissue, smaller spider-like creatures who have the ability to move quickly and the machine workers whose hands dwarf the rest of their bodies. And there are the slave laborers who are drugged and rendered immobile when not needed by their masters.

Cavor has learned to communicate with the Selenites and is eventually granted an audience with the Grand Lunar, who wants to know everything about human beings. But he makes the mistake of relating man's proclivity for war, which shocks the Grand Lunar. In his last message, Cavor realizes his blunder and tries to send the formula for Cavorite to Earth so others may travel to the moon and rescue him, but the transmission is interrupted. Bedford can only imagine what horrible fate may have befallen Cavor.

Like all of Wells' novels, *First Men in the Moon* includes the author's allegories relating to Victorian society and his philosophies about humanity in general. Wells believed that advances in technology were leading to a specialization among the masses that was harmful to humanity. In his novel, this kind of specialization reaches its definitive expression. As a result of the author's humanitarian priorities, the scientific details in his novels are not

**Bedford (Edward Judd) and Kate (Martha Hyer) escape from the Selenites.**

intended to be subject to close analysis. He was more concerned with the human condition and the injustice of humanity that he witnessed in his own society. Thus he used his novels to illustrate the inequalities and injustices of Victorian England through his creation of an alien world. The discriminations of his own world are magnified in a way that he hoped would educate those in power to be less arrogant and more considerate of those beneath their social level. However, these philosophical and social messages do not interfere with the storytelling. Though his novels are told in the style of the nineteenth century and contain antiquated language as well as outmoded science, they are still entertaining and provocative. Wells remains one of the founding fathers of science fiction for good reason.

In his book *Film Fantasy Scrapbook* (A.S. Barnes; 1972), Ray Harryhausen writes that he had always wanted to make a movie of *First Men in the Moon* since it was one of his favorite novels. However, Charles Schneer had argued that the story would lack credibility to modern audiences because of the advances in space science by the early 1960s. British writer Nigel Kneale, famed author of the *Quatermass* series, solved this problem when he developed the idea of the modern-day prologue with the main story told in flashback by the hero. This not only modernized the story but allowed the filmmakers to retain the period setting of the novel. The final screenplay, credited to Kneale and Jan Read, transforms the novel to the screen rather faithfully, though with some modifications. There are naturally some changes regarding life on and within the moon due to budget limitations, but the spirit of the novel is captured splendidly. One character, Katherine Callender, is added but Bedford and Cavor are perfect cinematic representations of their novel's counterparts. Kate may have been created for a romantic interest, but she makes the adventure more dramatically interesting. She is also the type of modern woman that Wells endorsed in many of his nonfiction writings.

*First Men in the Moon* begins in the present day with the first landing on the moon by a United Nations expedition composed of British, American and Russian astronauts. As the three men set foot on the surface of the moon, the world celebrates. However, while exploring the lunar surface, the astronauts are shocked to discover a British flag attached to a document claiming the moon for Queen Victoria. The document includes the name of Katherine Callender and this startling news sends British authorities in a panic as they try to locate the mysterious Miss Callender. Discovering that she died 10 years earlier, the investigators are directed to her husband, Arnold Bedford, who lives in a nursing home. Considered eccentric because of his letters to space agencies warning of the dangers of landing on the moon, Bedford greets his visitors politely until he is shown a picture of the British flag and realizes that men have landed on the moon. Knowing now that people will finally believe him, Bedford relates his story.

The setting then shifts back to 1899 England. Arnold Bedford, an indebted struggling playwright, is joined by his fiancée, Kate Callender, at his cottage. They meet their eccentric neighbor, Joseph Cavor, a scientist who has perfected a new substance called Cavorite, which defies gravity and which he plans to use to travel to the moon in a space-sphere he has designed. Cavor is so absorbed with his invention that he seems to have no regard for anything else, not even his health, since he frequently rushes from the heat of his laboratory out into the cold of the British coast. Bedford sees an opportunity to solve his financial problems, particularly after Cavor tells him that there may be gold on the moon. He invests money that he has fraudulently earned by conning Kate into signing a bill of sale for the cottage. When Kate learns that Bedford has lied to her about his financial problems, she rushes furiously to Cavor's cottage only to be pulled into the sphere as it blasts off for the moon.

The trip is successful and they endure a bumpy but triumphant landing on the surface of the moon. Unlike the novel, there is no atmosphere on the moon and the explorers use diving suits to traverse the terrain. They find the moon's surface to be uninhabitable but discover that a civilization inhabited by ant-like creatures called Selenites exists below the surface. The Selenites, who appear to have a complex system of labor with workers serving their elite masters, capture the humans. Cavor, who is beginning to sniffle due to his disregard for his health, finds the alien civilization fascinating, while Bedford and Kate are repelled by the strange creatures. By studying and analyzing the speech patterns of the humans, the Selenites are able to learn rudimentary English, at least enough to communicate.

Cavor is excited by communicating with the alien creatures and wants to share knowledge with them, while Bedford and Kate just want to escape. Cavor is taken to a creature that seems to be the supreme leader (he is not identified as the Grand Lunar in the movie). The leader is very curious about Earth and its inhabitants and Cavor is only too happy to answer all of his questions. Some of the information he provides, especially the concept of war, disturbs the leader who becomes determined to prevent other men from bringing death and destruction to the moon. Since Cavor tells the leader that no one else knows the secret of Cavorite, the leader then decrees that the three earthlings will never leave the moon. Bedford hears this pronouncement and, unable to operate the sphere, suddenly bursts upon the scene to rescue Cavor, even though the scientist doesn't want to be rescued. Bedford forces Cavor, resisting and periodically coughing, to return to the sphere. Realizing his obligation to Kate more than Bedford, Cavor repairs the sphere but refuses to return to Earth with them, craving to learn from the Selenites.

The movie then returns to the present day where Bedford, surrounded by the U.N. commission, watches on television as transmission from the moon records the exploration by the astronauts. Bedford recognizes the catacombs and tunnels but is surprised to see that they are all deserted and crumbling. There are no signs of life and only the remnants of a dead civilization is all that is left of the lunar city. It appears that an unknown virus (for which they had no immunity) killed the Selenites. Bedford can only smile as he rushes to his telescope to look up at the moon that he once visited. "Poor Cavor," he says with glee. "He did have such a terrible cold."

This is a memorable climax that still reverberates almost half a century later, while the framing story adds immeasurably to the film's effectiveness. Wells probably would have approved of the climactic revelation, a variation of his ending for *The War of the Worlds*. At one point in the novel, Cavor does develop a fever, though it is not mentioned again. Regardless, the bottom line is that the framing story with its surprise revelation works. Wells probably would also have approved of the depiction of the caste system depicted in the film, though it simplifies the intricate social system he devised for the novel. Instead of the multiple castes of creatures who are separated by their assigned tasks and surgically altered to perform a specific duty, the movie displays a less complex but equally authoritarian society of workers and managers. Retained is the principle of suspended animation by which workers are rendered immobile when not needed to perform their assigned tasks.

Although the voyage to the moon doesn't occur until almost an hour has passed, the story is never dull. The first part of the main narrative is filled with humor and warmth. The Victorian society is beautifully recreated in all

**Bedford fights the Selenites while Cavor (Lionel Jeffries) tries to avoid violence.**

details, from the clothing worn by the participants to the simplicity of the residences as well as the charming etiquette practiced by all of the characters. Most of the humor in the opening is due primarily to Cavor's characterization. He is genuinely amusing but he is never a clown. Beneath the clothing that doesn't seem to fit and the goggles that seem too large for him is a dedicated scientist who wants to learn, to explore and to enrich his mind, not his pockets. Arnold Bedford is an equally interesting character. He appears to be a bit of a scoundrel but a likeable one, and it is easy to see why Kate tolerates his irresponsibility, despite her independence.

Once the adventure begins, the tone of the movie becomes more serious. Many memorable scenes occur during this second half of the movie, particularly during the events leading to the climax. Bedford is revealed to have faults not usually associated with a standard hero and, like his novel's counterpart, he is too quick to use brute force against the Selenites. It is suggested that the Selenites are as frightened of him as he is of them and, in a way, he represents the kind of violence that the leader fears. One of the many questions left unanswered is whether, during their first encounter, Cavor might have communicated with the Selenites in a peaceful way if Bedford had not been provoked by the point of a spear and responded violently.

In one unsettling sequence, the Selenite leader shines a bright light into Cavor's eyes, displaying no concern when Cavor expresses pain. Later, Cavor believes that he is having a friendly discussion with the leader, not realizing that he is actually on trial. In the final scene of the main narrative, Cavor's last line to Bedford is poignant. "There's a lot to learn," he says anxiously, adding, "One day I'll explain." It is sad in retrospect because it is obvious from the framing story that he never got a chance to explain. Did he suffer the same horrible fate as his novel's counterpart, or did he die alone on the moon after witnessing the deaths of the Selenites due to the virus he carried? The answer will never be known and this makes the movie quite haunting.

The screenplay is so intriguing that it is regrettable that Nigel Kneale did not write the scripts for some of Harryhausen's earlier films. In view of his literate Quatermass series about invasions from space, he could have vastly improved *Earth vs. the Flying Saucers* and *20 Million Miles to Earth*. Co-writer Jan Read also provided valuable contributions to the script, just as he had done for *Jason and the Argonauts,* which he also co-wrote.

Nathan Juran directed *First Men in the Moon* and is his best film. Unfortunately, this isn't saying much, since he directed some pretty bad movies. These include such genre potboilers as *Attack of the 50-Foot Woman* (1958), *The Brain from Planet Arous* (1958), both under the name of Nathan Hertz, and *The Deadly Mantis* (1957). Juran started his film career as an art director in 1941 and shared an Academy Award for *How Green Was My Valley*. He received another Oscar nomination five years later for *The Razor's Edge*. He began directing in 1952 and spent most of the decade in B movies, including *20 Million Miles to Earth* for Harryhausen and Schneer. He directed other programmers for Schneer, who produced films apart from Ray, and collaborated again with the duo for *The 7th Voyage of Sinbad*. *First Men in the Moon* would be his last movie for the duo and his most successful, at least from an artistic perspective.

Juran was quoted as saying that, "I was just a technician who could transfer the script from the page to the stage and I could get it done on schedule and on budget." This attitude would account for his plodding efforts on so many potboilers. However, in *First Men in the Moon*, he was presented with an above-average script and fine actors. This may have perhaps inspired him to contribute more than his accustomed duties as a hired hand. As a result, the movie is visually quite interesting and moves along at a swift pace, quite unlike some of his earlier vehicles that seem to plod along at snail speed.

During the first half of the movie, despite the relatively benign proceedings, Juran keeps the story moving steadily without any unnecessary exposition. There are several interesting shots, including many in Cavor's laboratory, which help to maintain interest until the action begins with the blast off. Then the real drama begins and the director uses his camera quite effectively, particularly beneath the moon's surface. Some of these shots may have been necessitated by the miniature set pieces and traveling mattes, but they are still handled in a very imaginative manner. All things considered, Juran rises to the occasion with the material presented to him and deserves credit for his efforts. Indeed, his work on this film may account for his receiving a Life Career Award in 1999 from the Academy of Science Fiction, Fantasy and Horror Films, USA.

Of course, Juran had the advantage of very good actors in *First Men in the Moon*. Edward Judd is a very likeable leading man, a credit to his acting skill, since his character's actions are quite often not very admirable. The manner in which he hoodwinks Kate by taking advantage of her love for him is not very nice, to say the least, but yet his charm still invites begrudging understanding. Also, his Bedford tends to lose his temper a bit too quickly and his treatment of Cavor in one scene borders on abuse of the elderly man. And yet, he retains empathy, not just because there is some justification for his actions, but because of the qualities with which he imbues his flawed hero. During the first half of the movie, he always seems to have a twinkle in his eye, and in the second half he projects strength and resolve in his determination to protect Kate. Bedford is a more complex role than that of a nominal hero, and Judd captures all of his qualities.

Martha Hyer establishes warmth for Kate through her natural screen personality but she also gives her a fiery independence. Kate could have been just another stereotyped female romantic interest, but Hyer finds the genuine person created by the scriptwriters and elevates her to a sympathetic and credible level. When she is surrounded by Selenites, she could have just screamed as so many heroines in creature movies have done, but she instead believably projects anger as well as fear, especially when she finds the courage to berate them for apparently laughing at her. It is just this sort of added touch that makes so many scenes more interesting than they otherwise could have been.

However, with due respect to Judd and Hyer, the movie belongs to Lionel Jeffries as Cavor. Jeffries is a very gifted character actor who is perhaps chiefly known for his comic roles in such films as *Chitty Chitty Bang Bang* (1968), in which he believably played Dick Van Dyke's father, even though he was younger than Van Dyke. But he was equally impressive in dramatic roles, excelling as the Marquis of Queensbury in *The Trials of Oscar Wilde* (1960) and as a fraudulent braggart in *Tarzan the Magnificent* (1960). Additionally, Jeffries was a skillful director and writer. During the 1970s, he directed several charming family films, among them *The Railway Children* (1970), considered by many an unsung classic, and *The Amazing Mr. Blunden* (1972). He also proved to be quite astute with the adult drama, *Baxter* (1973).

Jeffries is marvelous as the wildly eccentric scientist whose superficial comic appearance and behavior masks the steely determination of a man who seeks knowledge above everything else. Initially, his Cavor appears to be a typically odd scientist, an object of humor and perhaps even derision. The

**Cavor is caught by a Selenite in a publicity shot from *First Men in the Moon*.**

actor's comic capabilities are in evidence in these early scenes, but yet beneath the surface, he also projects an almost neurotic obsession to explore the unknown. It is a carefully realized performance because, as the film progresses, this obsession and its accompanying hunger for knowledge gradually become more pronounced and ultimately eradicates all traces of humor.

Once they are on the moon, Cavor is no longer a figure of amusement. He is totally dedicated in his quest to learn from the alien creatures, even to the point of disregarding danger. The scene in which he and Bedford are being led away by the Selenites is unforgettable due to his conflicting expressions. He is frightened but yet eager to see more details of the lunar civilization, and he rushes along with his captors to see what lies ahead. But then, when Bedford starts fighting with the Selenites, Cavor pleads with Bedford to refrain from violence. When a Selenite jumps on Bedford, Cavor hesitates momentarily before almost reluctantly tearing the Selenite away from Bedford. The contradictory yet simultaneous emotions Jeffries displays in this scene are extremely effective. He doesn't want to add to the violence but yet feels that he must help a fellow human being. When he later says "I knew I should have come alone," there is some truth to his words and one of the major speculations of the movie is how different the journey would have been if he had indeed traveled to the moon alone.

**Bedford tries to rescue Cavor, who does not realize the danger he is in.**

However, it is in the concluding scenes that Jeffries really excels. Though furious with Bedford for taking him away from the Selenite leader, Cavor nevertheless feels an obligation to help Bedford and Kate escape. Once he repairs the sphere and helps them climb inside, the expression on his face reflects both fear and determination. By this time, he is aware of the danger to himself because of Bedford's violence as well as the Selenite leader's anger. But he still elects to stay because his desire for knowledge is stronger than his concern for his life. The desperation on his face when he makes this decision is mixed with both alarm and enthusiasm as he turns to face the armed Selenites, who are rapidly approaching. And the last shot of him as he tries to reach out to the creatures that surround him is agonizing. His expression suggests simultaneous enthusiasm and terror. With this scene, Jeffries fully transforms Cavor from a comic figure into a valiant figure and, ultimately, a tragic one. Indeed, he emerges as the real hero of the story.

Laurie Johnson's score, especially the title theme, is particularly noteworthy. Johnson composed extensively for British television with over 300 scores, his most famous work being perhaps his theme for *The Avengers*. He also scored numerous British films beginning in 1956, his most notable being *Tiger Bay* and *Dr. Strangelove*. Schneer and Harryhausen signed Johnson for *First Men in the Moon* when Bernard Herrmann, who had scored their previous four movies, became unavailable. Johnson had previously scored *East of Sudan* for Schneer and proved to be an excellent replacement, not only because of his own skills but because of his admiration for Herrmann. When he developed the Soundtrack Series for Varese Sarabande Records in 1980, the first volume (LP record) was a recording of Herrmann's score for *North by Northwest*.

Johnson's score necessarily lacks the vitality of Herrmann's scores for Schneer and Harryhausen because this film, unlike the previous ones, is decidedly more morose. After the ominous opening title theme, the early scenes are accompanied by a lighthearted approach that is perfectly appropriate for Victorian setting. However, the score eventually becomes suitably menacing and moody to suit the action onscreen. The difference in sound once the expedition is on—and in—the moon is deliberate, not only in tone but in instrumentation. As noted by Christopher Palmer in the liner notes for the 1980 re-recording of the score for Volume 2 in the Soundtrack Series, the scenes on Earth are scored for a conventional orchestra while the lunar scenes exclude upper string instruments and utilize to a large degree woodwind and brass instruments (oboes, trumpets, clarinets, bassoons, tubas, etc). The title theme returns for the finale and adds immeasurably to the emotional and dramatic impact of the conclusion.

Production qualities for *First Men in the Moon* are all first-rate, with the cinematography particularly noteworthy and even breathtaking at times. Of course, being a Harryhausen movie, the special effects are preeminent, especially considering the fact that they were created long before computerized digital effects took all of the fun out of effects. This was Harryhausen's first movie in a widescreen process—Panavision—and in his book he reports some difficulties adapting to the anamorphic screen. Although he expresses some dissatisfaction with the studio's mandate to utilize Panavision, the effects do look quite impressive on the wide screen.

The mooncalves are retained from the novel and provide an opportunity for Harryhausen to display his expertise. Children enclosed within alien suits mostly play the Selenites, except for two notably horrifying stop-motion specimens. The Selenites remain suitably gruesome. The modern-day moon landing is quite realistic and reproduces the actual NASA designs of the period. The separation of the landing capsule from the mothership is particularly prophetic. Cavor's space-sphere is a precise representation of the sphere that Wells describes in the novel.

However, most extraordinary is the Selenite civilization devised by Harryhausen and his technicians. The landscape of the moon was built at Shepperton Studios in England and the entire environment looks eerily alien. In his book, Harryhausen writes that since the film had a small budget, it was necessary to build all of the spectacle set pieces in miniature and then utilize traveling matte shots and split screens to incorporate the actors into the scenes.

**Bedford and Cavor discover that the surface of the moon is not hospitable.**

The breathtaking caverns, barren labyrinths and the lunar leader's dwelling all look like they were actually carved from rock. The depiction of the filtering of the sun's rays through gigantic crystals is also impressive, while the sparkling containers that produce air from water beneath the surface of the moon are equally imposing. All of the production personnel responsible for the sets above and below the surface of the moon deserve credit for creating a totally alien yet credible civilization. Unfortunately, the estimable efforts of all of the personnel on both sides of the camera were unappreciated upon the film's release.

*First Men in the Moon* perhaps suffered because of the timing of its release. Science fiction movies about extraterrestrial life had flourished in the 1950s and included the made-in-Hollywood classics *The Thing from Another World*, *The Day the Earth Stood Still*, *The War of the Worlds*, *This Island Earth*, *Invasion of the Body Snatchers* and *Forbidden Planet*. Great Britain had contributed admirable adaptations of Nigel Kneale's first two Quatermass serials entitled *The Quatermass Xperiment* (U.S. title: *The Creeping Unknown*) and *Quatermass II* (U.S. title: *Enemy from Space*). But by the 1960s, movies about space travel were not in fashion and the few that were produced were commercial failures. The fine British-made *Village of the Damned* (1961) should have been more popular at the box office than it was. Also from Britain,

*Quatermass and the Pit* (1967), based on Kneale's third Quatermass serial, did middling business in England and failed in the U.S. as *Five Million Years to Earth*. As a result, Hollywood tended to restrict its major science fiction forays in the 1960s to earthbound themes, such as of *The Time Machine* (1960), based upon the H. G. Wells novel. One exception was *Robinson Crusoe On Mars* (1964), which had been released five months earlier than *First Men in the Moon* and, despite being an intriguing take on Daniel Defoe's classic tale, still died at the box office. (In 1968, space travel movies would triumphantly return with *Planet of the Apes* and *2001: A Space Odyssey*, but that was in the future.)

In 1964, science fiction was still not a reputable genre and Columbia Pictures released *First Men in the Moon* as an exploitation movie. The main poster for the movie exclaimed, "Gasp and Thrill to the Seven Wonders of the Moon World!" while a montage of comic strip-type drawings promised such thrills as "The Forbidden Fungus Forest," "The Brain that Ruled the Moon-World," "Man-Eating Moonbeasts" and "Earthlings Battle Moonlings." The studio's promotion made the movie appear to be cheap and tawdry, similar to its dreadful William Castle potboilers churned out with depressing regularity. For instance, publicity material for the movie stated that "Columbia Pictures will award $10,000 to the man, woman or child who comes closest to guessing the exact time of day and year, to the second that an American astronaut first touches the surface of the moon." Additionally, the studio announced that "10 live moonlings will make theater tours." Not surprisingly, adults stayed away in droves.

The title also seemed uninteresting since the moon, unlike distant planets, didn't suggest danger. Unlike film versions of other novels by Wells, such as *The War of the Worlds* and *The Time Machine*, this title didn't appear to promise much excitement, despite the lurid advertisements. Most potential patrons missed the significance of the preposition "in," not that it would probably have made much of a difference. With careful promotion, the movie might have had a better opportunity to catch on with audiences. Adults would perhaps have responded to the movie if they had been made aware of the mature elements of the script, as well as the charming period detail of the early scenes. But the movie was dumped on the market and disappeared quickly.

*First Men in the Moon* was disappointing at the box office and its critical reception was disdainful. A typical example was the review by Howard Thompson in *The New York Times* who called it "dull" and "only the most indulgent youngsters should derive much stimulation from this tedious, heavy-handed science fiction vehicle." Thompson adds that the explorers from Earth "stumble around, colliding with some English-speaking moon people." This line is obviously designed to denigrate the movie, but Thompson must have fallen asleep because the so-called moon people are only able to communicate after they study the speech patterns of the explorers.

On *Variety*'s list of Top-Grossing Films of 1964, *First Men in the Moon* is last at Number 73. Its domestic theatrical rentals are a dismal $250,000 but, since the movie was still in release, *Variety* estimated anticipated rentals of $1 million, which is the minimum amount required to be listed. The only other science fiction drama on the list is *Children of the Damned* (the sequel to *Village of the Damned*) that is Number 63 with rentals of $1 million, while the fantasy *The 7 Faces of Dr. Lao* is Number 56 with $1.25 million. *Robinson Crusoe On Mars* did not earn the minimum amount to be included on the list. By means of comparison, *The Carpetbaggers*, a tacky adaptation of a lurid novel, was one of the top grossers of the year with over $15 million. Equally outrageous, a lame Disney science fiction comedy called *The Misadventures of Merlin Jones*, which has the appearance of a sub-par television show, is Number 16 with earnings of over $4 million. And yet the combination of H.G. Wells, Nigel Kneale and Ray Harryhausen had to struggle to make even a fraction of that amount.

The film's reputation has improved since its initial reception. James Robert Parish and Michael Pitts in *The Great Science Fiction Pictures* (Scarecrow Press; 1977) write that it is "a pleasantly entertaining fantasy" and "the definitive film version of the novel." Jeff Rovin, in *The Fabulous Fantasy Films* (A.S. Barnes; 1977), calls it "a colorful, marvelously anachronistic adventure that spits in the eye of technology." In *Things to Come* (Times Books; 1977), Douglas Menville and R. Reginald (pseudonym for Michael Burgess) describe it as "an amusing exercise in nineteenth century pseudo-science fiction." Leslie Halliwell in his annual *Film Guide* calls it "an enjoyable schoolboy romp with a good eye for detail and tongue firmly in cheek." And in his encyclopedic book *Science Fiction* (William Morrow; 1984), Phil Hardy summarizes it as "a hugely enjoyable piece of fluff."

The status of *First Men in the Moon* should continue to improve in the future. It is an exciting, adventurous and stimulating motion picture.

CREDITS: Producer: Charles H. Schneer; Associate Producer: Ray Harryhausen; Director: Nathan Juran; Screenplay: Nigel Kneale, Jan Read, Based Upon the Novel by H.G. Wells; Cinematographer: Wilkie Cooper; Editor: Maurice Rootes; Music: Laurie Johnson.

CAST: Edward Judd (Arnold Bedford); Martha Hyer (Kate Callender); Lionel Jeffries (Joseph Cavor); Miles Malleson (Registrar); Peter Finch (Bailiff); Eric Chitty (Gibbs); Betty McDowall (Margaret); Gladys Henson (Matron); Lawrence Herder (Glushkov); Marne Maitland (Dr. Tok); Hugh McDermott (Challis); Norman Bird (Astronaut Stuart); Gordon Robinson (Astronaut Martin); John Murray Scott (Cosmonaut Nevsky)

# THE CHASE

Every so often, a movie is made that has critics lining up to condemn it even before its release. In some cases, the movie justifiably deserves the negative reviews heaped upon it. But in other cases, the movie in question is attacked for reasons that have nothing to do with its quality. *The Chase*, released in 1966 by Columbia Pictures, is one of those movies.

Three-time Academy Award winner Sam Spiegel produced *The Chase*. It stars two-time Academy Award winner Marlon Brando, who is considered one of the greatest motion-picture actors of all time. Acclaimed playwright Lillian Hellman, who was a two-time Academy Award nominee and the winner of the New York Drama Critics Circle Award, wrote the screenplay. It is based upon a play and novel by celebrated dramatist Horton Foote, winner of the Pulitzer Prize and two Academy Awards. The director is Arthur Penn, winner of the Tony Award and nominated twice for an Academy Award. Nevertheless, critics pilloried the film upon its release.

For instance, Bosley Crowther in *The New York Times* called it, "a phony, tasteless movie," adding that it is "a calefied clutter of clichés" and that "the screenplay, emotional content, directing and acting are all overheated." The reviewer for *Newsweek* wrote that *The Chase* "constantly fobs off sensationalism for significance" while "the screenplay exhumes a whole potter's field of banalities." *Time*'s reviewer called it "a shockworn message film that expertly exploits the violence, intolerance and mean provincialism that it is supposed to be preaching against." Philip T. Hartung in *Commonweal* wrote that, "considering all of the talent connected with it, it is hard to imagine how the movie went so wrong." *The New Yorker* described it as a "conventionally opulent

melodrama" that had been "overproduced, overplotted to the point of incoherence and overdirected."

Its reputation has not improved since its release. Tony Thomas in *The Films of Marlon Brando* (Citadel; 1973) calls it "a hideous exaggeration" and "a lamentable disappointment." Leslie Halliwell in the annual reference book *Film Guide* calls it "a shoddy essay in sex and violence." There are a few dissents. One is by Tom Milne in *The Time Out Film Guide*, who writes that the movie "does manage to weave a credible pattern out of the tangled loyalties and enmities, which Penn's direction takes by the scruff and shakes into a firework display of controlled violence."

However, Robin Wood deserves credit for blazing a trail that champions the film. In his book *Hollywood from Vietnam to Reagan* (Columbia University Press; 1968), Wood calls it "a seminal work." Though his meticulous reasons for this assessment may be debatable, they illustrate the complexity of the film. Wood states that, *"The Chase* amounts to one of the most complete, all-encompassing statements of the breakdown of ideological confidence that characterizes American culture through the Vietnam period and becomes a major defining factor of Hollywood cinema in the late '60s and '70s." This may be a minority opinion but also a correct one. *The Chase* is a brilliant movie and a credit to all of the involved personnel, beginning with the original author.

After a struggling career as an actor in the early 1940s, Horton Foote started writing and achieved acclaim quickly. *Only the Heart*, his first play, premiered on Broadway in 1944. In the 1950s, he achieved renown as one of the artistic forces responsible for the Golden Age of Television drama. He eventually went to Hollywood and, in 1962, won his first Academy Award for his adaptation of Harper Lee's *To Kill a Mockingbird*. Throughout his career, he has been the recipient of awards that are too numerous to include here. Besides his second Academy Award for *Tender Mercies* in 1983, he also received a nomination for the film version of *The Trip to Bountiful* in 1985. In 1989, he received the William Inge Lifetime Achievement Award in the American Theater. In 1995, he received the Pulitzer Prize for Drama for his play, *The Young Man from Atlanta*.

Realistic characters are at the root of Foote's distinctive style—most of whom are Texans, and Foote focuses on the depiction of their unrealized hopes and dreams. A common theme in his works is the desire for roots and intimacy by sympathetic characters who tend to compare the remembered happiness of their past with the unfulfilled dreams of their present, as well as the bleakness of their futures. These themes are present in *The Chase*, which began life as a play that premiered at the Playhouse Theater in New York City in 1952. Academy Award-winning actor José Ferrer staged the play. The leading performers were John Hodiak, Kim Stanley and Kim Hunter. It is the story of a small town and the mob mentality that infects its citizens, most of whom project their own sins not only upon their most notorious lawbreaker but their sheriff as well.

The setting of the play is Richmond, Texas. Sheriff Hawes is an honest lawman tired of his menial job and the pettiness of the townspeople. He wants to resign, buy a small farm and live quietly with his wife Ruby. When chronic troublemaker Bubber Reeves escapes from prison, Hawes feel obligated to capture him. Bubber hides out with his wife Anna who is living with his friend Knub McDermont. Bubber doesn't care about his wife's infidelity and is only obsessed with killing Hawes, whom he blames for his imprisonment. As citizens start to panic and demand Bubber's death, Hawes resents the presumption that he is a hired killer and is determined to capture Bubber alive. Even Bubber's mother infuriates Hawes by trying to bribe him to prevent his killing her son.

It soon becomes clear that Bubber got a raw deal from quite a few people, including his mother who regularly whipped him. Many townspeople have reasons for wanting to see Bubber killed, including an upstanding citizen who committed a theft and let Bubber take the blame. When Knub and Anna tell Hawes that Bubber is hiding in their cabin, Hawes races to prevent the mob from lynching him. Hawes pleads with Bubber to give himself up, but Mrs. Reeves distracts him and, when Bubber charges toward him, Hawes shoots and kills him instinctively. Plagued by remorse, Hawes feels that he is no better than the townspeople. He wants to quit his job but Ruby convinces him to keep on doing what he believes is right.

Though the play received some good reviews, it closed after 31 performances. Foote subsequently adapted the play into a novel that Rinehart published in 1956. Some characters are added and others are fleshed out. In the novel, despicable and pathetic characters may suffer temporarily but emerge virtually unscarred. In contrast, the most admirable person, Sheriff Hawes, suffers irreparably and becomes even more of a scapegoat for the town's sins than his counterpart in the play.

The novel begins as the news of Bubber Reeves' escape from the penitentiary spreads through the town of Harrison, Texas. Sheriff Hawes hopes that he can capture Bubber alive. Mrs. Reeves, Bubber's mother, plans to sell her house and use the money to bribe Hawes, whom she believes wants to kill her son. Petty gambler and bootlegger Stub McDermont is worried that Bubber will want to kill him because he is living with Bubber's wife, Anna. Bank clerk Edwin Stewart is afraid that Bubber may want revenge for taking the blame for a theft Edwin committed years before. Frugal banker Mavis sees the crisis as an opportunity to make money off Bubber's parents. Deputy Rip hopes Bubber's escape will prove that Hawes is incompetent so he can become the next sheriff.

Fearful for his safety, Edwin invites people over to his house and everyone quickly gets drunk as they build up courage to hunt down Bubber. At the party, questions are raised about the sheriff's honesty. It becomes apparent that Hawes is disliked and distrusted by many of the townspeople, who resent him because he takes his position of enforcer of the law seriously. Meanwhile, Edwin is unaware that his friend Hawks Damon is having an affair with his wife Emily, until Damon's wife Minnie tells Edwin of the affair. This leads to Edwin's attack upon Damon, who beats him unmercifully.

After Bubber sends word to his mother asking for help, Mrs. Reeves tells Hawes that she will persuade Bubber to give himself up and Hawes agrees to give her time to do this. Rip quickly spreads word about the deal and the townspeople think that Mrs. Reeves has bribed Hawes. Mrs. Reeves does try to convince her son to surrender but Bubber tells her that, during the course of his escape, he committed a murder and will not return to prison to be executed. When he is informed of this, Hawes knows that he has to confront Bubber and surrounds the cabin, where he is hiding with his deputies. Distracted by Mrs. Reeves, Hawes fires at the charging Bubber and kills him, only to learn in shock that Bubber didn't have a gun.

Hawes is provided with more character detail in the novel. He has spent 15 years trying to do a good job but has little to show for his efforts. He has sorrowful memories of his father who lost his farm and died in poverty. He hopes to borrow money from banker Mavis to buy a small piece of land. Due to the pressure of his job, Hawes suffers from dizzy spells and wants to resign, but he knows that he has to capture Bubber first. After killing Bubber, he is consumed by guilt and succumbs to a crippling illness. Once he recuperates, he resigns and settles on a small piece of land with his family. But the memory of the killing never leaves him and he is, in effect, a broken man.

Following the novel's publication, producer Sam Spiegel purchased motion picture rights to both the play and the novel. He initially hired Michael Wilson to do the adaptation, but Wilson's treatments were all discarded for one reason or another. The project languished in limbo until 1965 when Spiegel asked Lillian Hellman to write a new screenplay. *The Chase* would be Spiegel's first production since winning his third Academy Award for *Lawrence of Arabia* (1963), following *The Bridge on the River Kwai* (1957) and *On the Waterfront* (1954).

Lillian Hellman achieved renown for her socially conscious plays, beginning with *The Children's Hour* in 1934. She worked in Hollywood for several years and wrote many screenplays, receiving Academy Award nominations for *The Little Foxes* (1941), based upon her 1939 play, and the pro-Soviet *The North Star* (1943). Indeed, Hellman was so enamored of the Soviet Union that, upon Hitler's invasion of Russia, she cried out, "The motherland has been attacked!" Due to her leftist causes and sympathies, she was subpoenaed to appear before

THE CHASE IS ON! A BREATHLESS EXPLOSIVE STORY OF TODAY...

From Sam Spiegel, the producer of
"The Bridge On The River Kwai"
and "Lawrence of Arabia"!

COLUMBIA PICTURES presents

MARLON BRANDO

in SAM SPIEGEL'S PRODUCTION OF

THE CHASE

ANE ROBERT E.G. ANGE JANICE MIRIAM MARTHA ROBERT RICHARD HENRY DIANA JAMS
FONDA REDFORD MARSHALL DICKINSON RULE HOPKINS HYER DUVALL BRADFORD HULL HYLAND FOX Filmed in PANAVISION TECHNICOLOR

Screenplay by LILLIAN HELLMAN Music composed by JOHN BARRY · Produced by SAM SPIEGEL · Directed by ARTHUR PENN · Based on a novel and play by HORTON FOOTE · A HORIZON PICTURE

the House of Un-American Activities Committee in 1952 and refused to identify former associates who were suspected of being Communists. As a result, she was blacklisted in Hollywood. Unfortunately, any sympathy she may derive from her status as a HUAC victim is negated by the fact that she remained a defender of Joseph Stalin long after knowledge of his atrocities had been revealed.

By the end of the decade, the power of the blacklist was eroding. Hellman had achieved more fame on Broadway for *Toys in the Attic* in 1961, for which she won her second New York Drama Critics Circle award. In 1965, when Sam Spiegel invited her to adapt *The Chase*, she welcomed the opportunity to explore the undercurrents of the savagery that led to unmitigated acts of violence. In the aftermath of the assassination of President John F. Kennedy, she was intrigued by the idea of analyzing the inhabitants of a small Texas town.

Problems began almost immediately. Reportedly, Hellman wanted to link speculation on the JFK assassination to the plot, specifically by illuminating the decadence and evil of Texas oil barons. Spiegel apparently wanted this theme to be less overt. The obsessions of some Texans with guns and vigilante justice would also be a key factor in the script and would have a direct impact upon the story's denouement, as well as the actual post-assassination murder of the accused assassin and designated patsy.

Author Joan Mellen gives emphasis to other factors that impacted upon the creation of the script. In her book, *Hammett and Hellman*, (HarperCollins;

1996), Mellen writes that returning to the film capital brought back painful memories of Dashiel Hammet, who had died in 1961. Because of this, Hellman is quoted as saying that she entered "the longest period of depression of my life." As a result, the relationship between Hellman and Spiegel became increasingly strained. Speigel subsequently became dissatisfied with her script and considered her to be "dysfunctional." He then hired Ivan Moffat to rewrite the script and eventually brought in original author Horton Foote to work on it.

Foote also appears to have had less than a cordial relationship with Spiegel. In a 2001 interview with John Guare, Foote states that director Alan Pakula, who had produced Foote's screenplay of *To Kill a Mockingbird*, wanted to film the play but Spiegel's purchase put an end to that proposed project. Foote agrees with Guare that, "(Spiegel) did it very badly." He adds that Hellman told him that she used his play as a departure and that the script was more or less completed when he was brought in. "There was nothing much I could do," he said," but fiddle a bit." While Foote fiddled, the production didn't burn down but commenced and proceeded.

After filming was completed, Spiegel refused to show Hellman a final cut of the movie before its release. This led to resentment from Hellman and probably affected her opinion of the completed film. In an interview in *The New York Times* one week after the film's release, she complained that the final screenplay, for which she received sole credit, did not reflect her intentions, explaining that revisions by other writers as well as by the director and producer resulted in a distortion of her work. "Decision by democratic vote is a fine form of government," she stated, "but a stinking way to create."

This brings us to the fourth major player in this clash of egos. Marlon Brando was indisputably the star of the movie. His name was the only one above the title and his billing was in impressively larger letters than those of his co-stars. According to Peter Manso's biography *Brando* (Hyperion; 1994), the actor had begun the picture with high expectations. He was happy to be working again with Sam Spiegel, with whom he had enjoyed a good relationship since *On the Waterfront* a decade earlier. He was also attracted to the project because of the reputation of Arthur Penn who was "not considered mainstream Hollywood." Another lure for Brando was the script by Lillian Hellman, "whose politics had lent the script a cutting-edge slant." Thus, Brando approached the film enthusiastically. However, Manso claims that Brando gradually lost his optimism during the course of filming and lays the blame on producer Spiegel's rewriting of the script which supposedly "destroyed the story's original spine."

Director Arthur Penn brought another ego to the mix and gives further credence to Spiegel's role as the spoiler. Penn began his theatrical career as an actor in the early 1950s and then wrote and directed dramas for television anthology series. His first movie, *The Left-Handed Gun* (1958), reflected the

**James Fox, Jane Fonda and Robert Redford pose for a publicity shot in the setting of the climactic junkyard scene.**

"French New Wave" films that he admired, which is probably why it flopped. He then went to Broadway and had huge successes directing *The Miracle Worker* and *Toys in the Attic*, which led to his friendship with Lillian Hellman. He returned to Hollywood and had his first commercial success with the film version of *The Miracle Worker* (1962), which brought him an Academy Award nomination. His third film, *Mickey One* (1965), was another attempt to emulate the European style and died at the box office. *The Chase* would be his next motion picture.

At this point, Spiegel perhaps needs a defense. According to the book *Sam Spiegel* by Natasha Fraser-Cavassoni (Simon & Schuster; 2003), Arthur Penn pressured his agency for months to get him the job of directing *The Chase*. Initially, Spiegel was not interested but began to consider Penn after Hellman praised him. Spiegel had also been frustrated by his inability to obtain such prominent directors as Elia Kazan and William Wyler. Once Penn was signed, he began to work with Spiegel and Hellman on the screenplay. Apparently, his relationship with Spiegel was initially cordial and he reportedly said that he never stopped liking the producer. Interestingly, he is less kind about his friend from New York who had helped to get him hired. "Lillian was pretty annoying," he is quoted as saying, "and not really functioning very well."

However, the final script that Spiegel approved seemed to please no one but himself. Hellman's disapproval has already been noted and, in addition, Penn and Brando were not pleased with frequent script revisions by Spiegel during shooting. Since Penn also disapproved of Spiegel's choice of cameraman Joseph La Shelle, the friction escalated. During filming, according to Peter Manso, the cast and crew split the production into two camps, one represented by Spiegel and Columbia Pictures and the other being the East Coast group. It was Hollywood versus New York and this tension escalated as filming progressed.

During post-production, Spiegel did not allow Penn to edit the film and took it to London where he supervised the editing with Gene Mitford. Penn did not approve of the final cut of the film, claiming that it lacked "his sense of rhythm." He adds that, "I'm not saying that the film would have necessarily been better if I had edited it, but I just knew the rhythm that was in my gut and it was not on that screen. The tempos were not right and I pride myself on the tempo and on the accumulating velocity that is part of the volume." Penn admitted that he was both "dismayed" and "pretty angry" about his experiences on the picture. He considered Spiegel and Mitford to represent old-style filmmaking as opposed to the New Wave, to which he aspired.

As a result of the off-screen problems that were highly publicized, it is not surprising that *The Chase* received so many terrible reviews and was a box-office failure. On *Variety*'s list of Top-Grossing Films for 1966, it was Number 45 with domestic theatrical rentals of approximately $2.1 million. This is particularly humiliating when the list reveals such movies as *The Ghost and Mr. Chicken* with Don Knotts to be higher at Number 34 with $2.7 million. And earning almost as much at $2 million was something called *Fireball 500* with Frankie Avalon, Annette Funicello and Fabian, not exactly the equivalent of Marlon Brando, Jane Fonda and Robert Redford.

The film did recoup some of its cost in 1972 when Columbia Pictures sold it to ABC television for $940,000 for two showings. For some inexplicable reason, the network sabotaged the first showing. It was originally scheduled to be televised on Sunday evening, the highest viewing period of the week, and was heavily advertised. The magazine *TV Guide* highlighted it and devoted half a page to the upcoming presentation. Then, without advance notice, ABC changed its schedule and presented it four days earlier. Viewers expecting to see it on Sunday found another movie instead, unaware that *The Chase* had already been televised.

However, now that all of the terrible and negative things that have been said about *The Chase* are out of the way, it is time to look at the movie itself. The differences and similarities to both the play and the novel will be emphasized to give an idea of the genesis and development of the final screenplay. Incidentally, a paperback edition of the novel was published by Signet in 1966 to coincide with the release of the movie. Though the cover of the book pictured Marlon Brando and claimed that the novel was "now a powerful motion picture," the novel has only marginal relationship to the movie.

A summary of the film clearly indicates that both the play and novel were used merely as guidelines for a more complex exploration of the roots of American society in the 1960s, which is what Hellman originally intended. The entire story takes place during the course of one hot day and night. Bubber Reeves escapes from prison with a fellow inmate who kills the driver of a car and leaves Bubber to take the blame. In the small Texas town of Tarl where he lived, news of his escape spreads rapidly. Sheriff Calder has the task of capturing Bubber and sending him back to prison. His larger task is to keep a lid on the cauldron of tensions that become increasingly explosive during the course of the day. Calder represents social order but, with the exception of his wife Ruby and his two deputies, no one else seems to have much respect for Calder.

Meanwhile, Bubber's escape has triggered various reactions among the town's citizens. Bubber's wife Anna is having an affair with Bubber's best friend Jake Rogers, son of Val Rogers, the oil baron and banker who owns the town. Many people insinuate that Rogers also owns Calder and Ruby. Jake Rogers is also married unhappily and is indifferent to his wife's knowledge of his affair. Bubber's mother seems to feel guilty for her son's fate and thinks that bribing Calder will keep her son alive. Edwin Stewart, a bank vice-president who committed a petty crime for which Bubber was blamed, is fearful of Bubber's vengeance. He also refuses to admit that his wife Emily is having an affair with his colleague Damon Fuller.

During the course of the day, passions become more heated. As the night approaches, the people congregate within their own social systems. At his estate, Val Rogers celebrates his birthday with other oil-rich Texans who try to impress one another with the size of their gifts to the college named after Rogers. In the suburban part of town, the Stewarts and Fullers have their usual Saturday night party that seems to involve various degrees of alcoholism and infidelities among their friends. But the subject on everyone's mind is Bubber Reeves. Fuller's friends include Lem and Archie and the three of them, all of whom carry guns, appoint themselves vigilantes to catch Bubber. Sexual games are not enough to alleviate their restlessness and they hope that Bubber's escape will provide an outlet for their frustration. Even the teenagers next door consider Bubber's escape exciting and want to be involved in the hunt for the fugitive.

When Calder informs Jake of Bubber's escape, Jake leaves his father's party hastily to go to Anna. Still fearful, Edwin interrupts Val's party to tell him of Jake's affair with Anna and Bubber's escape. Val becomes frantic and frightened that Jake's closeness to Bubber will get him harmed. Calder finds himself increasingly isolated as he tries to maintain law and order while trying

**Mary Fuller (Martha Hyer), Emily Stewart (Janice Rule) and Edwin Stewart (Robert Duvall) join the carnival-like atmosphere at the junkyard.**

to find the fugitive. Many townspeople, including the vigilantes, gather in front of the sheriff's office to watch, hoping for some pleasure to relieve their drab lives, looking at the unfolding human drama as entertainment.

Meanwhile, Bubber has taken refuge in a junkyard and asks a black friend, Lester Johnson, to get a message to Anna. The vigilantes catch Lester in Anna's room, but before they can beat information out of him, Calder takes him to jail. Informed that Johnson has knowledge of Bubber's whereabouts, Val is determined to force the information from Lester. Calder tries to stop him and this gives the vigilantes the opportunity to express their hatred of the sheriff by beating him brutally. Ruby frantically tries to get help for Calder as he emerges on the steps of the jailhouse covered with blood, but the townspeople look on dispassionately, enjoying the show. By this time, the social order has completely broken down and all semblance of a civilized society is extinguished.

Calder is hardly able to walk but drives to the junkyard where Bubber is hiding. He finds that the hysteria has reached full pitch in a carnival-like atmosphere, complete with eager onlookers throwing gasoline bombs. Amidst the broken-down cars and castaway junk, Bubber huddles in fear and confusion as Anna and Jake try to get him away from the bloodthirsty rabble. Val Rogers only wants to keep Jake safe while Calder tries to gain Bubber's trust before it is too late. But nothing can stop the mob and the hysteria escalates in a celebratory atmosphere. After Jake is seriously injured, Calder manages to convince Bubber to give himself up. Through the hysterical crowd, Calder reasserts his authority and brings Bubber back to town.

Arriving at the jail, Calder's task is almost completed as he walks the weary Bubber up the steps of the jailhouse amidst the crowd of onlookers. Suddenly, Archie steps out of the crowd and shoots Bubber repeatedly. Exploding in unquenchable fury, Calder pummels Archie but it is too late to save Bubber, whose lifeless body represents the end of the story that the mob always wanted. Calder, virtually alone against the entire town, had done everything in his power to keep Bubber alive but his efforts, so close success, were destroyed at the last moment. The next morning, Calder and Ruby leave the town in despair as Val tells Anna of Jake's death.

*The Chase* possesses a large gallery of characters, all of whom are brought believably to life. It is strange that so many of the film's reviews for the movie complained about the stereotyped Texans and the nastiness of their caricatures. In actuality, the major characters are given more admirable qualities than their counterparts in the original works. Calder is particularly commendable, but Bubber, Anna and Jake are all deserving of some sympathy and all will pay a frightful price for their integrity. This makes the movie far more of a tragedy than the play or novel.

Unlike the Bubber of the play or novel, the film's Bubber is not a criminal. He has never killed or harmed anyone. He didn't abandon his wife and baby, as his novel's counterpart did. He is not serving a life sentence as in the original works and only has a year to go on his sentence. But he just couldn't take the brutality of prison life anymore. He didn't escape to seek revenge and has no animosity toward Calder or anyone else. He just wants to be free and reach Mexico, but fate brings him back to Tarl. He is a victim of the town and all of its cruelties and crimes.

Sheriff Calder is the film's hero but, from the first scene, it is obvious that he is not comfortable with his position as the town's lawman. In his introduction, his expression and demeanor clearly indicate discontent. As the film progresses, it will become clear that he is not pleased with the perception of the townspeople that he owes his authority to the town patriarch. Unlike Hawes and Ruby of the novel, the Calders do not have a son. Ruby's wish that they could have had a child is another reminder to him that something is missing from his marriage, just as he realizes something is missing from his profession.

Sheriff Calder and Sheriff Hawes are both conscientious men who believe in the law. Both men have been forced to take the job of lawman after having lost their farms and want to return to farming. In the novel, Hawes has been legally elected to his position of sheriff. In contrast, Calder has been appointed by Val Rogers and is perceived by virtually everyone as having been bought and paid for by Rogers. But this perception is due to the moral failings of the townspeople, who want to drag Calder down to their level. Since they cannot hurt him with their words, they will physically punish him and nearly kill him. Calder is the second major sacrificial victim of the story, after Bubber.

In the play, Hawes is an honest man who tries to do right but ultimately fails due to an unforeseen distraction by Mrs. Reeves. In the novel, Hawes is similarly distracted but his loss of control is due more to his own fears and insecurities. Thus, the Hawes of the play can keep on trying to serve justice while the Hawes of the novel collapses physically. But at least he can retreat to the security of a small farm with his wife and son. Lawlessness and the corruption surrounding him defeats Calder and leaves behind him a community that has expressed its contempt for him in the most brutal way. He, in effect, takes the position of the outcast that Bubber formerly occupied.

Val Rogers and his son Jake are new characters that were not in either the play or novel. Val represents Hellman's symbol of the corrupt oil magnates who rule Texas. Val is initially not an evil man but he owns the town and he asserts his authority in numerous ways. He considers himself a law-abiding citizen, but when he learns that his son may be in danger, he breaks the law without hesitation. Fear for Jake's safety brings his corruption to the surface and his brutal beating of Lester Johnson reveals his actual lack of moral fiber. But even Val is eventually accorded sympathy because he loses his son.

The triangle is more complex in the film than it is in the novel or the play. Jake Rogers takes the place of Stub/Knub McDermont as Anna's lover. But while the McDermont is poor white trash, Jake is the son of the wealthiest man in the county. While McDermont and Anna have little affection between them, Jake and Anna have been in love since childhood. But they also both love Bubber. Jake and Anna never married because of Jake's reluctance to tell his father that he loved a girl from the wrong side of the tracks. Unlike the selfish Anna of the play and novel, this Anna is willing to sacrifice her happiness with Jake because she knows she has wronged Bubber. But she makes that decision when time is about to run out on all of them, just as Jake finally summons the moral strength to tell his father of his love for Anna after he is fatally injured.

Edwin Stewart remains the spineless bank clerk of the novel and play who let Bubber take the blame for his theft. But the act has more significance in the film because it results in Bubber's first commitment to a reform school. Edwin is more pitiable than contemptible since he is not evil or ignorant, just scared. It is this fear that drives him to tell Val Rogers of his son's indiscretions and this will lead directly to the revelation of Val's true nature. Emily Stewart's relationship with Edwin's colleague Damon Fuller, who is a replacement for Hawks Damon of the novel, seems to be known to everyone except Edwin. The promiscuity of Emily, only suggested in the novel, becomes more overt in the film. All of the infidelities that were kept secret in the novel are public knowledge in the film, an indication of the changing mores from the 1950s to

**Jake Rogers (James Fox) and Anna Reeves (Jane Fonda) share an intimate moment, blissfully unaware that it will be their last.**

the 1960s. However, there are indications that Emily is more complex than the stereotyped cheating wife. For brief moments, the sadness and loneliness are clearly visible beneath the flirtatiousness. Mr. Briggs replaces Mr. Mavis, the real estate agent of the novel who has kept every penny he ever made. Briggs and his equally self-righteous wife walk through the town with an air of moral superiority, commenting on the various happenings condescendingly, instigating trouble wherever and whenever they can.

Racism is not present in the play or the novel except for a suggestion in the latter. In the film, it is more blatant and seems on the verge of erupting into violence. Both blacks and Mexicans are clearly second-class citizens. Calder's defense of blacks will increase the enmity of the townspeople against him. The subject of civil rights is not directly raised but it is always lurking in the background. When the self-appointed vigilantes stop a black pedestrian walking on a street and he justifiably responds with a challenge to their actions, they are immediately ready to teach him a lesson, if only because of his temerity to question their authority.

The subject of the sexual revolution was also a controversial issue of the 1960s. Particularly Emily more directly addresses the sexual revolution, but it is also manifested through the behavior of many others, including Anna Reeves and Elizabeth Rogers. The relationship between Bubber, Anna and Jake is handled in an adult manner, quite unlike the deliberate sensationalism and pseudo-sophistication of so many films that would follow. The relationship also exposes the class differences that further divide the town.

Religion is not the usual supportive force seen in many portraits of small southern towns. In fact, the only religious person is Mrs. Henderson, who appears to be emotionally unstable. Transposed from the novel, she appears periodically to pray for everyone and is either ignored or ridiculed by the townspeople. Religion serves no purpose to these people and, while this would become a cynical cliché in later decades, it was unusual in a film of the 1960s.

It is obvious that Hellman followed through with her intent to portray the modern Tarl as a lawless town of the previous century, not in actuality but in the minds of the townspeople. Their obsession with guns, along with their resentment of government, will impact upon their actions. Hellman's indictment of this type of Texas mentality will serve as an illustration of the factors that led to actual events that occurred in Dallas in 1963.

Regardless of what Hellman, Foote or anyone else may say about the screenplay as filmed, it remains a fine achievement. It is possible that the artistic personnel who publicly disapproved of the completed screenplay were simply too close to the project to view it objectively. Or perhaps their egos prevented them from admitting that someone else could improve upon their individual contributions. Since Spiegel contributed many additions to the script, this fact alone could account for the disdain by the original writers. It must have been difficult for writers of renown, including Hellman and Foote, to admit that a Hollywood producer could actually improve upon their work.

This is not to say that Spiegel was a better writer than those two dramatists, but only that he perhaps sensed what would be more cinematic and added elements to achieve this end. Though Hellman deserves the credit for the basic concept and the body of the screenplay, the contributions of others add to its richness. As a result, the filmed script is an incisive piece of work that encompasses burning issues of the day in a story that builds gradually through a series of increasingly emotional scenes to a crescendo of exploding violence. In essence, the movie has far more resonance than either the play or the novel.

Of course, it is in some ways not fair to compare the three works. The movie is more ambitious in scope and essentially uses the play and novel as the basis for a different story. Hellman took many plot points from the novel and from the play but expanded upon them for the script. Furthermore, the film's setting of the 1960s is different than the setting of the 1950s and therefore reflects a different culture. Within the span of one decade, the country would be torn apart and the movie reflects this in a way that neither the play nor the novel could conceivably do. In essence, everyone who contributed to the script deserves a share of the credit, whether he or she wants it or not.

Arthur Penn has to be included in this group. Though he believed that the completed film did not represent his vision, it is nevertheless masterfully directed. There is a dark, pessimistic atmosphere throughout the movie that is only occasionally alleviated by the moral center, as exemplified by Sheriff Calder. The movie begins on a note of imminent danger, as illustrated by two figures racing through the night, pursued by cars whose police lights reveal that the men are fugitives. The nervous rhythm that Penn believes is missing from the film is conveyed increasingly as the tension of the chase builds to the mesmerizing closing scenes. The climactic apocalypse that seems to occur at the junkyard is presented in a skillful and enthralling manner.

Despite the controversial aspects of many of the thematic issues, Penn handles them with sensitivity. Regardless of what some critics claimed, the film is not exploitational and, in fact, is relatively restrained. The film realistically presents a microcosm of American society, not only in the mid-1960s but, more significantly, of the years that would follow. And it achieves this with dramatic coherence and emotional involvement. Regardless of what Penn feels about the movie, he should be proud of it. It may be a Hollywood movie, but it is not sleep-inducing like so many New Wave movies.

The film lingers in the mind because of the intense passion of some of its scenes, particularly the brutal beating of Calder. This image lingers not just because of its viciousness but because it signifies the final dissolution of law and order. Penn agreed with Brando that the sequence would have to be sufficiently brutal because it signified a main theme of the film, essentially the reversal of authority and the beginning of mob rule.

There are many other equally memorable scenes of raw emotional power. The scene at the junkyard in which Val Rogers reaches out for Jake's hand and touches him briefly only to lose him once again is heartrending, despite the fact that Val has just done something contemptible by beating Lester Johnson. Also, the reunion between Bubber and Anna is tender and even cathartic, which is unexpected due to the complexity of their relationship. And there is the almost quiet and restrained scene in which Bubber realizes that his wife is having an affair with his best friend. Equally memorable is the passage in which Bubber relates why he couldn't take prison life anymore. "I just came to the end of me," he says and his character achieves the level of poetic tragedy.

Of course, there is the powerful yet controversial scene of Bubber's murder which provoked so much disdain from critics who felt it was too similar to the murder of Lee Harvey Oswald by Jack Ruby, less than three years earlier. The scene is deliberately similar but that was Hellman's point. Regardless, the scene works within the context of the story. The theme of lynch mob mentality was apparent, especially during the party scene at the Stewarts' home when Archie makes his first appearance. Significantly, Archie does not have a single word of dialogue in the entire film. But his appearances at carefully chosen sequences hints at the role he would eventually play in the drama.

The reports of tension between Penn and cinematographer Joseph La Shelle are not reflected on the screen, since so many scenes are greatly enhanced by the photography that is often simultaneously both ominous and beautiful. The atmosphere of a small, steamy Southern town is vividly captured through the locations, from the town square to the back roads, from the sordid oppression of Anna's room to the opulence of the Rogers estate. It is irrelevant that some of the scenes were filmed on Columbia's backlot. They simply breathe authenticity.

Another distinct asset to the film is John Barry's powerful score that often seems to anticipate the tragedy that is about to unfold. Accompanying the credits and the initial hunt for the fugitives, the music suggests an uneasy energy, emphasized by a harmonica that assumes greater importance. During the beating, the music doesn't explode but remains foreboding as string instruments produce an unsettling effect, thus making the violence even more discomforting. The climactic scenes in the junkyard are initially accompanied by a deliberate murkiness to suggest the hopelessness of Bubber's situation, but gradually the orchestra builds into a harsh upsurge. And in the final scene the score conveys tranquility and resignation as Calder takes one last sad look at the town and then drives away. Incidentally, when originally released in theaters, a pulsating variation of the main theme accompanied Anna's final walk. But in current release prints, the serenity of Calder's departure continues through Anna's exit.

Central to the film's success is Marlon Brando's impeccable portrayal of Sheriff Calder. It is a very disciplined and defined performance. During the first part of the movie, his acting is restrained mostly, but it is clear from his expressions that Calder is suppressing his emotions. In the scenes in which his integrity is attacked, he doesn't overtly display his anger but still communicates a vital sense that he is having increasing difficulty controlling his fury. When Mrs. Reeves accuses him of being a killer as well as a lackey for Rogers, he conveys the distinct impression that he may lose control as his voice rises in anger and his eyes glisten with rage. His fury finally erupts when Bubber is murdered and the ferocity on his face as he pummels Archie is terrifying.

Brando's most memorable scene is the one that follows the beating. Calder, his face swollen and battered, with blood covering his face and shirt, stumbles out of the building but cannot keep from falling down the steps. He then struggles to his feet and weakly stands on the steps of the jailhouse, trying to maintain dignity and authority as he puts on his holster and hat and faces the indifferent crowd. The scene is extremely poignant and distressing at the same time. It is an artfully controlled piece of acting that Brando executes to perfection and it is his characterization that dominates the picture.

However, Brando had been out of favor with critics for most of the 1960s. During the previous decade, he received justifiably rave reviews for all of his movies, beginning with *A Streetcar Named Desire* in 1951. They perceived him as the antithesis of the typical Hollywood movie star, which gave him legitimacy in their biased opinions. But then, in 1961, his direction of *One-*

**Ruby (Angie Dickinson) and two deputies try to help a badly beaten Sheriff Calder (Marlon Brando).**

*Eyed Jacks* went way over budget and resulted in him being called extravagant and self-indulgent. The following year, MGM used him as a scapegoat for a myriad of production problems on *Mutiny On the Bounty* and he was depicted as egotistical and difficult. Formerly considered a Broadway actor who made movies, he was now viewed as having "gone Hollywood." With the release of *The Chase*, the critics pounced on him once again and blindly ignored a terrific performance.

The supporting cast perfectly compliments Brando. Robert Redford projects a distinct charisma as Bubber. Though his scenes are relatively few, his characterization permeates the movie and it is easy to see why he quickly became a major star. Jane Fonda, avoiding the mannered self-absorption that marred many of her other roles, gives an affecting performance and makes Anna a sympathetic figure, despite her character's behavior. James Fox has the difficult task of making Jake likeable, even though he is required to often be rude and abrupt; he accomplishes this because of the innate sadness that he imparts beneath his rough exterior. E.G. Marshall excels as Val Rogers; as his character deteriorates from supreme pomposity to absolute desolation, it is clear from his expression at the finale that he has lost any reason for living, despite his wealth and power. Robert Duvall is equally fine as Edwin Stewart, displaying the skills that would soon hail him as an accomplished actor. Henry

**Val Rogers (E.G. Marshall) tries to help his son Jake (James Fox) as Bubber (Robert Redford) and Anna (Jane Fonda) follow.**

Hull as Briggs and Miriam Hopkins as Mrs. Reeves also stand out in the large ensemble cast. Angie Dickinson as Ruby, Richard Bradford as Damon, Janice Rule as Emily and Martha Hyer as Elizabeth all make distinct impressions in their roles and contribute to the effectiveness of the film. Regrettably, not given a chance to make an impact is Lori Martin, four years after her memorable role in *Cape Fear*, in an insignificant role as a partying teenager.

*The Chase* suffered commercially and was destroyed by critics because of the torrent of bad publicity and negative comments from some of its creators that accompanied its release. This negativity preconditioned critics to heap scorn upon it. Since they deduced that the conflict was between what they perceived as crass Hollywood production executives and literary artists, they identified with the artists and were prepared to attack the film even before they viewed it.

Sam Spiegel subsequently produced five more movies, none of which recaptured his past glory, though his final film, *Betrayal*, was a critical hit in 1983. Horton Foote went on to write many more distinguished plays and screenplays. Lillian Hellman never wrote another Hollywood script or Broadway play, spending the rest of her life writing memoirs and teaching. Arthur Penn achieved acclaim and commercial success the following year with *Bonnie and Clyde*. Among his subsequent movies are two terrible Westerns,

*Little Big Man* (1971) and *The Missouri Breaks* (1976), the latter re-uniting him with Brando. He has since directed occasionally interesting but mostly undistinguished films. Marlon Brando gave another excellent and neglected performance in the otherwise-disappointing *Reflections in a Golden Eye* in 1967. Only in 1972 would his talent be once again accepted when he portrayed the title role in *The Godfather*. After *Apocalypse Now* (1979), he allowed his career to slowly disintegrate.

Today, the production problems are all history. The negative reviews are meaningless. Only the film itself remains and its many virtues can now be fully appreciated. *The Chase* is a highlight in the careers of its creators and an exceptionally powerful motion picture.

CREDITS: Producer: Sam Spiegel; Director: Arthur Penn; Screenplay: Lillian Hellman, Based Upon the Novel and Play by Horton Foote; Cinematographer: Joseph La Shelle; Editor: Gene Mitford; Music: John Barry

CAST: Marlon Brando (Sheriff Calder); Jane Fonda (Anna Reeves); Robert Redford (Bubber Reeves); James Fox (Jake Rogers); E.G. Marshall (Val Rogers); Angie Dickinson (Ruby Calder); Janice Rule (Emily Stewart); Robert Duvall (Edwin Stewart); Richard Bradford (Damon Fuller); Miriam Hopkins (Mrs. Reeves); Martha Hyer (Mary Fuller); Diana Hyland (Elizabeth Rogers); Henry Hull (Mr. Briggs); Jocelyn Brando (Mrs. Briggs); Clifton James (Lem); Steve Ihnat (Archie); Malcolm Atterbury (Mr. Reeves); Joel Fluellen (Lester Johnson); Bruce Cabot (Sol); Katherine Walsh (Verna Dee); Lori Martin (Cutie); Paul Williams (Seymour); Nydia Westman (Mrs. Henderson); Marc Skaton (Paul); Maurice Manson (Moore); Steve Whittaker (Slim); Eduardo Ciannelli (Mr. Sifftifieus); Pamela Curran (Mrs. Sifftifieus); Ken Benard (Sam)

# THE QUILLER MEMORANDUM

"Did you ever meet a man called Jones?"

This cryptic question, occurring at the finale of the 1966 film *The Quiller Memorandum* is the emotional and dramatic highpoint of the movie. Unlike other espionage films, this one doesn't climax with gunplay or any kind of physical confrontation. Instead, it climaxes with a simple question asked by the hero of his romantic interest. Her answer, brief and deceitful, concludes the movie on a note of sadness and cynicism. It is a highly poignant end to an unheralded and unjustly neglected film that derives most of its power from its sub-themes rather than its main theme, from what is *not* shown rather than what is shown, from what is *unsaid* rather than what is said.

*The Quiller Memorandum*, based upon the first of a series of novels by Adam Hall, features the British hero known by his code name of Quiller. Hall is the pseudonym of Elleston Trevor, who achieved considerable acclaim under this name with such novels as *The Flight of the Phoenix* and *Bury Him Among Kings*. He was a prolific and skillful author who wrote over 80 books under numerous pseudonyms. (He was born Trevor-Dudley Smith but later legally changed his name to Elleston Trevor.) However, his 19 Quiller novels, written from 1965 to 1995, made him one of the most popular and critically acclaimed writers of espionage fiction. Exceptionally entertaining, the novels are brimming with sharp characterizations, intricate plots, unrelenting tension, vigorous action and a protagonist who is quite unique. Elleston Trevor died in 1995 and his last Quiller novel was published posthumously.

Quiller is not an official secret agent for the British government. He is a "shadow executive" who works for The Bureau, an unofficial agency that is authorized to carry out missions that the authorized agencies cannot legally do. Quiller is highly proficient and has the number 9 attached to his code name, which signifies that he has endured torture without breaking. He doesn't carry a gun because he feels that weapons provide a false sense of security. He believes that he will have a better chance of survival if he has to depend upon his own wits and cunning. He does not drink or smoke since such habits would diminish his reflexes. He has no close relationships and no known relatives. In his will, the only person he mentions is someone named Moira, to whom he leaves a rose.

Quiller will only work alone because he doesn't trust anyone, though he understands the necessity of having a director in the field once he accepts a mission. He will accept the most dangerous missions because he can only experience life to its fullest by edging as close as possible to death. He is aware that his superiors use him to their advantage, but this is the life he has chosen and the only one for which he seems suited. He fears an unmarked grave or a squalid prison cell in some foreign country, but he knows that any other kind

Pursuer or Pursued—he played the most dangerous game in Europe...and he played it alone.

20th Century-Fox presents
IVAN FOXWELL'S
PRODUCTION of

the Quiller
Memorandum

STARRING
GEORGE SEGAL ALEC GUINNESS
MAX VON SYDOW SENTA BERGER
Guest Stars GEORGE SANDERS · ROBERT HELPMANN
Produced by IVAN FOXWELL Directed by MICHAEL ANDERSON Screenplay by HAROLD PINTER
PANAVISION® Color by DELUXE
Released by Twentieth Century-Fox Film Corp. in association with National General Productions, Inc.

of life would be dreary and intolerable. Somewhat arrogant and bitter, he has loyalty to the Bureau but he knows that he is expendable.

Quiller narrates his adventures and shares his innermost thoughts with the reader as he experiences them. He constantly has to re-evaluate characters,

ADAM HALL
The Quiller Memorandum
Quiller in Berlin

reassess situations and revise perceptions, thus taking the reader on a roller coaster ride during which one minor miscalculation could be fatal. The novels move at a rapid pace as Quiller edges closer and closer to completing his mission and always at the risk of losing his life. Yet his adventures are always tinged with realism and the sense that this is the way people operate in the world of modern espionage. Courageous but often ruthless, Quiller is not the most likeable agent, but he is certainly one of the most proficient.

Simon & Schuster published *The Quiller Memorandum* (its original title was *The Berlin Memorandum*) in 1965. The novel concerns the resurgence of Nazis in Germany and their plan to establish a Fourth Reich. Pol, a Bureau official, contacts Quiller, who just completed a mission in Berlin bringing war criminals to justice. According to the last report of agent Kenneth Lindsay Jones before his murder, a secret organization of neo-Nazis is on the verge of launching a massive operation, which could cause the deaths of millions. Quiller accepts the assignment, to locate the base of the neo-Nazis, partly because one of them is a man named Zossen, a hated enemy whom Quiller knew in the war.

Quiller meets Inga Lindt, whose childhood experiences have left her with obsessions of death and Hitler, and she tells him that she has defected from the neo-Nazi group called Phonix. She mentions the name of Rothstein, whom Quiller had also known during the war and is now working as a bacteriologist in Berlin. But after Rothstein is killed, Quiller learns that the scientist was developing a bacteriological virus and that he may have been working for Phonix. Quiller uses Inga to infiltrate Phonix but he is captured. Taken to an unknown location, he is interrogated and drugged by Oktober, one of the group's leaders. Before Phonix can proceed with its mission, Oktober has to learn the location of Quiller's Control and how much the opposition knows about its plan. Oktober is unable to break Quiller and orders him killed.

Quiller is surprised to survive but this is part of Oktober's plan to put him on a leash until he betrays his Control, while functioning under the sights of assassins who will kill him if he doesn't follow the plan devised for him. This begins a series of confrontations in which Quiller is helplessly "in the gap between two opposing Armies," being pulled in one direction or the other by each side, being used by his enemies and his superiors to further the ends of each organization. While trying to survive under such pressure, Quiller realizes that Jones had been as close to the base as he now is and he realizes that he is simply on a longer leash than his predecessor, but just as vulnerable.

Inga introduces Quiller to Helmut Braun, who gives him information on the location of the Phonix base and its plan to start a war in Europe. Quiller, however, has to confirm the plan by infiltrating the Phonix base. This leads to another cat and mouse game in which Quiller must try to survive the long night as he is trailed and surrounded by Oktober's men, each of whom has the power to kill him at a moment's notice if he deviates even slightly from what he is supposed to do. Through his skills, Quiller outwits his enemies and reports back to his base. He then exacts his own revenge upon Zossen, whom he recognized as a high political official while at the Phonix base.

Upon publication, *The Quiller Memorandum* received acclaim and was awarded the Edgar Allan Poe Award for Best Novel of the Year and the Grand Prix de Literature Policiere. It is exceedingly well written and moves at a swift pace, the suspense building with each chapter as Quiller and his enemies engage in an increasingly deadly battle of wills that severely tests Quiller's skills as a survival expert. The psychological interplay between Quiller and other characters, including his own superiors, increases the tension and highlights the realistic dangers and unromantic perils of modern espionage. Inga is an absorbing character and her seemingly frequent change of loyalties is both believable and intriguing because of the psychological traumas she endured as a child. Other characters are equally credible, which provides the novel with an aura of realism. As much as the plot or characterizations matter, however, it is the author's style that makes the book so enjoyable. Quiller's acutely detailed stream of consciousness and the breathtaking suspense, that is as much internal as well as external, keeps readers glued to each page. The characterization of the proficient agent struck a chord with readers, ensuring his return for more adventures.

*The Quiller Memorandum* has all of the ingredients, including an incisive hero, to make an absorbing motion picture. However, Quiller's introspections and inner conflicts would not be easily transferred to the screen, thus necessitating some alterations of the source material. Upon its release the following year, it was apparent that the film version was more an interpretation than a direct adaptation. But though it excludes some of the novel's main elements and simplifies the plot, the movie still manages to capture the essence if not the letter of the novel and, to some degree, its main character.

*The Quiller Memorandum* is a British production with American actor George Segal as Quiller. It is a presentation of The Rank Organization and was released in the United States by 20ᵗʰ Century Fox. Producer of the movie is Ivan Foxwell who deserves credit for bringing together so many disparate talents into a commendably cohesive work. Foxwell, who wrote many of his productions, was responsible for such previous films as *The Colditz Story* (1955) and *Tiara Tahiti* (1962). After this film, he would only produce one more movie. Of the 10 films he produced over a 20-year period, *The Quiller Memorandum* is the finest and ideally should have set the pattern for what could have been an illustrious series. This was probably Foxwell's intention but the movie's commercial fate determined otherwise.

Director is Michael Anderson who, having previously worked as an assistant to David Lean and Carol Reed, subsequently achieved a notable body of work. He had his first international success with *The Dam Busters* in 1954 and two years later directed the underrated first version of George Orwell's *1984*. He received an Academy Award nomination for *Around the World in 80 Days* (1956), but did not win, though the film won the Best Picture award. Other fine films include *The Wreck of the Mary Deare* (1959), *Shake Hands with the Devil* (1959) and *Operation Crossbow* (1965). While some of his later films are unremarkable, when he was presented with a script of quality and a good cast, as in *The Quiller Memorandum*, he brought a commendable flair to the project and this style is a significant factor in the film's achievement.

The screenplay is by acclaimed dramatist Harold Pinter, winner of the 2005 Nobel Prize for Literature, an unusual choice for what was perceived as a genre thriller. Pinter is a fascinating writer, as artistic as he is stylized. His screenplays based upon his own works, such as *The Caretaker* (1963), *The Birthday Party* (1968) and *Betrayal* (1983), are filled with ambiguous characters, introverted conflicts, obscure motivations and temporal irregularities that can be extremely perplexing. His screenplays based on the novels of other authors, including *The Servant* (1964), *The Go-Between* (1970), *The French Lieutenant's Woman* (1981) and *The Trial* (1993), are less mystifying but equally intriguing. In these adaptations, Pinter not only preserves the flavor of the original work but also imposes his artistic signature upon it in an unobtrusive manner that blends his style with that of the original author.

With *The Quiller Memorandum*, Pinter's imposition is somewhat more intrusive as his screenplay alters the emphasis of the novel and abridges the plot. The script is often considered one of the author's lesser works. Joanne Klein in *Making Pictures: The Pinter Screenplays* (Ohio State University Press; 1985) writes that "in comparison with Pinter's other screenplays, this adaptation exhibits signs of hack writing for popular markets." William Baker and Stephen Ely Tabachnick imply in their book, *Harold Pinter* (Harper & Row; 1973) that his reasons for writing it may have been simply financial or technical ones, adding that "the film offers little more than watered down James Bondisms." This statement is perplexing since the novel and film are the antithesis of the Bond novels and films, but it was representative of many other critiques. Such critics may be aware of the folly or trying to resolve Pinter's enigmas by subjecting them to standard formulas. However, they may perhaps be erroneous in imposing a "Pinteresque" formula upon all of his works. They confuse the issue by not recognizing that his writing cannot be restricted to a particular mold. While his themes may be recurrent, the manner in which he conveys those themes can be quite different.

While the screenplay does not contain any temporal distortions and other Pinter trademarks, it does share some themes with the writer's more highly acclaimed works. Katherine H. Burkman points out in *The Dramatic World of Harold Pinter: Its Basis in Ritual* (Ohio State University Press; 1971) that the film is "illuminating as further exploration of man as victim of forces he cannot subdue, as victim even when the victor." Arnold Hinchcliffe in *Harold Pinter* (Twayne; 1981) comments that "the whole story is set in Pinterland— lies, sex, violence and betrayal suit him perfectly." And Michael Billington in *The Life and Work of Harold Pinter* (Faber and Faber; 1995) calls it "a classic Pinter film, one concerned with the ambiguity of action, female resilience and mystery and the need for resistance to authoritarianism of whatever kind."

Quiller's alienation, failed dreams and lost hopes are conditions that regularly occur in Pinter's works. Perhaps having such themes in a genre film alienated some of Pinter's admirers who may have thought such material beneath him. But Quiller has much in common with other Pinter protagonists such as Stanley in *The Birthday Party*, Teddy in *The Homecoming* and Spooner in *No Man's Land*. Underlying his courage and exploits are feelings of despair and loneliness. This loneliness will be a motivating factor for most of Quiller's actions. It is a theme that pervades the entire film.

Pinter's script retains the basic plot of the novel but eliminates two major characters, as well as the potentially apocalyptic aspects of the story. Many readers of the novel were probably disappointed to see no trace of Zossen, the principal motivation for Quiller's actions in the novel, or Rothstein, whose deranged plan could have killed thousands. Also gone is the neo-Nazi plan to provoke the superpowers into worldwide conflagration. By discarding these elements, Pinter places more emphasis on the characters and their personalities. More significantly, by eliminating Quiller's past experiences in the war, Pinter reduces his characterization to some degree but expands upon it in other ways, specifically through dialogue and interpersonal relationships. This is typical of many of Pinter's plays in which the backgrounds and histories of his main characters are of no interest compared to what only is happening on the stage.

The film's Quiller, part Pinter and part Hall, is neither the fantasy hero of Ian Fleming's escapist novels nor the common everyman of purportedly realistic espionage novels, such as those by John LeCarre and Len Deighton. He is the total professional and survival expert created by Hall. He is also

**Quiller (George Segal) is surprised to be alive.**

just as cynical and bitter. But he is more romantic and optimistic, at least at the beginning of the movie. He accepts his role in a sordid profession but still maintains his sense of humor. He is hopeful that not everyone has been corrupted. By the end of the movie, the film's Quiller will be just as tired as the novel's Quiller, though for different reasons.

Quiller, like his counterpart in the novel, insists on working alone, using unorthodox methods that make him an outsider within his own profession. He is contemptuous of codes and signals and deliberately humiliates more obedient colleagues, including Hengel, who are supposed to protect him. He doesn't carry a gun and, except for a single shot in the first scene, there is no gunplay and very little physical action in the movie. There are no gimmicks and Quiller has nothing to rely on but his instincts and intellect, while trying to stay alive long enough to complete his mission. Though in the novel the mission is of primary importance to Quiller, the film emphasizes the fact that Quiller's professional life is secondary to his personal life and his emotional needs.

What remains from the novel is somewhat faithful to the source, despite the condensation. Quiller is offered the assignment by Pol to locate the neo-Nazi base after his predecessor, Kenneth Lindsay Jones, is killed. Though impatient with Pol's annoying manner, Quiller accepts the mission, which leads him to a variety of persons, including schoolteacher Inge Lindt (not Inga as in the novel, but Inge). After deliberately exposing himself to the opposition, he survives a brutal interrogation by Oktober and subsequently becomes romantically involved with Inge. After Oktober's men seemingly capture them, Quiller is released to decide whether to betray the location of Pol's base or forfeit his and Inge's life. As in the novel, Quiller almost loses his life, but unlike the novel, he emerges only partially victorious and loses what he needs the most.

The theme of loneliness is apparent in the first scene of the movie, as it is in John Barry's haunting melody that accompanies the main titles. A lone man walks down a dark, deserted street in Berlin looking anxiously around as he approaches a telephone booth hesitantly. After a moment of indecision during which he appears obviously frightened, he enters the booth and starts to dial. But a shot rings out and he is killed. This is Kenneth Lindsay Jones, Quiller's predecessor, only referred to slightly in the novel but a key character in the film, if only because of the setting of his single scene.

The scene shifts to an exclusive club in London where Gibbs and Rushington, two upper class intelligence executives, pompously discuss the death of Jones with little emotion other than a bit of annoyance, as they consume a hearty meal. In their two brief scenes, these characters provide a wry perspective on the life and death struggle being waged for them and their country by men below their social class. The murder of Jones and the decision on who will replace him seemingly is of relatively minor concern to them compared to the impressive surroundings in which they mingle with their distinguished social contacts.

Back in Berlin, Quiller's introduction makes it visually clear that he is the film's hero, his frame initially filling the screen. The most obvious change from the novel is that Quiller is not British but an American working for the British. However, other than a couple of remarks to Inge during their initial meeting that he uses to assess her feelings, his nationality becomes insignificant. During this scene, audiences four decades later are not so naïve to accept Quiller's statement to Inge that the United States doesn't want to dominate other countries. But politics are irrelevant to Quiller; he is just testing her. Also, though in the novel Quiller is in Berlin because he is completing a mission, in the film he is on vacation and in need of a rest. However, he accepts the mission even though he doesn't indicate enthusiasm or even interest. Perhaps, despite his apparent cynicism, he still harbors the hope that he can do some good.

It is more than likely that the profession that Quiller seems to abhor is his only connection to people and the only means of assuaging his needs. His sense of alienation from his work is established by his relationship to Pol, which appears to be based upon mutual contempt. Pol's kinship to Gibbs and Rushington is made clear by the fact that food is a part of all of their scenes.

These upper echelon executives are constantly satisfying their needs, while Quiller's will remain unfulfilled.

Quiller's investigation initially takes him to a bowling alley and a swimming pool. Though he assumes different guises, the people he questions seem to know that he is lying and he knows that they know. It is as though the charade is part of a game, a deadly game which is endless and no one ever really wins. Posing as a journalist, Quiller visits a school where a teacher accused of war crimes has recently committed suicide. He meets the headmistress, Frau Schroeder, who directs him to Inge, one of the teachers. Unlike the blonde and epicene Inga of the novel, Inge is brunette and feminine, though equally enigmatic. Inge's profession also endows her with a different symbolic significance. In the novel, her childhood experiences in the bunker with Hitler make her a symbol of the past. In the film, her position of teacher makes her a symbol of not only the present but of the future, because of the impression she will have upon her students.

Inge's personal effect upon Quiller is obvious at their first meeting and his needs are stirred when he meets her. In her presence, the otherwise brash agent is almost boyishly shy and uncertain, eventually shedding his professional role. He is not acting any longer and allows his genuine feelings to appear. Sensing that she shares his needs, he asks her softly, "Do you like living alone?" She replies that her life is empty without her work, though to what work she is referring is unclear at this point. In the novel, Inga's duplicity is ingrained and never fools Quiller. In the film Inge's motivations are more complex and she, like Quiller, has personal needs that may affect her loyalties.

Quiller's scenes with Inge are particularly ambiguous. Martin Esslin points out in *The Peopled Wound: The Work of Harold Pinter* (Doubleday; 1970) that as their relationship progresses from flirtation to love affair, "we sense that he knows she is not what she pretends to be, that she knows he knows, that he knows that too." But since they obviously like one another, there is the implication that Quiller, and possibly Inge as well, is hoping that the distrust will be groundless and that genuine emotions will predominate. The sincerity of the emotion they feel for one another is apparent in the scene in the deserted gymnasium. Though Quiller is hoping to meet a man named Hassler, who may know the location of the Nazi base, there is a tender moment as they hold onto one another in the deep end of the empty pool. For a moment, they seem like an ordinary couple, their happy expressions clearly indicating that they are enjoying the closeness of the moment and the hope of a future in which they will grow even closer. But then Hassler appears and the moment is lost.

Quiller's emotional need for Inge is established during the interrogation scene after Oktober captures him. Struggling to resist the drugs given him, Quiller can only think of Inge, causing Oktober to sense his vulnerability. Though the specific drugs are not identified (as Sodium Amytal and Benzedrine) as in the novel, their effect is quite clear. While the first drug

**Quiller shares a tender moment in an empty pool with Inge (Senta Berger).**

induces narcosis and weakness to interrogation, the second awakens him and makes talking and a willingness to answer questions a necessity. "You must be lonely," he perceptively tells Quiller, whose helplessness steadily increases. But he successfully fights the drug, though Oktober missed the significance of one remark. Trying another tactic, Oktober orders his henchman to again drug Quiller and then kill him. As he is drugged into unconsciousness, Quiller's face shows fully the horror of his expected fate.

In the midst of these sordid events during which Quiller is enduring torture and a promised death, the scene shifts back to Gibbs and Rushington, who casually discuss the progress of the mission. But it is of minor importance to them. Of prime importance is the fact that Gibbs is on his way to the Lord Mayor's Banquet and Rushington hasn't been invited.

Awakening on the muddy banks of a river, shocked and dejected, Quiller is surprised to be alive and is barely able to find his way to a hotel. As he enters the seedy hotel, the radio is playing the film's theme song, "Wednesday's Child," as sung by Matt Monro. The lyrics to the song, which refer to a child of woe sadly crying alone, clearly reflect Quiller's emotional state and why he reaches for the telephone. He calls Inge and, once with her, confesses the truth about his mission. Though he still harbors suspicions about her, he wants to be close to her, physically and emotionally. This is more important to him than the mission. "I thought you ought to know," he tells her twice to convince her of his sincerity, or perhaps to warn her. She only resists his caresses tokenly and, as they embrace, they are like two lonely souls reaching out in the darkness for someone to hold, escaping from their other lives and their work. Once again, Quiller is not playing a role and Inge is also allowing her genuine feelings to

**Quiller and Inge are two lonely souls reaching out to one another.**

appear. Now Quiller is Friday's child, loving and being loved, but the words of the theme song have already promised that this will not last because it is his fate to be alone. Nevertheless, it is a fate that Quiller is trying to prevent.

In the novel, author Hall makes it clear that after the shock of expecting to die, Quiller's fear of death and his will to live, exemplified by his libido, propel him to the woman he desires. Hall carefully details the extent of Oktober's plan and how experiments have clearly shown that, upon awakening, Quiller will want to see Inge, in view of his apparent interest in her during the interrogation. In the film, this drive is strengthened by Quiller's loneliness. Though Oktober has not explained the specifics of the plan, it is natural from what has been depicted that Quiller will go to Inge. The subtlety of this motivation escaped many critics, including Bosley Crowther, who derided Quiller's "dumb" actions.

Quiller's behavior is logical if his emotional needs and feelings for Inge mean more to him than his mission. Being a professional, he is obligated to complete the mission but it is not his primary concern. He is obviously hoping that Inge will be unable or unwilling to help him. Similarly, Inge appears to have genuine feelings for Quiller, but she agrees, reluctantly it seems, to help him locate the enemy base. The expression on Quiller's face as she leaves his arms indicate his disappointment, though not complete loss of faith in her since her motivation to help may be due to her feelings for him. She knows some people, including Frau Schroeder and Hassler, who may know the location of the enemy base. They appear to be equally helpful and even caution him against getting too close to the base. But he has his job to do and he has to confirm the information before reporting back to his Pol.

Once in sight of Oktober's base, Inge pleads with Quiller to stay with her and tells him that she loves him. Her words may be sincere because asking him to stay with her means she has either been truthful all along or, if she is leading him into a trap, that she is putting her feelings above her mission. And Quiller seems genuinely affected by her emotion, as she promises to wait for him. But he has his mission to complete, more out of a sense of personal pride and responsibility than loyalty or patriotism. He makes the decision that is correct for the mission but destructive of their relationship, but only if she is sincere.

In the novel, Inga accompanies Quiller to the house where she quickly expresses her loyalty to the neo-Nazi movement. But the lonely Inge of the film may not be the same deceitful Inga of the novel. In the film, Quiller enters the house alone and confirms that it is indeed the enemy base, and Oktober and his men surround him. Only this time, they have the threat of not only his death but Inge's as well for, as Oktober tells Quiller, they found Inge waiting in the car for him. Quiller is given until dawn to decide whether to give Oktober the information he wants or forfeit his and Inge's life. They have to let him leave the house to force him to signal his Control, which will alert them to its location. Pol and his team will then be killed immediately. At this point in the novel, Inga tries to convince Quiller that she was only pretending loyalty to the cause and expresses feelings for Quiller, but only to get him to lead her to his base. In the film, Inge appears to be helpless, fearful and alone.

After Quiller is allowed to leave, it becomes instantly clear to the viewer, though not to Quiller, just how perilous his situation is, for the dark street upon which he emerges is the same street that Kenneth Lindsay Jones walked down at the film's beginning. The impact of this recognition is startling for the viewer who now knows that Quiller is running through the same maze as Jones.

Thus begins the film's penultimate sequence that is a masterpiece of suspense and intrigue, as Quiller is openly followed through the streets of Berlin and gradually becomes convinced of the hopelessness of his situation. As Hall explains in the novel, Quiller is similar to a pigeon in trapshooting that has been released from its trap only to be shot down. The sequence is not only dramatically crucial but eerily atmospheric, as Quiller's long odyssey takes on an almost dreamlike and ritualistic quality. Wherever he goes, whether it is the phone booth in which Jones met his end or a railway station, a café or a deserted avenue, Oktober's men are either behind or ahead of him, nearby or watching from a distance. Surrounded and with the threat of death never further than a moment away, Quiller has never felt more alone and more helpless.

As in the novel, Quiller survives by exploding the bomb that was meant to kill him when he tried to escape by car. Physically and psychologically exhausted, he reports to his base where he is greeted by Pol, not with praise and gratitude, but with impatience and contempt. Significantly, the capture of

Oktober and his group is not shown, almost a violation of the genre's tradition, but this omission deliberately maintains the focus on Quiller and his inner needs rather than the mission.

Quiller's success with his mission doesn't improve his relationship with Pol, who invites him to share a celebratory breakfast in his room, rather belatedly and insincerely. Quiller is too tired to go upstairs and Pol's lack of concern for him is edged with sarcasm. In fact, his indifference to Quiller's state is quite similar to Oktober's coldness. However, Quiller is too concerned for Inge to be bothered by the patronizing Pol or the smug Hengel, who cheerfully follows behind Pol. However, that concern is shattered when he learns that Inge has not been found at Oktober's base. Any hope that Quiller may harbor for happiness ends with this revelation, which will lead the way for the film's real climax, Quiller's reunion with Inge. This essential meeting does not occur in the book.

In the final sequence, Quiller angrily approaches the school to confront Inge. Inside the schoolroom, their conversation is crisp, deceptively banal and especially ambiguous. Each line has a hidden or double meaning while each pause expresses what they decline to say. Each penetrating look conveys their actual feelings. Overlying Quiller's anger and Inge's guilt is a feeling of loss and bitterness because of emotions that were crushed before they could flourish. Quiller nourished the faint hope that his latent romantic idealism could be nurtured with Inge, who seemed to share the same hope. They both exposed their inner selves to one another and joined together on a different level, in a different world, one without deceit or treachery. Quiller shed his distrust and put his faith in Inge, not perhaps because he fully believed in her but because he wanted to believe in her. And she responded with genuine emotion, perhaps with genuine love. However, she had to complete her mission, just as he had to complete his.

Once again, neither Quiller nor Inge is saying what either of them is feeling. Beneath her guilt is just a suggestion of sorrow in her expression, a trace of regret and even concern for him. But those emotions, if they exist, are quickly replaced by defiance. She has her work to do, which is important to her, while Quiller's work is meaningless to him. He knows that, regardless of how many missions he completes, people will still die and nothing will change. Quiller's disillusionment is total now, his last hope for love destroyed by her betrayal. His partial victory is a hollow one and he is drained emotionally. He tells Inge that he is leaving Berlin, explaining dejectedly, "I'm a little tired." It is obvious that he is more than a little tired, due more to the emotional stress she has caused than to the physical stress caused by Oktober and, indirectly, by Pol. Though they have all used him, he has emerged victorious, but he doesn't feel like a winner, for there are no real winners in the deadly game they all have played. There are only losers.

**Quiller is bored with Pol's (Alec Guinness) condescending attitude.**

At the end of the conversation, a sudden closeup of Quiller's face fills the screen and, after a long pause, he asks, "By the way, did you ever meet a man called Jones?" A closeup of Inge's face follows immediately as she hesitatingly replies, "No. No, I don't think so." The emotional impact of the exchange is powerful, the implication of the words fully understood by both Quiller and Inge. Once again, it is apparent that Quiller knows that she is lying, that she knows he knows and that he knows this, too. But now there is no hope and no tenderness, only sadness and pain. Afterward, all that is left is to say good-bye.

After Quiller leaves, Inge walks out to the front steps of the school. As the children flock to her open arms, she happily welcomes them and then slowly raises her eyes to look beyond them, her smile disappearing as she sees Quiller walking away. In the distance, Quiller is no longer as large an imposing figure as in his introduction but a very small figure gradually becoming lost amidst the surroundings. He is truly Wednesday's child, born to be alone.

Harold Pinter's script for *The Quiller Memorandum* could not have been brought so faithfully to the screen if director Michael Anderson and cinematographer Erwin Hillier did not share a complete awareness of its obscure motivations and complex emotions. Anderson and Hillier infuse every shot with a visual style that is in total harmony with the spirit of despair

**George Segal, Senta Berger and Max Von Sydow**

within Quiller's soul. Lighting and composition create an expressive quality of heightened realism throughout the film that escalates to a nightmarish imagery during Quiller's long and tortuous night through the streets of Berlin. The film utilizes Berlin locations excellently—from the Olympic Stadium to the Tiergarten—but never even faintly assumes travelogue aspects. Anderson deserves credit for the steady pace of the film that permits the story to gradually build in both tension and pathos.

John Barry's brilliant score is a masterpiece of film composition. His atmospheric music reflects both the images on the screen as well as the obscure meanings beneath the surface. As a result, virtually every cue is infused with darkness. The hauntingly beautiful main theme, "Wednesday's Child," with lyrics by Hal David, captures the essence of Quiller's romantic desires, while also conveying his despair and loneliness. During many sequences, Barry's use of the flexatone, a dithering percussion instrument, augments the mood of suspiciousness and uncertainty, while also suggesting the duplicity that imbues the other characters. Even during scenes of action and suspense, when the score assumes a pulsating tempo, there is a suggestion of hopelessness (particularly when contrasted with Barry's energetic James Bond scores). The poignancy of the final sequence is enhanced immeasurably by the main theme, which due to differences in instrumentation and rhythm, underscores the cynicism as well as sadness of the protagonist. In a career that has spanned four decades and five Academy Awards, this is one of John Barry's most accomplished scores. (Matt Monro's recording of "Wednesday's Child," as heard in the film and several instrumental versions were released on single records while a soundtrack album was also released.) Ironically, Barry won two Academy Awards for the year in which this movie was released, but they were for *Born Free*.

All of the efforts of so many talented artists behind the camera would be to little avail if not for the restrained and intelligent performance of George Segal in the title role.

Segal started his career in television and on stage in the early 1960s. In the mid-1960s, he began appearing in films and, in 1965, his starring performance in *King Rat* signaled the emergence of a major star. The following year, he accepted a supporting role in *Who's Afraid of Virginia Woolf?* and received an Academy Award nomination. *The Quiller Memorandum* was released later in the year and features one of his finest performances, but one that is difficult to appreciate because of the subtleties of the portrayal, which are in perfect accordance with the script's conception of his character.

Segal portrays the consummate agent who exudes an assertive self-confidence in his profession, while harboring inner anguish. In view of the script's deliberate ambiguities, Segal must convey Quiller's feelings and motivations in subtle ways and, as a result, manages to bring extraordinary empathy and nuances to his role. The scene in which he awakens from a promised death is just one example of his artistry. Wearily approaching the hotel, struggling up the stairway to his hotel room and sitting on his bed, he projects an image of total despondency. His body language communicates all the viewer needs to know to understand why he calls Inge instead of Pol. He is also extremely convincing as a more aggressive agent, particularly in the interrogation scene in which he is given the two drugs in succession with opposite effects upon his system. And in the final scene, he conveys outer victory and inner defeat, professional triumph and personal desolation. All of this can be discerned from his expression, which conveys sadness and disillusionment—from his tone which is soft yet accusatory and his manner which suggests that everything he has endured has little meaning. The sheer virtuosity of Segal's portrayal is indicative of a superb performance.

Austrian actress Senta Berger is strikingly effective as Inge, evoking a mysterious aura for her character that is initially somewhat sympathetic despite her ultimate betrayal of Quiller. Beneath the ambivalence is an innate sadness, as well as inner tension, which suggests that she may be genuinely wavering in her loyalties. In the film's most important scene, she recites her climactic lines with the just the right amount of deceit tinged with remorse. It is a highly compelling portrayal of a complex character.

In support, Britain's Alec Guinness gives his usual infallible performance as Pol, projecting pomposity as well as bureaucratic disdain for anyone beneath him. In the biography, *Alec Guinness* by Piers Paul Read (Simon & Schuster; 2003), Guinness dismisses the film as "cliché-ridden," perhaps because he only had four scenes in it. However, he makes each scene stand out because of his expressions and intonations that convey the callousness beneath the artificial concern. Sweden's Max von Sydow is equally compelling as the "German gentleman" he professes to be and as a symbol of ruthlessness. George Sanders and Robert Flemyng submerge themselves within their characters of Gibbs and Rushington, making the desired impact despite the brevity of their roles.

There is not a false performance in the film with the international cast investing commitment to even the smallest parts, but particular mention should be given to Peter Carsten as Hengel, Gunter Meisner as Hassler and Edith Schneider as Frau Shroeder.

*The Quiller Memorandum* was given a positive review in *Variety* by "Rich" who called it "an intelligent, credible secret-service adventure (that) hits the mark effectively and entertainingly." Box-office success seemed to be assured but proved to be elusive, despite equally favorable reviews upon its release in England in November 1966. *The London Times* called it "extraordinarily refreshing (and) a thriller in classic tradition." *The Daily Express* commented that "we could stand more spy films if they were all like this one." And *The Daily Mirror* hailed "at last a spy you can believe in." The movie would eventually receive three BAFTA nominations for Best Screenplay, Best Art Direction and Best Film Editing.

When it opened the following month in the United States, however, the film was pilloried. Bosley Crowther in *The New York Times* called it "a fraud (and) a hackneyed spy picture," while Rex Reed called it "an exercise in simple-mindedness." Philip Hartung observed in *Commonweal* that it was "just another exercise in violence and espionage claptrap." And the reviewer for *Time* called it "a B movie (with) an aimless plot." Such negative and misguided reviews are difficult to understand and may be an indication not of the film's quality but of the inability of the critics to comprehend the subtlety of the film and the deliberate obscurity of its themes. Perhaps some critics didn't feel that a genre film deserved the type of analytical assessment reserved for films they perceived as having more significance.

*The Quiller Memorandum* film was a box-office failure in the United States, in part because it was released during a period in which the market was inundated with spy movies. The previous year, the latest Bond movie *Thunderball* had broken box-office records. Other commercial successes of 1965, though not in the same financial league, included two other "serious" espionage films: *The Spy Who Came In from the Cold* with Richard Burton made $3.6 million in domestic theatrical rentals and *The Ipcress File*, with Michael Caine as Len Deighton's nameless hero, called Harry Palmer in the movie, earned $3.3 million. By 1966, the year *Quiller* was released, the abundance of spy movies had begun to exhaust the market. On *Variety*'s annual list of Top Grossing Films of the Year, the hits included Alfred Hitchcock's *Torn Curtain* with $6.5 million. Two Bond spoofs, *The Silencers* with Dean Martin as Matt Helm and *Our Man Flint* with James Coburn, scored with more than $7 million. Even the abysmal *Murderers' Row*, the second Matt Helm movie, earned $6 million. And the second Harry Palmer film, *Funeral in Berlin*, made $3 million. *The Quiller Memorandum* was at the bottom of the list with only $1.5 million, below such tripe as *Dr. Goldfoot and the Bikini Machine*.

Ironically, since the artists responsible for *The Quiller Memorandum* had been aware of the numerous espionage films with which it would compete, they attempted to create a spy film that was unique and would not fit into the mold of all of the others, whether serious or fantastic. And they succeeded triumphantly. Unfortunately, that isn't what the public wanted. Genre fans that saw it were not prepared for either the film's ambiguities or the emphasis on characterization

**Quiller gives in to his libido.**

over action and emotion over sex. The intricacies of the multi-leveled storyline combined with an unconventional hero and a melancholy ending doomed the film to obscurity.

Due to the financial losses, plans for a series were cancelled. Although the paperback edition of the second Quiller novel, *The 9th Directive*, stated that "it would soon be a 20th Century Fox movie," such a project never materialized. However, while later novels in the series are highly intriguing and would make fine motion pictures, they would have to be different in conception than the first one. While Adam Hall's Quiller has the qualities to make a frequent screen hero, Pinter's Quiller was perhaps destined to make just one screen appearance and fade into memory after his single adventure. Somehow, that seems appropriate for the unique and lonely hero of the film version of *The Quiller Memorandum*.

It is understandable why Elleston Trevor did not like the movie upon its release (which he stated to this writer in a 1993 conversation) and particularly did not appreciate Harold Pinter's adaptation. The script's radical changes in the storyline and the characterization of Quiller could not have been welcomed by the author of the original work for obvious reasons. However, it is possible that his disapproval of the film may have lessened (he seemed to be amused when asked about this possibility) in view of a passage in one of the later novels. In the 13th Quiller novel entitled *Quiller KGB*, published in 1989, Quiller is talking to the director of his mission when the author writes, as part of Quiller's narration, "The conversation was Pinteresque, loaded with all the things that couldn't be said." Also, one of the characters referred to in the novel is named Foxwell. Nevertheless, the creator of Quiller probably remained pleased that

**George Sanders is perfectly cast as the pompous Gibbs.**

20ᵗʰ Century Fox cancelled plans for a second film.

Quiller did reappear—in name only—on British television in 1975 as a series entitled *Quiller* with Michael Jayston in the title role. Except for one episode adapted by Trevor from the fifth novel in the series, *The Tango Briefing*, the episodes were original stories and had little, if any, relationship to the author's creation. As an indication of just how ill-conceived the series was, the title theme was a fast-paced tune that combined rock and jazz elements, suggesting a "hip, cool" action-based hero. Produced by the BBC, the series lasted for only 13 episodes. They were eventually broadcast in the United States on the ABC network in the midnight hour and induced sleep.

In 1993, Paramount Pictures announced that it had purchased an option on the Quiller novels for the purpose of starting a series, but it never developed, which probably pleased Elleston Trevor who had privately expressed misgivings about the option due to concerns over what Hollywood might do to his solitary but beloved agent. It was subsequently reported that United Artists had acquired the rights to all of the Quiller novels but, though various directors were reported as working on the series over the next few years, none of the various plans reached fruition. In 2000, MGM announced intentions to film *Quiller Solitaire*, the 16ᵗʰ novel in the series, but the project was cancelled which is extremely fortunate in view of the fact that John Travolta was announced for the role. This would have been ludicrous—and disastrous—miscasting.

Thus, to date, there has been only one motion picture featuring the character of Quiller and, over four decades after its release, the movie remains unique and memorable. *The Quiller Memorandum* is both a superb film about espionage and a sensitive portrait of human complexities and frailties. It remains distinctive because the espionage theme is subordinate to the familiar Pinter themes of alienation and betrayal. And this betrayal is not of Queen and Country but of the heart and soul that comprises the human condition. Of the film's many virtues, none has quite as much impact upon the heart and mind as that moment when Quiller's face fills the screen and he asks plaintively:

"Did you ever meet a man called Jones?"

CREDITS: Producer: Ivan Foxwell; Director: Michael Anderson; Screenplay: Harold Pinter, Based on the Novel by Adam Hall; Cinematographer: Erwin Hillier; Editor: Frederick Wilson; Music: John Barry; Song "Wednesday's Child" by John Barry and Mack David, sung by Matt Monro

CAST: George Segal (Quiller); Alec Guinness (Pol); Max von Sydow (Oktober); Senta Berger (Inge); George Sanders (Gibbs); Robert Flemyng (Rushington); Robert Helpmann (Weng); Peter Carsten (Hengel); Edith Schneider (Frau Schroeder); Gunter Meisner (Hassler); Herbert Stass (Kenneth Lindsay Jones); Paul Hansard (Doctor); Victor Beaumont (Dorfmann); Ernest Walder (Grauber); Claus Tinney (Hughes)


# THE QUILLER NOVELS

1)  *The Quiller Memorandum*; Original title: *The Berlin Memorandum* (1965)
2)  *The 9ᵗʰ Directive* (1966)
3)  *The Stryker Portfolio* (1968)
4)  *The Warsaw Document* (1971)
5)  *The Tango Briefing* (1973)
6)  *The Mandarin Cypher* (1975)
7)  *The Kobra Manifesto* (1976)
8)  *The Sinkiang Executive* (1978)
9)  *The Scorpion Signal* (1979)
10) *The Pekin Target*; U.S. title: *The Peking Target* (1981)
11) *Northlight*; U.S. title: *Quiller* (1985)
12) *Quiller's Run* (1988)
13) *Quiller KGB* (1989)
14) *Quiller Barracuda* (1990)
15) *Quiller Bamboo* (1991)
16) *Quiller Solitaire* (1992)
17) *Quiller Meridian* (1993)
18) *Quiller Salamander* (1994)
19) *Quiller Balalaika* (1996)

# AFTERWARD

## I.

The specter of the Hollywood blacklist has a long shadow. In 1986, when Lorimar-Telepictures purchased the MGM studio lot, one of the buildings acquired was called the Robert Taylor Building, named in honor of one of the film capital's most popular stars. A couple of years later, radicals who worked in the building circulated a petition demanding that Taylor's name be removed. The petitioners believed that Taylor should not be honored because he had been a cooperative witness before the House Un-American Activities Committee and had "named names." Taylor was a patriotic man who believed in his country. But his name was extinguished.

Robert Taylor was beloved in old Hollywood and probably wouldn't have wanted to be associated with the kind of fanatics who inhabited the building that once bore his name. Ironically, the former Robert Taylor Building became the George Cukor Building. Cukor, who directed Taylor in *Camille*, stated in 1983: "Robert Taylor was my favorite actor. He was a gentleman." This is one way of saying that Taylor had class.

It is curious that the asinine whiners didn't extend their vengeance to other cooperative witnesses. Shouldn't similarly minded protesters who worked at

Franchot Tone, Robert Taylor, Margaret Sullavan and Robert Young in a posed photo for *Three Comrades*.

Warner Bros. have demanded that the name of Warner be removed from the name of the studio since Jack Warner was also a friendly witness? Shouldn't the name of Mayer have been removed from M-G-M since Louis Mayer was also cooperative with the committee? Well, if the extremists have their way that could still happen.

In 1999, similar malcontents disrespected Elia Kazan—another cooperative witness—by remaining seated and grimacing angrily for the benefit of television cameras when Kazan was honored with a Lifetime Achievement Academy Award. Kazan ignored the protestors and graciously accepted his award. He had class.

Those incredibly ridiculous curmudgeons had no idea what it was like in Hollywood during the blacklist. And they didn't care to learn the truth. Nor were they interested in trying to understand how difficult and precarious it was during that era. And they certainly were not willing to tolerate anyone who had ideas or beliefs that differed from their own. They were—and remain—only determined to display their politically correct mindsets so they can be accepted by Hollywood's left-wing ideologues. They have no class.

They could learn a lot from some illustrious predecessors. Humphrey Bogart was a noted liberal. Indeed, he was one of the members of the Committee for the First Amendment that went to Washington to protest HUAC. But after the Hollywood Ten were convicted and their radical views became known, Bogart was compelled to write an article in a film magazine titled "I Am No Communist" to distance himself from the Ten. Bogie remained committed to his liberal beliefs but, like Bob Taylor, he did not want to be associated with the reactionaries who had become increasingly omnipresent in the film industry. Bogart and Edward Dmytryk, the member of the Ten who became a cooperative witness, also harbored no recriminations against one another, despite their conflicting positions; the actor and director worked together twice after Dmytryk's friendly testimony. Bogart and Dmytryk both had class.

Dalton Trumbo also had class. In 1970, upon receiving the Laurel Award for Lifetime Achievement from the Screen Writers Guild, his acceptance speech included the following words of pacification: "The blacklist was a time of evil. No one on either side who survived it came through untouched by evil. Caught in a situation that had passed beyond the control of mere individuals, each person reacted as his own nature, his needs, his convictions and his particular circumstances compelled him to. There was bad faith and good, honesty and dishonesty, courage and cowardice, selflessness and opportunism, wisdom and stupidity, good and bad on both sides. It will do no good to search for villains or heroes or saints or devils because there were none; there were only victims. In the final tally, we were all victims because almost, without exception, each of us felt compelled to say things he did not want to say, to do things that he did not want to do, to deliver and receive wounds he truly did not want to exchange. That is why none of us—right, left or center—emerged from that long nightmare without sin."

## II.

Dick Powell did it all, long before it became fashionable. He sang, danced, acted, directed and produced. And yet, despite his skills in all of these departments, he never received an Academy Award nomination and is generally unrecognized for his talents. The fact that the multi-talented Mr. Powell today

**Dick Powell and Ruby Keeler in _Footlight Parade_**

does not have the reputation he deserves is one of the many injustices that I have attempted to address in this book.

It is also unfair that Frank Lovejoy and Lloyd Bridges still do not receive acclaim for the performances of their careers or that Cy Endfield, Michael Anderson and Roy Ward Baker are comparatively unknown directors. It is equally unjust that Robert Taylor never received an Academy Award nomination. George Segal, due to the commercial failures of too many of his starring films, had his movie career as a leading man cut short, but that doesn't diminish his tremendous talent. And Edmund Purdom deserves to be rescued from obscurity.

At least actors such as Humphrey Bogart, Marlon Brando, Kirk Douglas and Dirk Bogarde, as well as directors such as Richard Brooks, Robert Aldrich, J. Lee Thompson and Michael Curtiz have received acclaim for movies other than the ones discussed in this book. But that didn't save them from critical condemnation. For instance, in the late 1980s, while reviewing one of J. Lee Thompson's later movies, film critics Gene Siskel and Roger Ebert on their television show casually dismissed the director as "a hack." This indicated an appalling and pompous ignorance of Thompson's film career.

Fortunately, the factor of time can correct such injustices. Years after its release, a movie may be in a better position to be appreciated, divorced from the social and political factors that may have impacted its reception. DVDs are an accessible means for most people to be introduced to great movies retrieved from oblivion. This technology allows past injustices to be rectified by supplementing these movies with commentaries by film historians and the surviving creative personnel. Nevertheless, the best way to see a great movie is in a theater.

The few revival theaters that are still in existence remain a wonderful outlet for correcting grievances of the past. Of the many excellent series of films presented by The American Cinematheque at the Egyptian Theater in Hollywood, one of the most memorable occurred in 2000. As part of the 2nd Annual Festival of Film Noir, _Pitfall_ was shown in a new 35mm print. Following the movie, Lizabeth Scott, Jane Wyatt and André de Toth appeared on stage. It is gratifying that they finally received praise for the movie from an appreciative audience. Such praise came just in time for de Toth and Wyatt, who have since passed away, respectively in 2002 and 2006. Dick Powell wasn't as fortunate, having died in 1963.

In February 2000, the Film Forum Theater in New York City presented *Cape Fear* as part of its Neo-Noir festival. In 2001, a special DVD edition of the movie was released, accompanied by a documentary on its production and commentaries by J. Lee Thompson, who died in 2002, and Gregory Peck, who died in 2003. And in October 2009, the Egyptian Theater presented *Cape Fear* (on a double bill with *The Night of the Hunter*) as a tribute to Robert Mitchum, who died in 1997. It may have taken almost half a century, but the movie finally has received the respect it deserves.

There are other optimistic signs. In 2003, Martin Scorsese presented his own personal print of *Try and Get Me!* to "Noir City: The Annual San Francisco Film Noir Festival," presented at the Castro Theater. It is nice to realize that Scorsese is a fan of this neglected film. It is unfortunate that he didn't have an equal amount of respect for the original *Cape Fear,* to refrain from debasing it. Incidentally, in 1996, Gregory Peck appeared at the Bushinell Auditorium in Hartford, Connecticut to talk about his career. *Cape Fear* was the subject of several questions and Peck was asked to comment on the two versions. Always the gentleman, he stated that he didn't like to criticize the work of others and only mentioned the differences in characterizations for the two films. His reluctance to elaborate seemed to speak volumes.

In April 2004, a newly restored 35mm print of *In a Lonely Place* was presented at the Egyptian Theater. In December 2006, the Egyptian presented it again as part of a tribute to its director, called appropriately, "In a Lonely Place: the Rebellious Cinema of Nicholas Ray." In July 2009, the Film Forum Theater presented it for a week as the opening feature of another tribute called simply "Nick Ray." The director's widow, Susan Ray, hosted the first night's showing. During her introduction, she mentioned two scenes in the movie—the kitchen scene and the restaurant scene—reflecting what the director called an

Anne Haywood, Gregory Peck and F. Lee Thompson on the set of *The Chairman* (1969).

"Involuntary Performance," in which the actor and the character he/she is playing merge so completely that it is difficult to tell which one is on the screen. In these two scenes, Ray felt that Bogart's raw emotion—tender in one scene, brutal in the other—was so palpable that it was impossible for him to know if it was Bogart or Dix Steele in front of his camera. The film was so popular that it returned the following month for another week's engagement. It is unfortunate that Ray, who died in 1979, and Bogart, who died in 1957, could not witness the belated acclaim given to a movie into which they invested so much personal commitment.

In July 2005, Ray Harryhausen appeared in person at the Aero Theater in Santa Monica to host two of his movies. The main feature was *First Men in the Moon* and anyone fortunate enough to view it on the large screen saw it the way it was meant to be seen. This movie was designed to be nothing more than an entertaining motion picture and it still succeeds in that objective today. It was also gratifying to hear words of appreciation for Lionel Jeffries, who died in February 2010.

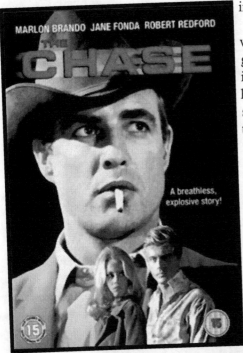

Since *The Quiller Memorandum* was unknown for so long, it is gratifying that it saw a DVD release in 2006 with commentary by two film historians. This is a welcome first step in bringing belated recognition to this haunting drama. Michael Anderson, whose name is never listed among great film directors, is deserving of overdue acclaim. In March 2009, the Egyptian Theater presented a memorial weekend of films written by Harold Pinter (who died in December 2008) but, unfortunately, *Quiller* was not included. Hopefully, if there is another tribute, this omission will be corrected. George Segal, still working quite regularly though in supporting roles, would probably be happy to attend. Hopefully, Michael Anderson would also be able to participate.

*The Chase* was given less respect on its DVD presentation. It was released without any supplements in 2004 and the erroneous liner notes were obviously written by someone who either didn't watch the movie or didn't understand it. Future releases will hopefully correct this. Perhaps someday Arthur Penn will even be able to view the movie objectively and recognize its numerous virtues.

*The Last Sunset* is still disparaged, but, there is no denying a lyrical beauty that reaches culmination in its concluding scenes. Kirk Douglas is still with us and would no doubt appreciate overdue praise for his film. *The Singer Not the Song* is also still ridiculed but it is difficult to forget the conflicting emotions that pervade the climax of this neglected film. Perhaps even Roy Ward Baker would be amenable to recognizing its virtues. Also memorable is the heartbroken expression on the title character's face at

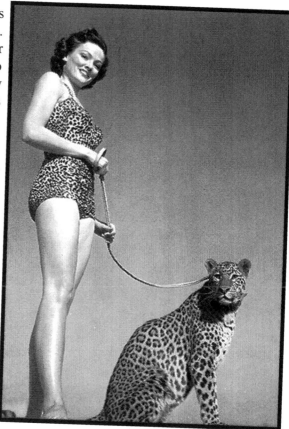

*The Egyptian* **is a beautiful film in more ways than one!**

the end of *The Egyptian*, a rich and beautiful film that should not be exiled like its title character. Finally, one of the most haunting closing images in film history has to be the one that fills the screen in *The Last Hunt* and, just as the buffalo has been rescued from extinction, this marvelous film hopefully will also be rescued from oblivion.

Optimistically, it is my hope that with the passage of even more time, all of the films discussed in this book will be increasingly appreciated, enjoyed and perhaps even loved by more people. The artists on both sides of the camera who were responsible for the movies deserve nothing less.

**IF YOU ENJOYED THIS BOOK
PLEASE CALL, WRITE OR E-MAIL
FOR A FREE CATALOG**

**MIDNIGHT MARQUEE PRESS
9721 BRITINAY LANE
BALTIMORE, MD 21234**

**WWW.MIDMAR.COM
410-665-1198
MMARQUEE@AOL.COM**

16462865R00114

Made in the USA
Charleston, SC
21 December 2012